VISUAL FACTFINDER

DINOSAURS &
PREHISTORIC LIFE

First published by Bardfield Press in 2005
Copyright © Miles Kelly Publishing 2005

Bardfield Press is an imprint of
Miles Kelly Publishing Ltd,
Bardfield Centre, Great Bardfield, Essex, CM7 4SL

This material also appears in the *1000 Facts* series

4 6 8 10 9 7 5 3

Editorial Director: Belinda Gallagher

Art Director: Jo Brewer

Copy Editors: Stuart Cooper, Sarah Doughty

Editorial Assistant: Bethanie Bourne

Designer: Tom Slemmings

Picture Researcher: Liberty Newton

Production Manager: Elizabeth Brunwin

Indexers: Charlotte Marshall, Jane Parker

Reprographics: Anthony Cambray, Mike Coupe, Ian Paulyn

British Library Cataloguing-in-Publication Data
A catalogue record for this book is available from the British Library

ISBN 1-84236-541-X

Printed in China

www.mileskelly.net
info@mileskelly.net

VISUAL FACTFINDER

DINOSAURS &
PREHISTORIC LIFE

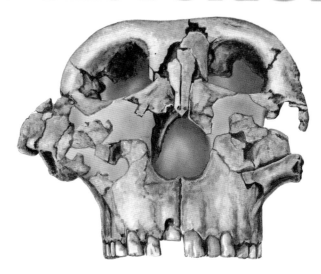

Andrew Campbell
Steve Parker
Consultants: Steve Parker, Dr Jim Flegg

**BARDFIELD
PRESS**

Contents

Dinosaurs

6

7

Humans

DINOSAURS &
PREHISTORIC LIFE

What was the biggest dinosaur?

Which invertebrate was as long as a human?

Who found the most famous hominid fossil?

The answers to these and many other questions can be found in this amazing book of almost 2500 facts. Beginning with the earliest forms of life on Earth, the pages span the evolution of plants, invertebrates, birds, reptiles and humans – as well as the rise and fall of the dinosaurs.

The book is divided into sections that examine the development of prehistoric life and consider its relationship with modern-day animals.

Prehistoric time

- **Time since the Earth formed** is divided into large units called eras, which are in turn divided into periods. Some periods split further into epochs. These units of time relate to the formation of rock layers.

- **The Precambrian Era** ran from 4600–542 million years ago (mya). It saw the beginning of life in the seas. In the Cambrian Period (542–490 mya) the seas were dominated by the first vertebrates.

- **During the Ordovician Period** (490–435 mya) plants spread to land. In the Silurian Period (435–410 mya) the first jawed fish appeared, together with the first upright-standing land plants.

- **The Devonian Period** (410–355 mya) witnessed the development of bony fish in the seas, and trees and insects on land.

- **The Carboniferous Period** (355–298 mya) was the time of the great tropical forests and the first land animals with backbones.

- **During the Permian Period** (298–250 mya) reptiles became the major land creatures.

- **The Triassic Period** (250–208 mya) saw the rise of the dinosaurs and the first small mammals. In the Jurassic Period (208–144 mya) reptiles dominated the land, sea and sky.

- **The Cretaceous Period** (144–65 mya) saw the proliferation of flowering plants, but its end also saw the extinction of the dinosaurs.

- **The Tertiary Period** (65–1.6 mya) saw the successful development of mammals and grassland habitats, and cooling temperatures.

- **The Quaternary Period** (1.6 mya–present) has witnessed the most recent series of ice ages and the rise of modern humans.

▼ *Even though many kinds of animals and plants died out 65 mya, other groups lived on. Insects, worms, fish, birds and mammals all survived the mass extinction – and these groups are still alive today.*

Plant fossils

- **The earliest plant fossils** are found in stromatolites, which are limestone deposits formed by algae. Some stromatolites are over 3 billion years old.

- **The earliest fossils** of land-living plants, such as liverworts and mosses, come from the Late Ordovician and Early Silurian periods (around 440–430 mya).

- **By the Mid-Silurian Period** (around 420 mya), plant fossils begin to show more features of upright plants, such as parts of branching stems and water-carrying tubes.

- **Plant fossils** are very rare because plants have delicate structures. However, pollen, fruits and seeds are much more durable – it is more common for fossil hunters to find their remains.

- **Pollen, fruit and seed fossils** can be distributed over a very wide area, so it is a real challenge for scientists to match them to particular plants.

- **Most plant fossils** are just the impressions of plants left in rock layers, but some can be preserved as three-dimensional structures.

- **Plant fossils found in Rhynie** in Scotland are three dimensional. Scientists think that the area where they grew was flooded by hot spring water rich in the mineral silica. The silica then turned to rock, preserving the plants' shape.

- **Scientists count** the number of growth rings in tree trunk fossils to tell how old the tree was when it died.

- **Some plant fossils** exist with fossils of plant-eating animals and predators in the same rock zone. This enables scientists to work out prehistoric food chains, listing which animals depended on what.

- **Plant fossils** can demonstrate climate change. For example, a desert in Arizona contains fossilized trees that, millions of years ago, were part of a huge forest.

▲ *Stromatolites such as these exist off the coasts of western Australia, southern Africa, eastern Greenland and parts of Antarctica. They are made up of the fossils of algae and bacteria.*

Earliest plants

▲ Lichens such as these are made up of an alga and fungus. Early lichens – like modern-day ones – grew on rocks and, over time, eroded part of the rock and helped form soil.

- **The very first** living things on Earth were single-celled bacteria and cyanobacteria, also known as blue-green algae.

- **Blue-green algae** emerged around 3500 mya.

- **Although it is not** a plant, blue-green algae contains chlorophyll and was the first living thing to photosynthesize (make energy from sunlight).

- **Photosynthesis** also produces oxygen. Over millions of years, the blue-green algae produced enough oxygen to enable more complex life forms to develop.

- **True algae**, which are usually regarded as plants, developed around 1000 mya.

- **By about** 550 mya, multi-celled plants had begun to appear, including simple seaweeds.

- **Algae and lichens** were the first plants to appear on land.

- **Bryophyte plants** (mosses and liverworts) emerged on land around 440 mya. Bryophytes are simple green seedless plants.

- **Bryophytes** cannot grow high above the ground because they do not have strengthened stems, unlike vascular plants, which emerged later.

. . . FASCINATING FACT . . .
Liverworts grew on mats of blue-green algae, which trapped nitrogen from the air. Liverworts used this nitrogen to grow tissues.

Vascular plants

- **Vascular plants** are more suited to living on drier land than mosses and liverworts.
- **They have branching stems** with tubelike walls that carry water and nutrients.
- **These stems** and walls also mean the plants can stand tall. Vascular plants have spores (reproductive cells, like seeds) – the taller the plant the more widely it can disperse its spores.
- **One of the first known** vascular plants was *Cooksonia*. It was about 5 cm tall, with a forked stem.
- **Scientists** called palaeontologists discovered fossil remains of *Cooksonia* in Wales. Palaeontologists study fossils of prehistoric plants and animals to see how they lived and evolved.
- **One site** where lots of vascular plant fossils have been found is Rhynie in Scotland.
- **The plants** at Rhynie would have grown on the sandy edges of pools in the Early Devonian Period (about 400 mya).
- **One plant fossil** found at Rhynie is *Aglaophyton*, which stood around 45 cm high.
- *Aglaophyton* had underground roots and tissues that supported the plant stem. It also had water-carrying tubes and stomata (tiny openings) that allowed air and water to pass through.
- **Land-living plants** were essential for providing conditions for animals to make the transition from the seas to land. They created soil, food and ground cover for shelter.

▶ *The* Cooksonia *plant had forked stems ending in spore-filled caps. The earliest examples of* Cooksonia *have been found in Ireland, dating to around 430 mya.*

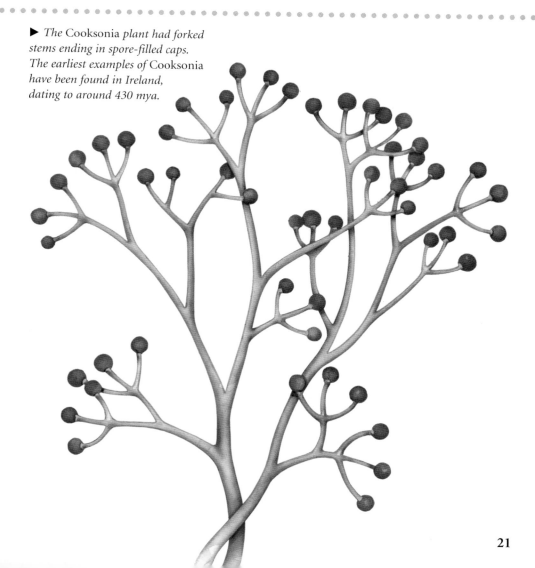

Ferns

- **Ferns** are flowerless, spore-producing plants, with roots, stems, and leaves called fronds.
- **They developed** from the earliest vascular plants, such as *Cooksonia*.
- **Ferns** first appeared in the Devonian Period (410–355 mya).
- *Cladoxylon* was an early, primitive fern. It had a main stem, forked branches and leaves, and fan-shaped structures that contained spores.
- **During the Carboniferous Period** (355–298 mya), ferns became some of the most abundant plants on Earth.
- **Prehistoric ferns** would have looked similar to modern ones, but they could grow much larger. Large ferns are called tree-ferns.
- **Sometimes palaeontologists** find many fossilized fern spores in a single layer of rock. These 'fern spikes' show that there were a lot of ferns around at a particular time.
- **There is a major fern spike** from rock layers that are around 65 million years old, when many other plants had died out, along with dinosaurs and other animals. This fern spike shows that ferns were not affected by the extinctions.
- **Ferns** are great survivors – after volcanic eruptions, they are the first plants to grow again in a landscape.

...FASCINATING FACT...
Ferns remain successful plants today – there
are over 12,000 living varieties.

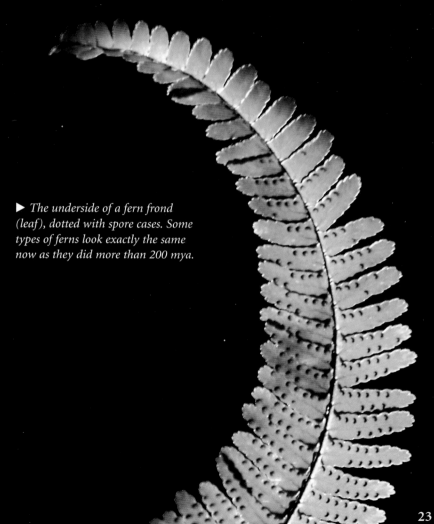

▶ *The underside of a fern frond (leaf), dotted with spore cases. Some types of ferns look exactly the same now as they did more than 200 mya.*

23

Clubmosses

- **Clubmosses** are covered with tiny spiral-patterned leaves. Near the top of the stem are club-shaped structures that produce spores.

- **Clubmosses** started to grow on moist ground in the Devonian Period (410–355 mya).

- **Early clubmosses** included *Protolepidodendrum, Baragwanathia* and *Sawdonia*.

- **Another early clubmoss** was *Asteroxylon*. It had forked branches with tiny leaves called leaflets.

- **By the Late Devonian Period**, clubmosses evolved into much bigger forms and produced the first tree-sized plants, such as *Lepidodendron*.

- *Lepidodendron* **trees** could grow more than 30 m high. The diameter of their trunks could be over 2 m.

- *Lepidodendron* grew all over the world in the Carboniferous Period (355–298 mya).

- **It produced** large spores inside cone-shaped containers.

- **Some clubmosses** survive to this day, including *Lycopodium*.

> ...FASCINATING FACT...
> Along with tree-ferns, clubmosses were the first tree-sized plants.
> They were supported by the first well-developed underground roots.

▶ *Fossilized* Lepidodendron *bark shows that the trunks of these giant clubmosses were covered in diamond-shaped patterns.* Lepidodendron *leaves could be up to 1 m long, and its roots stretched out for up to 12 m.*

Forests

- **The Carboniferous Period** (355–298 mya) was the time of the greatest forests on Earth.

- **The damp climate** of this period suited forests, as did the huge number of swamps in which many trees grew.

- **Carboniferous forests** contained huge clubmosses, growing up to 50 m tall, as well as tree-ferns and primitive conifers, such as *Archaeopteris*.

- **The huge numbers** of enormous trees in this period produced the highest levels of oxygen there has ever been on Earth.

- **Dead forest trees** fell and formed mats of rotting wood, which over time turned into peat.

- **Layers of sandstone** or other rock formed over the peat. The pressure of these new layers eventually caused the peat to dry and harden into coal.

- **Coal deposits** are rich sources of fossilized animals.

- **In later periods,** following the Carboniferous Period, plant-eating dinosaurs ate their way through huge areas of forest.

- **Forests** were home to many prehistoric animals, including the first small mammals, such as *Megazostrodon* and *Morganucodon*, which could hide from predators amongst the trees.

● **By the Tertiary Period** (65–1.6 mya), forests contained many more deciduous (leaf-shedding) trees, such as magnolias, than evergreens, such as conifers.

▼ *Two plant-eating sauropod dinosaurs (Jobaria left, and Janenschia right) eating the branches at the tops of trees in a forest of the late Jurassic Period (159–144 mya). These forests had developed millions of years earlier, during the Carboniferous Period.*

Grasslands

- **In the Oligocene Epoch** (37–24 mya), the Earth's climate became cooler, causing the ice cap covering Antarctica to increase in size.

- **As a result**, tropical rainforests began to decline and grasslands became increasingly common.

- **Grasslands** are called many things in different parts of the world: plains, savannahs, steppes, veldt and prairies.

- **The change** from one ecosystem to another, such as forest to grassland, is called succession. It is a continual process and in central Australia, for example, prehistoric grasslands have been succeeded by desert.

- **Grasses** provided an abundant source of food.

▼ *Etosha National Park, Namibia, South Africa. Grasses did not appear on Earth until around 50 mya. Their ability to withstand drought, fire and grazing are part of the reason why they spread so successfully across the world.*

- **Unlike many** other plants, grasses can be cropped without destroying the plant itself, so they provide animals with a constant supply of food.

- **Grasses** are tougher than soft forest plants. This meant that plant eaters had to develop stronger teeth and better digestive systems.

- **The open nature** of grasslands meant that mammals had to become faster runners, too – to chase after prey or to escape predators.

- **About 11,000 years ago** temperatures began to rise and many grasslands dried out. Lush, mixed grasses gave way to much coarser grasses and scrub – or to desert.

- **This change** led to the extinction of many prehistoric herbivores, such as camel and horse species.

Invertebrate fossils

- **Invertebrates have left** a very rich fossil record. One reason for this is because many of them lived in the sea – the best environment for fossilization.

- **Some of the most common** invertebrate fossils include those of trilobites, ammonites, corals and sponges.

- **Many invertebrates** have also left trace fossils, which include tracks, trails and burrows.

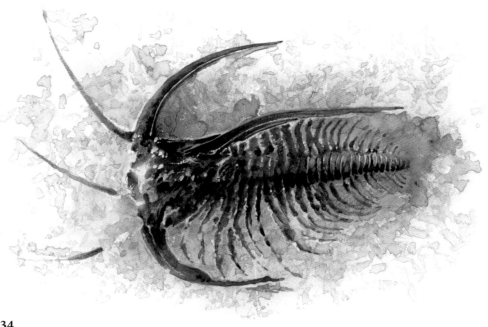

- **For many** soft-bodied invertebrates, such as worms, trace fossils may be all palaeontologists have as evidence of their existence.

- **Fossilized ammonites** clearly demonstrate the evolution of the species over time, showing early, middle and later stages of development.

- **Examining trilobite fossils** has taught palaeontologists much about this invertebrate. They reveal that trilobites could see in all directions.

- **They also reveal** that trilobites shed their skin from time to time, in order to add another segment to their body.

- **Palaeontologists can estimate** the age of a trilobite from the number of segments on its fossilized body.

- **As well as fossils**, invertebrates can be preserved in other ways. Amber (ancient tree resin) is very effective at preserving the remains of small creatures, such as insects and spiders.

> ...FASCINATING FACT...
> Sometimes palaeontologists cannot place invertebrate fossils in any category of known species – perhaps because the animal is so unusual or because so little of its body is preserved. Palaeontologists call these animals 'problematica'.

◀ *Trilobite fossils such as this are found in rocks around the world from the Cambrian, Ordovician and Silurian periods, between 542 and 410 mya. Many trilobite fossils are actually the remains of shed outer shells, or exoskeletons.*

35

The first invertebrates

▲ Charnia *was a prehistoric animal that grew in feather-like colonies attached to the seabed, like living sea pens.* Charnia *fossils date to around 700 mya.*

- **An invertebrate** is an animal that does not have a spinal column. Invertebrates were the first animals to live on Earth, in the prehistoric seas.

- **The very first animal-like** organisms that fed on other organisms or organic matter were single-celled and sometimes called protozoans.

- **Only prehistoric protozoans** with hard parts survive as fossils. The earliest fossils are around 700 million years old.

- **One of the earliest-known fossils** of a multi-celled animal is around 600 million years old. This is a creature called *Mawsonites*, which may have been a primitive jellyfish or worm.

- **Most of the earliest** invertebrate fossils are from extinct groups of animals.

- **Some of these animals** had segmented bodies that looked a bit like quilts.

- **One such invertebrate** is *Spriggina*, which is named after Reg Sprigg, a geologist. He discovered its fossilized remains near Ediacara in southern Australia in 1946.

- **Palaeontologists** have unearthed the fossils of many other jellyfish-like invertebrates from Ediacara.

- **Another famous** invertebrate discovery was made by Roger Mason, an English schoolboy, in 1957. This was the fossil of *Charnia*, an animal that was similar to a living sea pen.

> ...FASCINATING FACT...
> *Spriggina* has a curved, shieldlike end to one part of its body.
> Some palaeontologists think this was its head, while others
> think it was an anchor that secured it to the sea bed.

More early invertebrates

- **The early, quilted invertebrates** were extinct by the beginning of the Cambrian Period (542–490 mya).

- **Palaeontologists** regard their extinction as a loss that compares with the death of the dinosaurs at the end of the Cretaceous Period (around 65 mya).

- **Small, shelled invertebrates** emerged in the Early Cambrian Period.

- **These creatures included** the archaeocyathids, which had bodies that were like two cups, one inside the other.

- **Living animals** that most closely resemble archaeocyathids are sponges and corals.

- **Other small, shelled invertebrates** included animals such as *Tommotia* and *Latouchella*. They may have been early molluscs, the ancestors of snails and clams.

- ***Tommotia* and *Latouchella*** left behind fossils of their shells, which have strange-looking horns and tubes on the surface.

- **Other Early Cambrian invertebrates**, such as wormlike creatures, did not live in shells. Once predators began to appear, they would have made easy pickings.

- **Invertebrates** therefore evolved defences against hunters, such as a tough exoskeleton (outer skeleton).

- **Another defence** was hiding. Many invertebrates, from worms to arthropods, began to burrow into the sea floor.

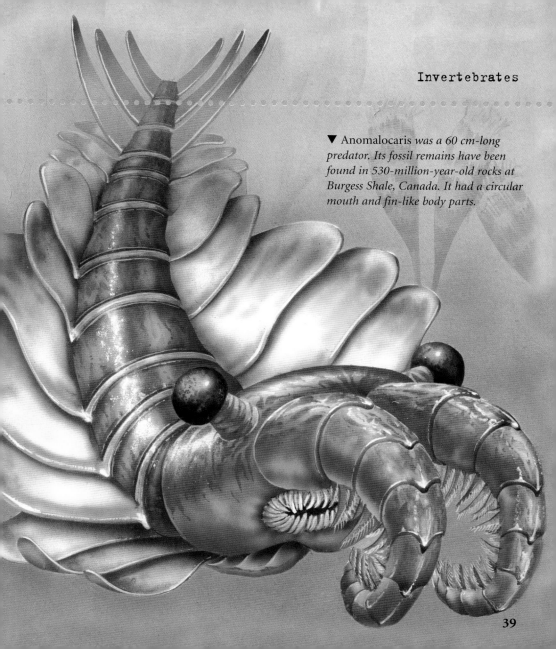

▼ Anomalocaris *was a 60 cm-long predator. Its fossil remains have been found in 530-million-year-old rocks at Burgess Shale, Canada. It had a circular mouth and fin-like body parts.*

Arthropods

- **Arthropods form** the largest single group of animals. They include insects, crustaceans (crabs or lobsters), arachnids (spiders) and myriapods (millipedes) – any creature with a segmented body and jointed limbs.

- **The earliest known remains** of arthropods come from the 530-million-year-old mudstone deposits of the Burgess Shale in Canada.

- *Marrella* is one of the most common fossils that were discovered at the Burgess Shale. It was about 2 cm long and had a head shield and two antennae.

- **Its body was divided into segments**, each of which had a jointed leg for scurrying over the seabed.

- **At first**, palaeontologists thought Marrella was a trilobite, but they now regard it as an entirely different type of arthropod.

- **Arthropods were one of the first** – if not the first – groups of animals to emerge from the sea and colonize the land, some time between 500 and 400 mya.

- **Arthropods** were well suited for living on land. Many of them had exoskeletons (outer skeletons) that prevented them from drying out. Their jointed limbs meant they could move over the ground.

- **Woodlice** may have been the very first arthropods on land. They feed on rotting plant material, which they would have found on seashores.

- **The largest-ever land arthropod** was a millipede-like creature called *Arthropleura*, which was 1.8 m long.

- ***Arthropleura* lived on the floor** of forests during the Carboniferous Period (355–298 mya). Like woodlice, it ate rotting plants.

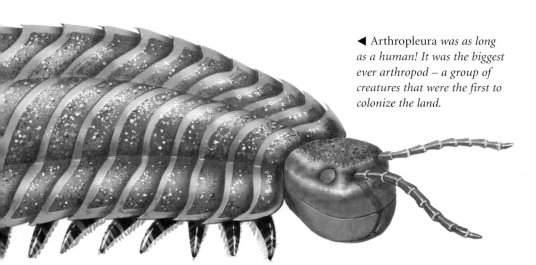

◀ Arthropleura *was as long as a human! It was the biggest ever arthropod – a group of creatures that were the first to colonize the land.*

Molluscs and graptolites

- **Modern molluscs** include gastropods (slugs, snails and limpets), bivalves (clams, oysters, mussels and cockles) and cephalopods (octopuses, squids and cuttlefish).

- **Modern and prehistoric molluscs** represent one of the most diverse animal groups ever to have lived.

- **The first molluscs** were tiny – about the size of a pinhead. They appeared at the beginning of the Cambrian Period, about 542 mya.

- **The first cephalopod molluscs** emerged towards the end of the Cambrian Period, around 490 mya.

- **One early cephalod** was *Plectronoceras*, which had a horn-shaped shell divided into different chambers.

- **Graptolites** had tentacles that they used to sieve food particles from water or the seabed.

- **Gastropod molluscs** (snails and slugs) were one of the first groups of animals to live on land.

- **Snails and slugs** are limited to where they can live on land as they require moist conditions.

- **Cephalopods** are the most highly developed of all molluscs. Squids and octopuses evolved big brains, good eyesight, tentacles and beaklike jaws.

- **Graptolites are an extinct group** of molluscs that lived in string-like communities, like lines. Graptolite means 'written stone' because the fossils of the lines of these creatures resemble scrawled handwriting.

◀ *This snail is a mollusc. Its features include a muscular foot, a head with eyes and tentacles and a shell. Today there are more than 100,000 living species of molluscs but many more times this number have lived in the past. They are very important as their shells make good fossils and some types evolved quickly, so their rapid-changing shapes are used as 'marker fossils' to date rocks.*

43

Ammonites

- **Ammonites** belong to the cephalopod group of molluscs.

- **They were once** widespread in the oceans, but, like the dinosaurs, died out at the end of the Cretaceous Period (about 65 mya).

- **The number** of ammonite fossils that have been found proves how plentiful these animals once were.

- **Ammonites** were predators and scavengers. They had very good vision, long seizing tentacles and powerful mouths.

- **Their mouths** consisted of sharp beaks, poisonous glands and a tooth-covered tongue.

- **Ammonites** had multi-chambered shells that contained gas and worked like flotation tanks, keeping the creatures afloat.

- *Stephanoceras* was an ammonite with a spiral, disc-shaped shell, 20 cm across. It was very common in the seas of the Mesozoic Era (250–65 mya).

- **The closest living** relative of ammonites is *Nautilus*, a cephalopod that lives near the seabed and feeds on shrimps.

- **People once thought** that ammonite fossils were the fossils of curled-up snakes.

- **Builders** have traditionally set ammonite fossils into the walls of buildings for decoration.

▶ *This shell protected the soft-bodied ammonite that lived inside it. Its tentacles would have poked out of the shell as it moved over the seabed, looking for food.*

Chambers

▶ *A rock containing an ammonite fossil, clearly displaying the shell's division into different chambers. The innermost chamber was the home of a newborn ammonite. As it grew, it built a bigger chamber and moved into it. When it outgrew that chamber it built another one, and so on, to form a spiral-patterned shell.*

45

Worms

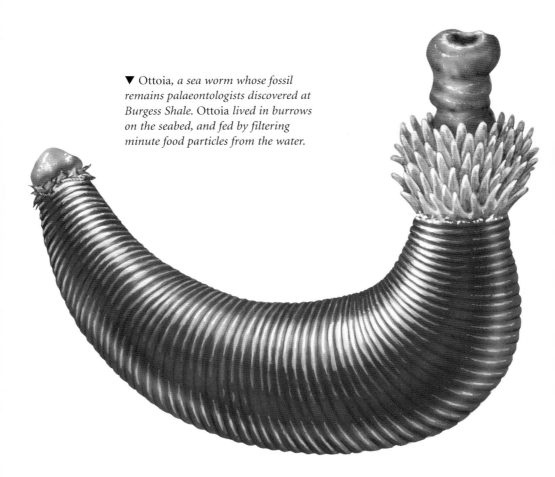

▼ Ottoia, *a sea worm whose fossil remains palaeontologists discovered at Burgess Shale.* Ottoia *lived in burrows on the seabed, and fed by filtering minute food particles from the water.*

- **Worms** are invertebrates that usually have long, soft, slender bodies.

- **They were among** the earliest multi-celled animals to live in the prehistoric seas.

- **The soft bodies** of worms means that they do not make good fossils.

- **Much of our knowledge** of prehistoric worms comes from trace fossils, which include tracks, tunnels and the impressions of their bodies in fine-grained rocks.

- **The tracks and trails** of early worms show that they were mobile creatures, which probably grazed the microbes that covered the sea floor.

- **The 530 million-year-old mudstone** deposits of the Burgess Shale in Canada contain the fossil impressions of worms.

- **Some of the Burgess Shale worms** like *Canadia* and *Burgessochaeta*, had thousands of hairlike bristles.

- *Canadia* is an annelid worm. In this type of worm, the body is divided into segments. Palaeontologists think that millipedes and other arthropods evolved from annelids.

- **Some types of worms,** such as serpulid worms, secrete tubes, which they live in and which contain durable minerals.

- **Remains of serpulids' tubes** are quite common in rocks of the Mesozoic and Cenozoic Eras (250 mya to the present).

Trilobites

- **Trilobites** belonged to the invertebrate group called arthropods – animals with segmented bodies and hard outer skeletons.

- **Trilobite** means 'three lobes'. Trilobites' hard outer shells were divided into three parts.

- **The first trilobites** appeared about 530 mya. By 500 mya, they had developed into many different types.

- **Trilobites** had compound eyes, like insects' eyes, which could see in many different directions at once.

- **Some trilobites** could roll up into a ball, like some woodlice do today. This was a useful means of protection.

- **Trilobites** had long, thin, jointed legs. They moved quickly over the seabed or sediment covering it.

- **Trilobites** moulted by shedding their outer skeletons. Most trilobite fossils are the remains of these shed skeletons.

- **One of the largest trilobites** was *Isotelus*, which grew up to 44 cm long.

- **Trilobites** could also be much smaller, such as *Conocoryphe,* which was about 2 cm long.

- **Trilobites** became extinct around 250 mya – along with huge numbers of other marine animals.

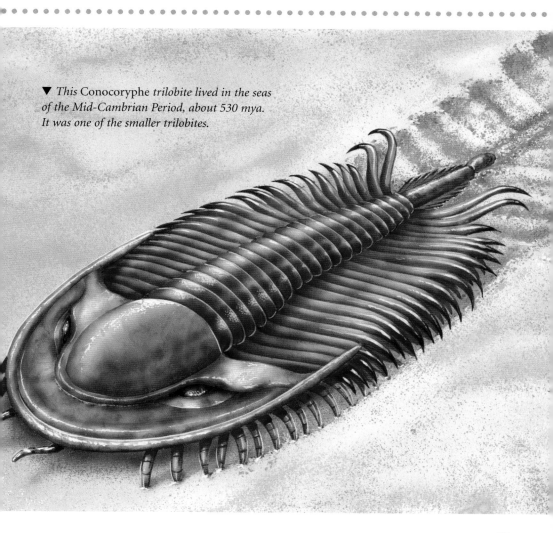

▼ *This* Conocoryphe *trilobite lived in the seas of the Mid-Cambrian Period, about 530 mya. It was one of the smaller trilobites.*

Pterygotus

- *Pterygotus* was an enormous water scorpion that grew up to 2.3 m long.

- **Fossils of** *Pterygotus* have been found in rocks of the Silurian Period (435–410 mya).

- *Pterygotus* was a fearsome hunter, equipped with large eyes and long claws.

- **It had two huge claws** (called chelicerae) for grasping prey, two paddles for swimming, and eight legs for chasing victims over the seabed and digging them up from the sediment.

- *Pterygotus* belonged to the group of invertebrates known as eurypterids (water scorpions).

- **Eurypterids** lived between 490 and 250 mya.

- **Not all eurypterids** were giants – some were only 10 cm long.

- **They were not** true scorpions, because their tail parts (called the opisthosoma) served as swimming paddles, not stinging weapons.

- *Pterygotus'* opisthosoma was long and ended in a flattened paddle. Palaeontologists think it swam by beating this paddle up and down.

> ...FASCINATING FACT...
> Dolphins swim by beating their tails up and
> down – which is how palaeontologists think
> *Pterygotus* swam.

▼ Pterygotus, *which was bigger than a human, was the largest arthropod (an animal with a segmented body and a hard outer skeleton) ever to have lived.*

Insects, centipedes and millipedes

- **Insects** evolved from sea-dwelling arthropods, such as trilobites. Like them, insects have segmented bodies, jointed legs and exoskeletons (external skeletons).

- **The first land-living insects** appeared in the Devonian Period (410–355 mya).

- **Insects** made the transition to breathing air on land by developing small tubes called tracheae in their bodies.

- *Rhyniella* was the first known land insect. It was a springtail – an insect still alive today, which eats rotting plants and flips itself into the air if disturbed.

- *Latzelia* was an early centipede that lived on damp forest floors in the Carboniferous Period (355–298 mya).

- *Latzelia* had poisonous fangs, which it used to kill worms and other insects.

- **Insects** were the first animals to achieve flight. Early flying insects had stiff wings, which stuck out from their bodies – similar to dragonflies' wings.

- **The Cretaceous Period** (144–65 mya) saw a big rise in the number of flying insects, because of the emergence of flowering plants.

- **Many flowering plants** rely on flying insects to spread their pollen, while flying insects, such as bees, rely on flowers for food (nectar and pollen).

- **Beelike insects** date back to the Late Cretaceous Period, while modern bees first appeared around 30 mya.

▲ *The evolution of winged, pollinating insects such as these honey bees is closely linked to the evolution of flowering plants. Bees, as well as other flying insects, help these plants to spread by carrying pollen from the male part of one flower to the female part of another as they feed off nectar.*

Spiders

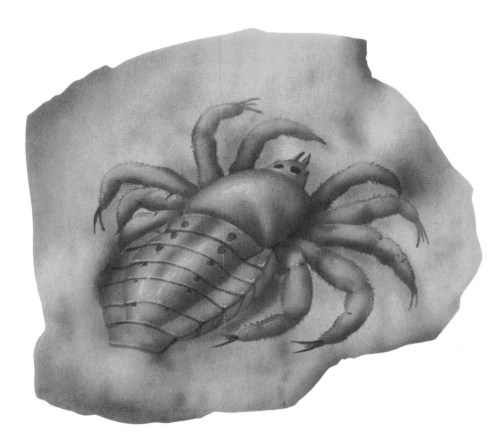

▲ Palaeocharinus *preserved in amber. Early spiders such as* Palaeocharinus *were among the first creatures to live on land.*

- **Spiders were among** the first land-dwelling animals.

- **One of the earliest-known spiders** is *Palaeocharinus*, which was discovered in 400-million-year-old rocks in Rhynie, Scotland.

- *Palaeocharinus* was 0.5 mm long. It would have hunted tiny mites that fed on rotting plant matter.

- **A later – but still early** – spider was *Arthrolycosa*, which lived in the Carboniferous Period (355–298 mya).

- *Arthrolycosa* had eight legs and eight eyes. It had poisonous chelae (claws) in front of its mouth, which it used to kill its prey.

- **Many early spiders** could spin only basic webs, which they may have used to cover their eggs or to line holes where they lived.

- **Spiders evolved** their silk-spinning skills during the Mesozoic Era (250–65 mya).

- **In order to catch** the increasing variety of flying insects, spiders began to spin intricate sheetlike and mazelike webs on the ground and between plants.

- **Spider experts** have an abundance of information about spiders from the Tertiary Period (65–1.6 mya) because so many were trapped in amber (ancient tree resin).

. . . FASCINATING FACT . . .
Amber spider fossils show that spiders have
changed little for the past 30 million years.

Monster mini-beasts

- **The biggest insects** ever known lived in the forests of the Carboniferous Period (355–298 mya).

- **The size** of flying insects increased with the size of trees in the Carboniferous forests. One explanation for this is that they needed to fly higher to feed on the insects that lived in the tall trees.

- *Meganeura* was the largest-known winged insect, with a wingspan of up to 70 cm. It lived during the Late Carboniferous Period.

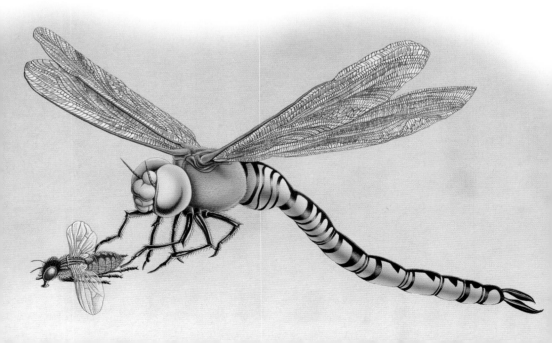

> ...FASCINATING FACT...
> Another huge Carboniferous dragonfly is known as the
> 'Bolsover dragonfly', since its remains were discovered
> in Bolsover, England. It was the size of a seagull.

- **Like modern dragonflies**, *Meganeura* was unable to fold back its wings when it was resting.

- **The Carboniferous forests** were also home to enormous millipedes. They are known to palaeontologists because of fossilized traces of their footprints. Some of these millipedes might have been as long as a human is tall.

- **Some millipedes** had poisonous fangs. A human-sized, poisonous millipede must have been a terrifying predator.

- **Mega-insects** did not live only in the Carboniferous Period. *Formicium giganteum* was a giant ant that lived about 45 mya.

- **Worker giant ants** grew up to 3 cm long, but queens were nearly 6 cm, with a wingspan of 13 cm – bigger than some small birds!

- ***Formicium giganteum's*** closest living relative is the red wood ant.

◀ *Like this modern-day dragonfly,*
Meganeura *had large bulging eyes that
allowed it to spot the movements of potential
prey. However,* Meganeura *could be up to
15 times the size of a living dragonfly, and
had much stronger legs.*

Fish fossils

▼ *A fossilized tooth from a prehistoric* Megalodon *shark (left), compared to a tooth from a modern great white shark (below). The most common fossil remains of fish, like many other vertebrates, are teeth because they are made of long-lasting enamel.*

- **Fish fossils** include bony plates, spines, scales, backbones and teeth.
- **Complete fish skeletons** are rare, especially in the earliest fish, which had gristly bones that do not fossilize well.
- **Some early fish** called ostracoderms were covered in body armour that does preserve well.

- **Ostracoderms' bony plates** are plentiful in rocks from Europe and North America that date from the Late Silurian and Early Devonian periods (420–400 mya).

- **Fish fossils can show** how the distribution and level of seas around the world has changed over time.

- **As well as the remains** of bones and scales, trace fossils of fish include spiral coils of their faeces (waste matter) and their intestines.

- **Palaeontologists** can estimate how old a fish was when it died by counting the number of growth rings in its fossilized scales.

- **It is rare** to find fossils of shark skeletons, because they are made of cartilage, which does not preserve as well as bone.

- **Prehistoric shark teeth** are much more common than skeletons. Many of them show what effective killers prehistoric sharks were – like their modern descendants.

. . . FASCINATING FACT . . .
In Wyoming, USA, more than one kilometre above sea level, fossil-hunters have found the remains of hundreds of different fish that once lived in a sea in the area.

Pikaia

- *Pikaia* was a small, wormlike creature that is thought to be the ancestor of all backboned animals.

- **Its fossil remains** were found in the 530 million-year-old mudstone deposits of the Burgess Shale in Canada.

- *Pikaia* was the first-known chordate, a group of animals with a stiff supporting rod, called a notochord, along their back. All vertebrates belong to this group, as well as marine animals called tunicates and acraniates.

- *Pikaia* was 5 cm long with a notochord (stiffening rod) running along its body – a kind of primitive spine that gave its body flexibility.

- **The notochord** also allowed the animal's simple muscles to work against it, and the animal's body organs to hang from it.

- *Pikaia* is very similar to a modern creature called *Branchiostoma,* a small, see-through creature that lives in the sand at the bottom of the sea.

- **As it lacks** a bony skeleton, a backbone, ribs, paired fins and jaws, *Pikaia* is not really a fish.

- *Pikaia* is a more complex creature than many other animals found in the Burgess Shale. It suggests that other complex creatures must have lived before it, although there is (as yet) no fossil evidence for this.

- **The head** of the *Pikaia* was very primitive, with a pair of tentacles, a mouth and a simple brain (a swelling of the nerve cord) for processing information.

- *Pikaia* swam in a zig-zag fashion, similar to a sea snake.

▲ Pikaia *looked a little like an eel with tail fins. The stiff rod that ran along its body developed, in later animals, into the backbone.*

61

Jawless fish

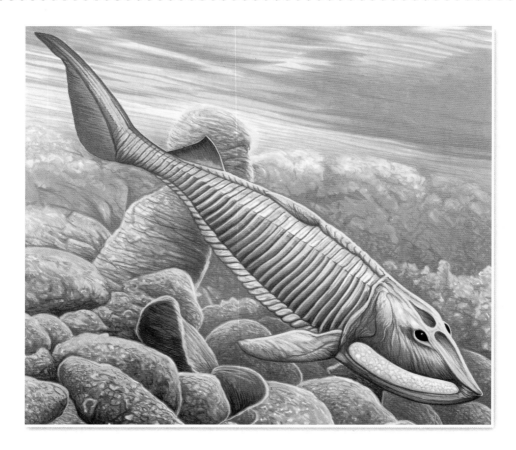

▲ *Early jawless fish such as* Hemicyclaspis, *could swim much farther and quicker than most invertebrates. This meant they could more easily search for and move to new feeding areas.*

- **The first fish** appeared in the Late Cambrian Period, about 500 mya.

- **These fish** had permanently gaping mouths – as they had no jaws they could not open and close their mouths.

- **Early fish** were called agnathans, which means 'jawless'.

- **Agnathans** ate by sieving plankton through their simple mouth opening, as well as scooping up algae on the seabed.

- **Among the oldest** complete agnathan fossils are *Arandaspis,* which comes from Australia, and *Sacabambaspis*, which comes from Bolivia.

- *Hemicyclaspis* was another agnathan. It was a very flat fish, with a broad head shield and a long tail.

- **Later jawless fish** had more streamlined, deeper bodies and eyes at the front of their heads. This suggests they were not restricted to the seabed.

- **Most jawless fish** died out by the end of the Devonian Period (around 350 mya).

- **Living relatives of agnathans** include lampreys and hagfish, which have soft bodies and look like eels. Like agnathans, they are also jawless.

> ... **FASCINATING FACT** ...
> *Hemicyclaspis* had eyes on top of its head. This
> suggests it lived on the seabed, and used its eyes to
> keep a lookout for predators above.

Jawed fish

- **The first jawed fish** emerged in the Early Silurian Period (about 430 mya).

- **Palaeontologists** call jawed fish acanthodians, a name that comes from the Greek word *akantha,* meaning 'thorn' or 'spine'.

- **Jaws and teeth** gave acanthodians a huge advantage over jawless fish – they could eat a greater variety of food and defend themselves more effectively.

- **Jaws and teeth** allowed acanthodians to become predators.

- **Acanthodians' jaws** evolved from structures called gill arches in the pharynx, the tube in vertebrates that runs from the mouth to the stomach.

- **Gill arches** are bony rods and muscles that surround the gills, the breathing organs of a fish.

- **As acanthodians developed** jaws, so they developed teeth, too.

- **The earliest** fish teeth were conelike shapes along the jaw, made out of bone and coated with hard enamel.

- **The teeth** of early acanthodians varied greatly. In some species they were sharp and spiky, in others they were like blades while in others they resembled flat plates.

...FASCINATING FACT...
Another difference between jawed and jawless fish was that jawed fish had a pair of nostrils, while jawless fishes only had one.

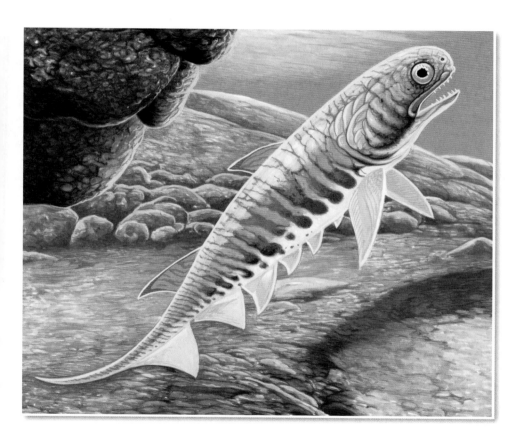

▲ A Climatius, *a type of acanthodian or jawed fish, that lived around 400 mya. Another name for acanthodians is 'spiny sharks' – although they were not sharks, many had spines on the edges of their fins.*

Placoderms

- **Placoderms** were jawed fish that had bony plates covering the front part of the body.

- **They appeared** in the Late Silurian Period (about 415 mya) and were abundant in the seas of the Devonian Period (410–355 mya).

- **Placoderm** means 'plated skin'. The plating provided placoderms – especially the smaller species – with protection against predators.

- **Most placoderms** were larger than acanthodians (the first jawed fish). They ranged in size from 30 cm to 10 m in length.

- **There were two groups** of placoderms – arthrodires and antiarchs.

- **Arthrodires** had a ball-and-socket joint between the head and the front part of the body, which meant they could turn their head in many directions.

◄ Bothriolepis *had eyes on the top of its head. Its mouth was lined by a set of cutting plates and was situated under the head. These features lead alaeontologists to believe that* Bothriolepis *was a bottom-dwelling sediment feeder.*

● **Arthrodires** were predators, armed with powerful jaws and sharp teeth. They were very fast swimmers.

● **Antiarchs** were much smaller than arthrodires. Like arthrodires, antiarchs' head and the front part of its body were covered in bony plates.

● **Antiarchs** also had a pectoral (front end) fin connected to its head plates. Palaeontologists think they might have used this fin as a leg, to help it move over the seabed.

> **. . . FASCINATING FACT . . .**
> *Dunkleosteus* was an arthrodire. It was a huge fish, which could grow up to 10 m long. It was probably the biggest animal of its time, and is named after the man who discovered it, Dr David Dunkle.

Sharks

◄ Hybodus *was a blunt-headed prehistoric shark that lived between 250 and 125 mya, in the time of the dinosaurs. It looked quite similar to modern sharks, but had very different jaws.*

...FASCINATING FACT...
Prehistoric sharks' jaws were fixed to the side of their skull, while modern sharks' jaws hang beneath their braincase, which gives them a more powerful bite.

- **The earliest-known** shark fossils come from rock layers of the Early Devonian Period (410–355 mya).

- **Sharks** belong to the group known as cartilaginous fish, which also includes rays and skates. Their skeletons are made from cartilage, not bone.

- *Cladoselache* was a prehistoric shark, which could grow up to 2 m long.

- *Cladoselache* appears to have been quite similar to a modern shark – it had a streamlined body, a pair of dorsal (back) fins and triangular-shaped pectoral (front end) fins.

- **Early sharks** hunted squid, small fish and crustaceans.

- *Stethacanthus* was a prehistoric shark that looked nothing like a modern one. It had an anvil-shaped projection above its head, which was covered in teeth.

- *Stethacanthus* lived in the Carboniferous Period (355–298 mya).

- **Sharks** are at the top of the food chain in modern seas, but this was not the case during the Devonian Period.

- **Placoderms**, such as *Dunkleosteus,* dwarfed even the biggest sharks, and ate them for breakfast!

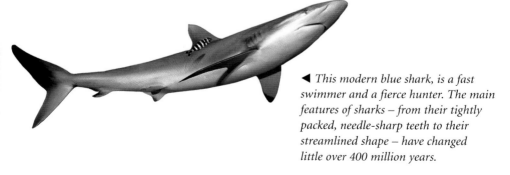

◄ *This modern blue shark, is a fast swimmer and a fierce hunter. The main features of sharks – from their tightly packed, needle-sharp teeth to their streamlined shape – have changed little over 400 million years.*

Bony fish

- **Bony fish** have internal skeletons and external scales made of bone.

- **They first appeared** in the Late Devonian Period (around 360 mya).

- **Bony fish** evolved into the most abundant and varied fish in the seas.

- **There are two types** of bony fish – ray-finned fish and lobe-finned fish.

- **There were plenty** of prehistoric lobe-finned fish, but only a few species survive today. They belong to one of two groups – lungfish or coelacanths.

- **Amphibians** – and, ultimately, reptiles and mammals – evolved from lobe-finned fish.

- **Ray-finned fish** were so-called because of the bony rays that supported their fins. Most early ray-finned fish were small, ranging in size from about 5 cm to 20 cm long.

- *Rhadinichthys* and *Cheirolepis* were two early ray-finned fish. They were small predators, equipped with good swimming ability and snapping jaws.

- **Around 250 mya,** ray-finned fish lost many of the bony rays from their fins. The fins became less stiff and more flexible – and the fish became better swimmers.

- **New types of ray-finned fish,** called teleosts, also developed more symmetrical tails and thinner scales.

▶ *This modern-day coelacanth is a direct descendant of the lobe-finned bony fish that lived 350 mya. Coelacanths were thought to be extinct until a fisherman caught one off the coast of South Africa in 1938.*

Fins

- **The earliest fish** did not have fins. The first fish to have them were acanthodians (jawed fish).

- **Acanthodians** were the first fish predators. Fins gave them manoeuvrability, which they needed when chasing their prey.

- **Fins allow fish** to make quick or subtle changes in direction.

- **They also help fish** to stay afloat and counter the pull of gravity, since their bones and muscles are denser than water.

- **This explains why** most agnathans (jawless fish), which lacked fins, lived on the bottom of seas – it meant they did not have to struggle against gravity.

- **Pectoral fins,** at the front end of a fish, help to keep it level and counteract its tendency to pitch forward at the front because of the weight of the head.

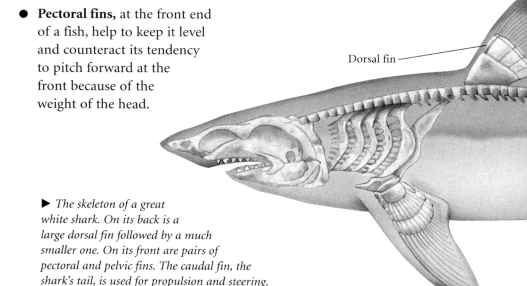

Dorsal fin

▶ *The skeleton of a great white shark. On its back is a large dorsal fin followed by a much smaller one. On its front are pairs of pectoral and pelvic fins. The caudal fin, the shark's tail, is used for propulsion and steering.*

Pectoral fin

- **Dorsal fins**, on a fish's back, and pelvic and anal fins at its rear, stop it from rolling over.

- **The first acanthodians** to have fins had a pair of dorsal fins, a single anal fin beneath the tail and a varying number of pairs of fins on their undersides.

- **Later bony fish** developed pairs of fins that were borne by lobes, or projections, of bone and muscle. They were called lobe-finned fish.

- **The fins** of lobe-finned fishes evolved into the limbs of amphibians.

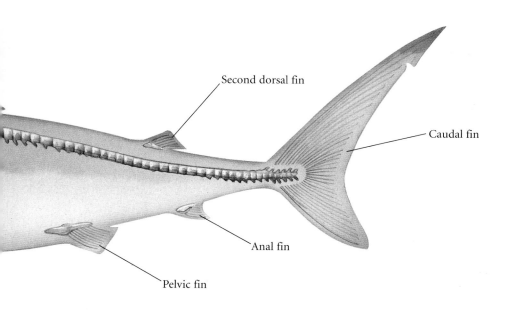

Second dorsal fin

Caudal fin

Anal fin

Pelvic fin

Amphibian fossils

- **A fossil of an animal** from which amphibians probably evolved has been found in Lode, Latvia. This is *Panderichthys*, a fish with paired muscular fins, from which limbs developed.

- **The skull** of *Panderichthys* is nearly identical to that of later amphibians.

- **Fossil remains** of *Acanthostega* and *Ichthyostega*, two of the earliest amphibians, come from river and lake deposits in Greenland dating to the Late Devonian Period (370–355 mya).

- **One of the most important sites** for amphibian fossils was discovered in East Kirkton, Scotland, in the 1980s.

- **The East Kirkton fossils** include early salamander-like amphibians such as *Balanerpeton woodi*.

- **They also include** several animals that combine amphibian and reptile features, particularly *Westlothiana lizziae*, named after the West Lothian region of Scotland.

- **Another important amphibian fossil** site was discovered in Iowa, USA, in 1985. Like East Kirkton, this site dates from the Early Carboniferous Period (355–315 mya).

- **The fossils from Iowa include jaws** with teeth, pelvic and shoulder bones, backbones and ribs.

- **Some of the Iowan fossils** are of amphibians as large as alligators, while others are as small as salamanders.

- **Like spiders and insects**, small amphibians such as frogs could also be trapped in amber (ancient tree resin).

▶ *Fossil remains of* Acanthostega. *Palaeontologists had to work hard to figure out what the animal looked like and how it moved from the jumbled-up bones they found.*

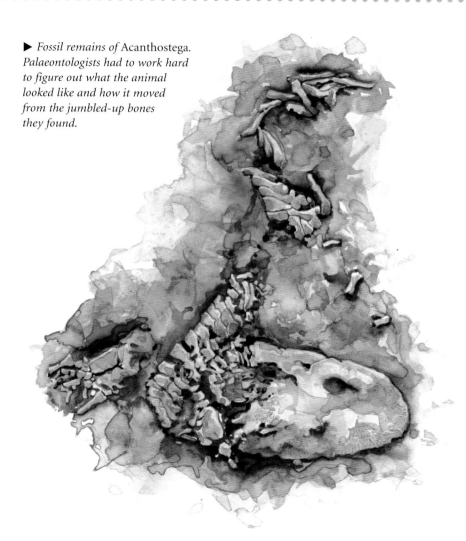

From fins to limbs

- **The first land-dwelling** backboned animals were called tetrapods. They needed legs to hold up their bodies and move around in search of water and food.

- **Tetrapods** evolved from lobe-finned fish, which had all the right body parts to develop arms and legs.

- **The fossil skeleton** of the lobe-finned fish *Eusthenopteron* shows that the organization of bones in its front and rear fins was similar to the arrangement of limbs in tetrapods.

- *Eusthenopteron* lived in shallow waters. It could use its fins as primitive legs and move over the land if the waters dried out.

- **Recent research suggests** that another lobe-finned fish, *Panderichthys*, could more effectively use its fins as limbs than *Eusthenopteron*. According to scientists, *Panderichthys* was more like a tetrapod than a fish.

- **The front fins** in lobe-finned fish connected to a shoulder girdle, while the rear fins connected to a hip girdle. These girdles connected to the backbone.

- **These hip and shoulder** connections meant that the limbs of future tetrapods were connected to a skeleton, which prevented the limbs from pressing against the inside of the body and damaging it.

... FASCINATING FACT ...
Suitable fins were not the only feature that meant lobe-finned fish could evolve into land-dwelling animals. They also had lungs for breathing air!

- **The shoulder girdle** of lobe-finned fish also connected to their heads. Tetrapods, however, developed heads that were separated from their shoulders and joined instead by a neck.

- **Necks** were a great advantage to land-living animals. They could use them to bend down to feed, to reach up for food, and to turn around to see.

▲ Eusthenopteron *using its fins to move out of the water.* Eusthenopteron, *which means 'good strong fin', was once thought to be the closest ancestor to tetrapods. However palaeontologists have recently discovered that another fish,* Panderichthys, *was an even closer relative.*

Tetrapods

- **Tetrapod** means 'four-legged'. All early tetrapods were amphibians as they were animals that could survive in water and on land.

- **The first tetrapods** emerged in the Late Devonian Period (about 360 mya).

- **They lived in warm**, shallow freshwater lakes and rivers. They developed limbs and lungs to cope with the waters drying out and this enabled them to move to new habitats.

- **The size of tetrapods** increased during the Carboniferous Period (355–298 mya). This may have been because there was more oxygen in the atmosphere, produced by the huge Carboniferous forests.

- **Tetrapods** adapting to the land had to face a range of challenges such as greater temperature variations, and more ultraviolet radiation from the Sun.

▶ Eogyrinus
was an amphibious
tetrapod that lived around
310 mya. It grew up to 4.5 m long
and had a skull similar to a crocodile's
and a body similar to an eel's.

- **The early tetrapod**s were called labyrinthodonts, because of their labyrinth-like tooth structure. These animals include *Ichthyostega, Protogyrinus, Eogyrinus* and *Diadectes*.

- ***Diadectes*** is the earliest-known plant-eating vertebrate. It was 3 m long and had small jaws with blunt teeth.

- **Modern amphibians** can be less than 10 cm long, while early tetrapods could grow up to 2 m.

- **Like their living descendants**, frogs and newts, early tetrapods laid eggs in water that hatched into tadpoles

---

. . . FASCINATING FACT . . .

Some early tetrapods had seven digits (fingers and toes). Others had six or even eight. Eventually all tetrapods evolved to have five digits.

Breathing air

- **Fish** breathe oxygen in water through their gills. When a fish is out of the water, these gills collapse.

- **For creatures to adapt** to living on land, they had to develop air-breathing lungs.

- **Tetrapods** were not the first creatures to develop lungs – this step was taken by lobe-finned fish.

- **Lungfish** are lobe-fins that still exist today. They live in hot places and, when rivers dry out, bury themselves in mud and breathe through lungs.

- **Early tetrapods,** such as *Ichthyostega* and *Acanthostega,* had gills and lungs, which suggests they could breathe in both air and water.

- **Later tetrapods** breathed through gills when they were first born, but, like modern frogs and newts, their gills shrank when they got older and were replaced by lungs.

- **Modern amphibians** also take in oxygen through their skin, which is soft and moist.

- **Early tetrapods** had tougher skin, so were unable to breathe through it.

- **Breathing through skin** limits an animal's size, which is why modern amphibians are much smaller than many of their prehistoric ancestors.

> ...FASCINATING FACT...
> Animals could only evolve to live on land because of the
> work of plants over millions of years, producing oxygen
> that became part of Earth's atmosphere.

▼ *Prehistoric lungfish had lungs as well as gills. Like these modern lungfish, they were able to breathe air if the pools or rivers they lived in dried out.*

Acanthostega

▲ Acanthostega *may have evolved from lobe-finned fish such as* Eusthenopteron *and* Panderichthys. *It shared a number of features with these fish, including a similar set of gills and lungs, as well as tail fin and braincase.*

- *Acanthostega* was one of the earliest tetrapods. It had a fishlike body, which suggests it spent most of its life in water.

- **Its fossil remains** were found in rock strata dating from the Late Devonian Period (around 370 mya).

- *Acanthostega's* **body** was about 1 m long.

- **It had a wide tail**, which would have been useful for swimming but inconvenient for moving on land.

- **Its legs** were well-developed, however, with eight toes on the front feet and seven on the rear ones.

- **The number of toes** on its feet surprised palaeontologists – they had previously thought all tetrapods had five toes.

- *Acanthostega's* **legs and toes** would have helped give its body a thrusting motion when it swam. They would also help it move through underwater plants at the bottom of rivers and lakes in search of prey.

- *Acanthostega* had a flattened skull, and its eye sockets were placed close together on the top of its head.

- **A complete** but jumbled-up *Acanthostega* fossil was discovered in hard rock in Greenland. Palaeontologists had to work very carefully to prise the fossil from the rock.

· · · **FASCINATING FACT** · · ·
Acanthostega had fishlike gills for breathing
water as well as lungs for breathing air.

Ichthyostega

- *Ichthyostega* was another early tetrapod. Like *Acanthostega,* it was discovered in Greenland in rock that was 370 million years old.

- **Its body** was around 1 m long. Palaeontologists think it was probably covered in scales.

- *Ichthyostega* had a flat head, a long snout, large jaws and teeth.

- **Its body** was barrel shaped. It had short, strong legs and a fishlike tail.

- **This tetrapod** ate small fish and shellfish, but would have been prey for large fish.

- *Ichthyostega* had a skull that was completely solid apart from its eye sockets. This meant that there were no holes around which jaw muscles could attach.

- **Without proper jaw muscles,** *Ichthyostega* and other early tetrapods could do little more than snap their jaws open and shut.

- **Like *Acanthostega***, *Ichthyostega* was more suited to swimming than walking. It used its legs for paddles, and its tail for manoeuvrability.

- *Ichthyostega* also used its limbs and feet for holding onto plants and digging for shellfish.

- *Ichthyostega* and *Acanthostega* show how animals were slowly adapting from a life in water to one on land.

▼ Scientists think that Ichthyostega's *shape and behaviour were similar to that of seals. Like seals, it could probably tuck its limbs alongside its body when swimming. On land, it might have used its forelimbs to drag the rest of its body over the ground.*

Temnospondyls

- **Temnospondyls** were a group of tetrapods that emerged in the Carboniferous Period (355–298 mya). They were some of the biggest early tetrapods.

- *Gerrothorax* was a temnospondyl. It grew up to 1 m or more long and had a flattened body shape and a very wide, flat head, with eyes on top.

- *Gerrothorax* looked a little like an enormous tadpole. It probably spent most of its time in water rather than on land.

- **Its flat body shape** suited it to a life spent hunting by lying at the bottom of swampy waters and ambushing passing fish.

- **Other temnospondyls,** such as *Paracyclotosaurus* and *Cyclotosaurus,* had rounder bodies and thinner, sharper heads with powerful teeth and jaws – like an alligator's.

▶ Gerrothorax *was an aquatic temnospondyl of the Late Triassic Period (215–208 mya). Like most other temnospondyls, it was a predator.*

- *Gerrothorax*, *Paracyclotosaurus* and *Cyclotosaurus* were all suited to watery habitats, but other temnospondyls show more adaptations for living on land.

- **One temnospondyl** that had a land-adapted body was the sturdily built *Cacops*, which grew to about 40 cm long.

- **A much bigger** land-living temnospondyl was *Eryops*, which grew to about 2 m in length.

- **Temnospondyls** were the most successful land predators of their day.

- **They were all** destined for extinction, however. Temnospondyls were not the ancestors of reptiles – this role belonged to smaller tetrapods.

Lepospondyls

- **Lepospondyls** were another group of early tetrapods. Like temnospondyls, they first appeared between 350 and 300 mya.

- **Lepospondyls** were small animals, often about the size of modern-day newts (10–15 cm long).

- **Their backbones** differed from temnospondyls' backbones.

- **Lepospondyls** also had simpler teeth and fewer bones in their skulls than temnospondyls.

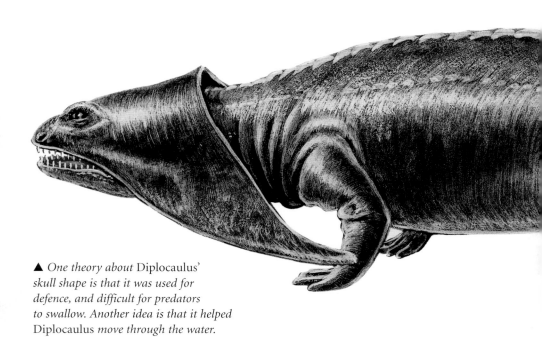

▲ *One theory about* Diplocaulus' *skull shape is that it was used for defence, and difficult for predators to swallow. Another idea is that it helped* Diplocaulus *move through the water.*

- *Diplocaulus* was a lepospondyl with strange wing shapes, which looked a bit like a boomerang, protruding from its skull.

- **It lived** in the Mid Permian Period (about 275 mya).

- **One *Diplocaulus* fossil** was found in Texas, USA. It was 0.8 m long.

- *Diplocaulus* lived in freshwater streams. Its oddly shaped head probably increased its manoeuvrability in the water, like the rudder on a submarine.

- **Lepospondyls** were controversial creatures. Some palaeontologists argue that they were the ancestors of modern amphibians.

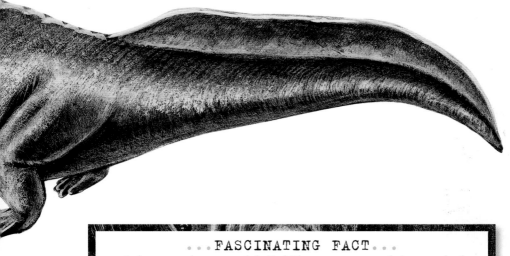

...FASCINATING FACT...
At least one lepospondyl, *Ophiderpeton*, reversed the trend of the tetrapods by losing all its legs so that it resembled an eel.

Frogs and salamanders

- **Modern amphibians,** such as frogs, toads, salamanders and newts, all belong to the group called the lissamphibians.

- **Lissamphibians** evolved later than the early tetrapods, between the Late Carboniferous and Early Triassic Periods (300–240 mya).

- ***Triadobatrachus*** lived in the Early Triassic Period, in Madagascar and was 10 cm long.

▼ Triadobatrachus *was the earliest-known frog.*
Frogs and salamanders are descendants of a group
of amphibious temnospondyls known as dissorophids.

- **Triadobatrachus** had a froglike skull. Compared to earlier amphibians, it had a shortened back, with fewer spinal bones, and a shortened tail.

- **Evolution** did not stop with *Triadobatrachus* – modern frogs have even fewer spinal bones and no tail at all.

- **Triadobatrachus**' hind legs were roughly the same size as its front legs. Again, this is different to modern frogs, which have long hind legs for hopping.

- **Karaurus** is the first known salamander. It lived in the Late Jurassic Period (around 150 mya) in Kazakhstan. It was 19 cm long, with a broad skull.

- **More modern-looking frog** and salamander fossils have been discovered in Messel, Germany. They date from the Early Eocene Epoch (around 50 mya).

- **Some Messel frog fossils** have their legs bent, as if they were in mid-hop. There are even tadpole fossils from Messel.

> ...FASCINATING FACT...
> *Andrias scheuchzerii* was a salamander from the Miocene Epoch (24–5 mya). It was named after the Swiss scientist Johannes Scheuchzer, who discovered it in 1726.

Reptile fossils

- **The first reptile** fossils exist in rock strata (layers) of the Carboniferous Period (355–298 mya).

- **The fossil record** for reptiles shows that all reptile groups – from pelycosaurs to dinosaurs – lived all over the world during their time.

- **Far fewer** early reptile fossils have been found in South America or Australia than in other parts of the world. Palaeontologists believe this is because they were not well preserved or have not yet been discovered.

- **Reptile fossils** can be preserved in very dry conditions, such as deserts, or can be buried under sediment.

- **Reptile fossils** discovered in desert conditions include entire dinosaur skeletons, found in sandstone in Mongolia.

- **The *Ichthyosaurus*** and *Plesiosaurus* fossils were discovered in Lyme Regis, England in the early 19th century. They forced many scientists to realize that creatures that had once existed had become extinct.

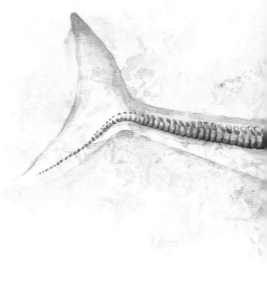

- **The fossil record** shows that numbers of flying reptiles and sea reptiles, together with some groups of dinosaurs, were in decline before the end of the Cretaceous Period (144–65 mya).

- **Messel**, near Frankfurt in Germany, is an important site for reptile fossils from the Early Tertiary Period, about 50 mya.

- **Reptile remains** from Messel include snakes, iguanas and an armoured lizard called *Xestops*.

...•**FASCINATING FACT**•...
When the fossils of the large sea reptiles *Ichthyosaurus* and *Plesiosaurus* were discovered, people thought they were sea dragons.

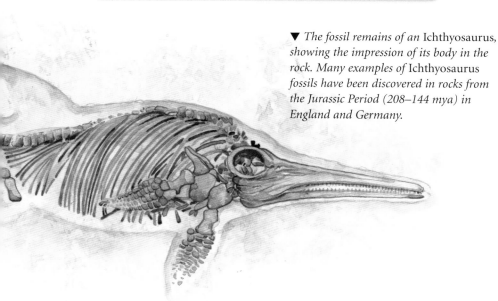

▼ *The fossil remains of an* Ichthyosaurus, *showing the impression of its body in the rock. Many examples of* Ichthyosaurus *fossils have been discovered in rocks from the Jurassic Period (208–144 mya) in England and Germany.*

First reptiles

- **Reptiles** evolved from amphibians during the Carboniferous Period (355–298 mya).

- **Unlike amphibians,** which usually live near and lay their eggs in water, reptiles are much more adapted for a life on land.

- **Compared to amphibians**, reptiles had better limbs for walking, a more effective circulatory system for moving blood around their bodies, and bigger brains.

- **They also had more powerful** jaw muscles than amphibians and would have been better predators. Early reptiles ate millipedes, spiders and insects.

- **One of the earliest reptiles** was a small creature called *Hylonomus,* which lived in the Mid Carboniferous Period.

- *Hylonomus* lived in forests on the edges of lakes and rivers. Fossil remains of this reptile have been found inside the stumps of clubmoss trees.

- **Another early reptile** was *Paleothyris*. Like *Hylonomus*, it was about 20 cm long, and had a smaller head than amphibians.

- **One animal** that represents a staging post between amphibians and reptiles is *Westlothiana lizziae,* which was discovered in Scotland in the 1980s.

- *Westlothiana lizziae* lived in the Early Carboniferous Period (about 340 mya).

- **At first** palaeontologists thought that *Westlothiana lizziae* was the oldest reptile. But its backbone, head and legs are closer to those of an amphibian.

▶ Hylonomus, *meaning 'forest mouse', was one of the earliest reptiles. Fossil hunters discovered its remains in fossilized tree stumps at Joggins in Nova Scotia, Canada.*

Eggs

- **Reptiles' eggs** are a major evolutionary advance over amphibians' eggs.

- **Early amphibians,** like modern ones, laid their eggs in water. This is because their eggs were covered in jelly (like modern frogspawn) and would dry out on land.

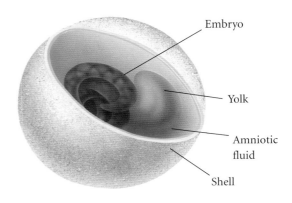

▲ *Amphibians lay their eggs, such as this frogspawn, in water.*

- **Reptiles** evolved eggs that were covered by a shell. This meant they could lay them on land and they would not dry out.

- **One advantage** of shelled eggs was that reptiles did not have to return to water to lay them.

- **Another advantage** was that reptiles could hide their eggs on land. Eggs laid in water are easy pickings for hungry animals.

- **Reptiles' embryos** complete all their growth phases inside eggs – when they hatch they look like miniature adults.

▶ *Reptiles broke the link between reproduction and water by laying hard-shelled eggs on land. This snake shell contains the developing young (the embryo), a food store (the yolk) and a protective liquid (the amniotic fluid).*

Embryo

Yolk

Amniotic fluid

Shell

- **In contrast**, baby amphibians hatch out of their eggs as larvae, such as tadpoles. They live in water and breathe through gills before they develop lungs and can live on land.

- **Reptile shells** are hard, and protect the growing reptile embryos. They also provide them with food while they develop.

- **During the evolution** from amphibians to reptiles, some tetrapods laid jelly-covered eggs on land.

- **A number** of living amphibians lay jelly-covered eggs on land, including some tropical frogs and mountain salamanders.

▼ *A female snake protecting her eggs. Eggs laid on land are easier to protect than those laid in water.*

Skulls

- **The jaws of reptiles** are another feature that shows the evolutionary progression from amphibians.

- **Amphibians' jaws** are designed to snap but not to bite together tightly.

- **In contrast**, reptiles had more jaw muscles and could press their jaws together more firmly. This meant they could break insect body casings and chew through tough plant stems.

- **By the Late Carboniferous Period** (about 300 mya), reptiles developed openings in their skulls, behind the eye socket. These openings allowed room for more jaw muscles.

- **Four types of reptile skull** developed. Each belonged to a different type of reptile.

- **Anapsids** had no openings in their skull other than the eye sockets. Turtles and tortoises are anapsids.

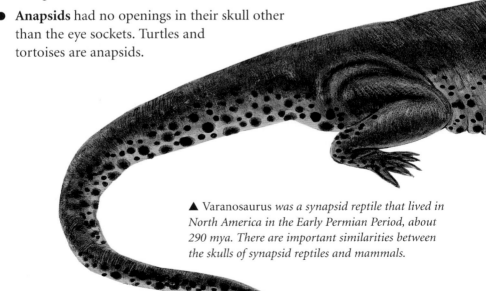

▲ Varanosaurus *was a synapsid reptile that lived in North America in the Early Permian Period, about 290 mya. There are important similarities between the skulls of synapsid reptiles and mammals.*

- **Euryapsids** had one opening high up on either side of the skull. Sea reptiles, such as ichthyosaurs, were euryapsids, but this group has no surviving relatives.

- **Synapsids** had one opening low down on either side of the skull. Mammals are descended from this group.

- **Diapsids** had two openings on either side of the skull. Dinosaurs and pterosaurs were diapsids; so too are birds and crocodiles.

...FASCINATING FACT...
Plants developed tough stems and leaves, spines and poisons to protect themselves frum hungry reptiles.

Synapsids

- **Synapsids** were a group of reptiles that had a pair of openings on their lower skull, behind the eye socket, onto which their jaw muscles attached.

- **Synapsids** are the ancestors of mammals, which explains why they are sometimes called 'mammal-like reptiles'.

- **These reptiles** first appeared in the Late Carboniferous Period (about 310 mya). They became the dominant land animals in the Permian and Triassic Periods (298–208 mya).

- **The first synapsids** are called pelycosaurs. They were large, heavy-bodied animals that walked a bit like modern-day crocodiles.

- **The fierce meateater** *Dimetrodon* and the plant-eating *Edaphosaurus* – both of which had long, fanlike spines on their backs – were pelycosaurs.

- **Later synapsids** are called therapsids. The earliest therapsids had bigger skulls and jaws than pelycosaurs, as well as longer legs and shorter tails.

- **Later therapsids** are divided into two subgroups – dicynodonts and cynodonts. Dicynodont means 'two dog teeth' – cynodont means 'dog tooth'.

- **Dicynodonts** were herbivores. Most had round, hippopotamus-shaped bodies and beaks that they used to cut plant stems.

- **Cynodonts** were carnivores. They used different teeth in their mouth for different tasks – for stabbing, nipping and chewing.

- **Cynodonts** were the most mammal-like of all reptiles. Some had whiskers and may even have been warm-blooded.

▶ Diictodon *was a mammal-like reptile that lived about 260 mya. A plant-eater and a burrower,* Diictodon *was an advanced form of a synapsid known as a dicynodont.*

Dimetrodon

- *Dimetrodon* was an early synapsid reptile called a pelycosaur.

- **It was a carnivore,** and was one of the first land animals that could kill creatures its own size (about 3.5 m long).

- *Dimetrodon* had a tall, skinny fin – a bit like a sail – running along its backbone. This fin was formed by a row of long spines that grew out of separate vertebrae.

- **Blood flowing** inside this sail would have been warmed by the early morning sun and carried to the rest of the body. The sail could also have radiated heat out, preventing overheating.

- **As a result**, *Dimetrodon* would warm up more quickly than other reptiles, so it could hunt them while they were still sluggish, cold or asleep.

- *Dimetrodon* had a deep skull and sharp, dagger-like teeth of different sizes. Its name means 'two shapes of teeth'.

- **In contrast with** other sail-backed pelycosaurs such as the herbivore *Edaphosaurus*, *Dimetrodon* had lightly built limbs and was a fairly fast mover.

- *Dimetrodon* was one of the dominant land predators between 280 and 260 mya.

- **After that time**, however, other reptiles, known as archosaurs, began to eclipse *Dimetrodon* because they were even bigger and better hunters.

- *Dimetrodon* was extinct by the beginning of the Triassic Period (about 250 mya).

▼ *As well as allowing its body to quickly warm up or cool down,* Dimetrodon's *large fin might have helped it to attract mates or ward off rivals.*

Moschops

- *Moschops* was a later synapsid reptile called a therapsid. It also belonged to a group of reptiles called dinocephalians (meaning 'terrible heads'), because it had a very big skull.

- **It was a plant eater**, and was probably preyed upon by large flesh-eating dinocephalians, such as *Titanosuchus*.

- *Moschops* lived in the Permian Period (298–250 mya) in southern Africa.

- **It grew up to 5 m long**. It had a squat body and a short tail. Stocky limbs held it well off the ground.

- *Moschops* had many peglike, chisel-edged teeth, which were adapted for biting and uprooting plant matter.

- **Its back** sloped downwards from the front, rather like a giraffe's.

- **It had enormous limb girdles** for both its front and rear legs, to support its heavy weight.

- *Moschops* had a high skull with a thick bone on top, which it may have used to head-butt its rivals or enemies.

- **Its skull bones** became thicker as it got older. This thickening of the skull is called pachyostosis.

- **While *Moschops'* skull** was very big, its brain was not. 'Bone head' might be a good nickname for it!

▼ *The bones on the top of* Moschops' *skull could be up to 10 cm thick – enough to withstand the blows from head-butting rivals or enemies.*

105

Cynognathus

- **Cynognathus** was a therapsid reptile called a cynodont.
- **It lived** in the Early to Mid Triassic Period (250–220 mya).
- *Cynognathus* was the size of a large wolf, and weighed between 40 and 50 kg.
- **Its skull** was about 40 cm long, and its total body length was around 2 m.
- **Like modern wolves**, *Cynognathus* was an active predator.
- *Cynognathus* had some very mammal-like features. Palaeontologists think it may have been warm-blooded, may have had hair on its skin, and may have given birth to live young.
- **One of the many features** *Cynognathus* had in common with mammals was a bony palate that separated the mouth from the nasal cavity, and allowed it to breathe while it was eating.
- **Its teeth** were similar to a dog's. It had incisors (front teeth) for cutting, canines (teeth next to incisors) for piercing and molars (cheek teeth) for slicing.
- **The legs** were designed for fast running – they were tucked underneath and close to its body unlike the legs of *Moschops*, which stuck out more at the sides.
- **Fossil skeletons of *Cynognathus*** have been found in South Africa. Palaeontologists think that it favoured hunting in dry, desert-like areas.

◀ Cynognathus *means 'dog jaw'. Like other synapsid reptiles, it had strong muscles for opening and closing its jaws, which made it a powerful killer.*

Thrinaxodon

- **Thrinaxodon** was part of a broad group of mammal-type reptiles called Cynodontia.

- **Fossil hunters** discovered *Thrinaxodon* in rocks from the Early Triassic Period (250–235 mya) in southern Africa.

- **Thrinaxodon**, which means 'trident tooth', was a small carnivorous reptile about 50 cm long.

- **Like other** cynodonts such as *Cynognathus*, *Thrinaxodon* had many mammal-like features.

▼ Thrinaxodon *had three different types of teeth. These were small front teeth for nipping and biting, larger canines for stabbing and rough-edged cheek teeth for shearing. It used these to good effect when preying on smaller creatures.*

- ***Thrinaxodon* is the first-known** vertebrate to have a distinct thorax (chest) and lumbar (lower back) region.

- **This structure** of its skeleton, for example, suggests that it had a diaphragm – a major breathing muscle that all modern mammals possess.

- **Small holes** in *Thrinaxodon's* snout bones suggest that it might have had whiskers – and even hair on the rest of its body. Hair is a very mammal-like feature.

- ***Thrinaxodon*** also had a heel, which had evolved from one of its foot bones. This made it a more efficient runner because the heel could help lift the foot right off the ground.

- **Its toes** were all the same length, which meant that its body weight was evenly spread between them.

... • FASCINATING FACT • ...
Thrinaxodon had a stronger jaw than other cynodonts because its teeth were set into a single bone.

Crocodilians

- **The first crocodile-like reptiles** were called eosuchians, meaning 'dawn crocodiles'. They appeared in the Permian Period (298–250 mya).

- **The first true crocodiles** appeared at the end of the Triassic Period (about 215 mya). They were called protosuchians, and lived in pools and rivers.

- *Protosuchus* was, as its name suggests, a protosuchian. It had a short skull and sharp teeth, and would have looked quite like a modern crocodile.

- **Other early crocodiles**, such as *Terrestrisuchus*, looked less like modern crocodiles.

- *Terrestrisuchus* had a short body and long legs. Its name means 'land crocodile', because palaeontologists think it may have been more at home on land than in water.

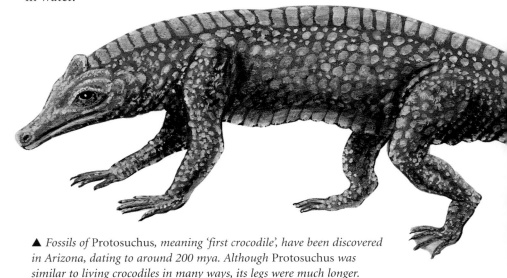

▲ *Fossils of* Protosuchus, *meaning 'first crocodile', have been discovered in Arizona, dating to around 200 mya. Although* Protosuchus *was similar to living crocodiles in many ways, its legs were much longer.*

> ...FASCINATING FACT...
> Modern crocodiles are living fossils. They look similar
> to the crocodiles that were alive 100 mya.

- **The next group** of crocodilians to evolve were the mesosuchians, which lived in the sea.

- *Metriorhynchus* was a marine mesosuchian. It had flippers instead of limbs, and very sharp, fish-stabbing teeth. It lived in the Late Jurassic Period (around 150 mya).

- **One subgroup** of mesosuchians, the eusuchians, are the ancestors of modern crocodiles.

- *Deinosuchus* was an eusuchian. It was thought to be the largest-ever crocodile at 11 m long until a recent discovery of a *Sarchosuchus* fossil which is estimated to measure 15 m.

Archosaurs

- **The archosaurs** (meaning 'ruling reptiles') were a group of reptiles that came to dominate the land, seas and skies in the Mesozoic Era (250–65 mya).

- **Archosaurs** included crocodilians, dinosaurs and the flying reptiles called pterosaurs.

- **Archosaurs** are the ancestors of modern birds and crocodiles.

- **Archosaurs** were diapsid reptiles – they had two openings in the skull to which jaw muscles were attached, which meant their jaws were very powerful.

- **The first archosaurs** appeared in the Permian Period (around 255 mya). They would have looked quite like lizards, but with shorter bodies and longer legs and necks.

- **One early archosaur** was *Chasmatosaurus*. It had a large, heavy body, and probably spent most of its time hunting in rivers.

- *Lagosuchus* was another early archosaur. Some palaeontologists think it might have been the direct ancestor of the dinosaurs.

- *Lagosuchus* was very small. It was about 30 cm long and weighed about 90 g. It had a slender body, and ran on its hind legs.

- **The name** *Lagosuchus* means 'rabbit crocodile' – palaeontologists think it may have moved like a rabbit by hopping.

> ...**FASCINATING FACT**...
> Like many later dinosaurs, some early
> archosaurs were bipedal (two-legged walkers),
> leaving their arms free.

▲ Chasmatosaurus *was an early archosaur and a forerunner of the dinosaurs. It lived about 250 mya and grew up to 2 m long.*

Turtles and tortoises

- **Turtles** and tortoises both have shells that cover and protect their bodies. Because of this, they both belong to a group of reptiles called chelonians.

- **Chelonians' shells** evolved from belly ribs that grew outside of their bodies.

- **The earliest** chelonian fossils come from the Triassic Period (250–208 mya). They have been found in Germany and Thailand.

- *Proganochelys* was a very early chelonian.

- *Proganochelys* had a well-developed, heavily-armoured shell, but palaeontologists think that it could not pull its head, legs or tail inside it.

● **The ability** to pull the head, legs and tail inside the shell is important for turtles and tortoises, because it provides them with maximum protection.

● **The protective shells** of turtles and tortoises may have helped them survive at the end of the Cretaceous Period, 65 mya, when so many other reptiles became extinct.

● **Tortoises** have bigger shells than turtles. This is because tortoises are very slow-moving land creatures – unlike the swimming turtles – and need more protection.

● **A huge number** and variety of turtle fossils have been discovered at Riversleigh in Australia, dating from the Miocene Epoch (25–4 mya).

> **. . . FASCINATING FACT . . .**
> Turtles and tortoises evolved a toothless
> beak for slicing meat or plants.

◀ Proganochelys, *an ancestor of modern turtles and tortoises, had a 60-cm-long shell, but it was unable to pull its head or legs inside.*

115

Archelon

▲ Archelon *fossils show that it was similar to, but much bigger than, modern leatherback turtles. Its front limbs were thinner and longer than its hind ones and were of more use to it in the water. Females used their back limbs to dig nests for their eggs, which they laid on land.*

> **. . . FASCINATING FACT . . .**
> Archelon means 'ruling turtle'. It could
> measure over 4 m in length, and was twice
> the size of modern turtles.

- *Archelon* was a giant sea turtle and the largest turtle ever to have lived.

- **It lived** in the seas off North America during the Cretaceous Period (144–65 mya).

- **It weighed** about 2.3 tonnes and fed on the different types of squid that swam in the Cretaceous seas.

- *Archelon* had very powerful front flippers that propelled it through the water.

- **Like other turtles** and tortoises, *Archelon* had a thick, bony shell to protect it.

- **Some experts** suggest that this shell was actually made of thick leather, to help give Archelon added buoyancy in the water.

- **The largest** *Archelon* skeleton was found in South Dakota, USA, in the mid-1970s. It now stands in the National Natural History Museum in Vienna, Austria.

- **The Vienna specimen** is 4.5 m long from beak to tail and 5.25 m wide from the end of one outstretched front flipper to the end of the other.

- **This turtle** was approximately 100 years old when it died, during a period of hibernation. It was then buried in mud on the sea floor.

Snakes

▲ *Some scientists argue that modern snakes, like this mangrove snake, are related to the prehistoric sea reptiles, mosasaurs. Like snakes, mosasaurs' limbs were reduced in size, and their bodies were long and flexible.*

- **The first-known snake** is *Dinilysia*, which was found in Argentina and lived in the Mid-Cretaceous Period, about 80 mya.

- **There are earlier** snakelike fossils, but palaeontologists generally think these were reptiles and not snakes.

- **The ancestor** of snakes was a lizard. Palaeontologists think it would have been a varanid lizard, of which the modern monitor lizard is an example.

- **Snakes** are an evolutionary triumph. They are one of the few land-living animals to survive – in fact to flourish – without arms or legs.

- **Compared to other reptiles**, snake fossils are rare. This is because snake bones are delicate and do not fossilize well.

- **Snakes evolved** into a huge variety of types in the Tertiary Period (65–1.6 mya). Today, there are more than 2000 snake species, living in nearly every type of habitat.

- **The 50 million-year-old fossil** finds from Messel in Germany include the well-preserved remains of *Palaeopython*, an early python that grew to 2 m long.

- **Early snakes** killed their prey by strangling or squeezing them to death. Modern boas and pythons also use this method to hunt.

- **Poisonous snakes**, such as vipers, adders and cobras, did not evolve until the Miocene Epoch (25–4 mya).

...FASCINATING FACT...
Snakes are one of the few groups of reptiles
that had their main evolutionary
development after the time of the dinosaurs.

Placodonts

- **After adapting** so well to life on land, some groups of reptiles evolved into water-dwelling creatures.

- **Placodonts** were early aquatic (water-living) reptiles. They lived in the Mid Triassic Period (about 240–220 mya).

- **The name placodont** means 'plate tooth'. These reptiles had large cheek teeth that worked like large crushing plates.

- **Placodonts** appeared at about the same time as another group of aquatic reptiles, called nothosaurs.

- **They had shorter**, sturdier bodies than the nothosaurs but, like them, did not survive as a group for a very long time.

- *Placodus* was a placodont. It had a stocky body, stumpy limbs, and webbed toes for paddling. It may have had a fin on its tail.

▶ Placodus *grew up to 2 m long, and probably used its sticking-out front teeth to scrape up molluscs from the seabed. Its platelike side teeth would then make short work of crunching the molluscs.*

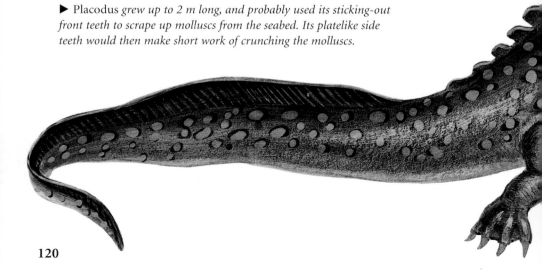

- *Placodus* means 'flat tooth'. It probably used its flat teeth, which pointed outwards from its mouth, to prise shellfish off rocks.

- *Psephoderma* was a turtle-like placodont. Its body was covered in a shell, which in turn was covered by hard plates.

- *Psephoderma* also had a horny beak, like a turtle's, and paddle-shaped limbs.

- *Henodus* was another turtle-like placodont. It also had a beak, which it probably used to grab molluscs from the seabed.

Nothosaurs

- **Nothosaurs** were another group of reptiles that returned to live in the seas.

- *Nothosaurus* was, as its name implies, a nothosaur. Its neck, tail and body were all long and flexible.

- **Its total length** was about 3 m and its approximate weight was 200 kg.

- **Impressions** left in some *Nothosaurus* fossils show that it had webs between its toes.

- *Nothosaurus'* **jaw** had many sharp, interlocking teeth, which would have crunched up the fish and shrimps on which it fed.

- *Ceresiosaurus* was another nothosaur. Palaeontologists think it swam by swaying its body and tail from side to side, like a fish.

- *Ceresiosaurus* means 'deadly lizard'. It was bigger than *Nothosaurus* at 4 m in length and 90 kg in weight.

- **Nothosaurs emerged** in the middle of the Triassic Period (250–208 mya), but were extinct by the end of it.

- **The place left by the extinct nothosaurs** was taken by the plesiosaurs – another group of marine reptiles, but ones that were better adapted to life in the seas.

◄ Nothosaurus *was an aquatic reptile that could use its webbed feet to move over land. The long-necked nothosaurs were probably the ancestors of plesiosaurs, many of which also had long necks.*

...FASCINATING FACT...
Nothosaurus had nostrils on the top of their snouts, which suggests that they came to the water's surface to breathe, like crocodiles.

123

Plesiosaurs

- **Plesiosaurs** were marine reptiles that were plentiful from the Late Triassic to the Late Cretaceous Periods (215–80 mya).

- **They were better suited** to a marine lifestyle than nothosaurs or placodonts. Their limbs were fully-developed paddles, which propelled their short bodies quickly through the water.

- **Many plesiosaurs** had a long, bendy neck, which ended in a small head with strong jaws and sharp teeth.

- **The diet** included fish, squid and probably pterosaurs (flying reptiles), which flew above the water in search of food.

- **The first** Plesiosaurus fossil was discovered at Lyme Regis, on the south coast of England by Mary Anning in the early 19th century. The fossil, which is in the Natural History Museum, London, is 2.3 m long.

- *Plesiosaurus* was not a fast swimmer. It used its flipper-like limbs to move through the water but it had a weak tail that could not propel it forward very powerfully.

- *Elasmosaurus*, the longest plesiosaur, lived in the Cretaceous Period (144–65 mya). It grew up to 14 m long and weighed up to 3 tonnes.

- **One group of plesiosaurs** were known as pliosaurs. They had much shorter necks and much larger heads, with huge jaws and enormous teeth.

- **Research suggests** that plesiosaurs may have caught their prey with quick, darting head movements.

▶ Plesiosaurus *was an early plesiosaur. It was about 4.5 m long – but most of that length was its huge neck.*

...FASCINATING FACT...
One large pliosaur was *Rhomaleosaurus*, another was *Liopleurodon*. Both could grow up to 15 m long.

Ichthyosaurs

- **Ichthyosaurs looked similar** to sharks, which are fish, and to the later dolphins, which are mammals. When one type of animal evolves to look like another, scientists call it convergence.

- **Unlike plesiosaurs**, which relied on their paddles to propel them forwards, ichthyosaurs swayed their tails from side to side, like fish.

- **Hundreds of complete skeletons** of the ichthyosaur *Ichthyosaurus* have been discovered. This reptile could grow up to 2 m long, and weighed 90 kg.

- *Ichthyosaurus* had very large ear bones, which it may have used to pick up underwater vibrations caused by prey.

- **Some fossilized skeletons** of *Ichthyosaurus* and other ichthyosaurs have embryos (unborn infants) inside. This shows that ichthyosaurs gave birth to live young, as opposed to laying eggs.

- **One of the largest ichthyosaurs** was *Shonisaurus,* which was 15 m long and weighed 15 tonnes.

- **Ichthyosaurs** were plentiful in the Triassic and Jurassic Periods (250–144 mya), but became rarer in the Late Jurassic and in the Cretaceous Periods (144–65 mya).

- **Ichthyosaur** means 'fish lizard'.

- **Fossil-hunters** have found ichthyosaur remains all over the world – in North and South America, Europe, Russia, India and Australia.

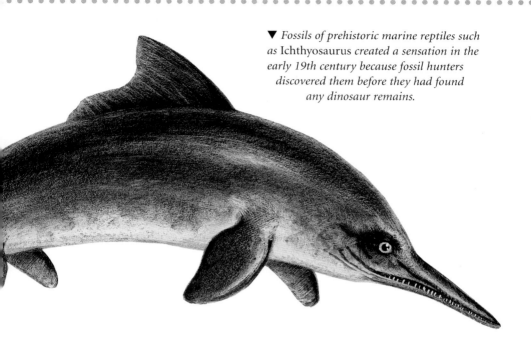

▼ *Fossils of prehistoric marine reptiles such as* Ichthyosaurus *created a sensation in the early 19th century because fossil hunters discovered them before they had found any dinosaur remains.*

... FASCINATING FACT ...
The first *Ichthyosaurus* fossil was found in 1811 by the English fossil-hunter Mary Anning. It took seven years before scientists identified the skeleton as that of a reptile.

Mosasaurs

- **Mosasaurs** were another group of large sea reptiles. They appeared between 160 and 120 mya, at the time when ichthyosaurs were less common.

- **Mosasaurs** were diapsid reptiles, a group that included dinosaurs and pterosaurs. All other large sea reptiles belonged to another group, the euryapsids.

- **Unlike the other** giant prehistoric sea reptiles, mosasaurs have living relatives. These include monitor lizards, such as the Komodo dragon.

- **The best-known mosasaur** is *Mosasaurus,* which could be up to 10 m long and 10 tonnes in weight.

- **The huge jaws of *Mosasaurus*** were lined with cone-shaped teeth, each of which had different cutting and crushing edges. They were the most advanced teeth of any marine reptile.

- **So distinctive** are *Mosasaurus'* teeth that palaeontologists have identified its tooth marks on the fossils of other animals, in particular the giant turtle *Allopleuron*.

- **The jaws of a *Mosasaurus*** were discovered in a limestone mine in Maastricht, in the Netherlands, in 1780. The fossil disappeared in 1795 when the French invaded Maastricht, but later turned up in Paris.

- **At first,** scientists thought the jaws belonged either to a prehistoric whale or a crocodile, until they decided they were a giant lizard's.

- ***Mosasaurus*** means 'lizard from the River Meuse', because it was discovered in Maastricht in the Netherlands, through which the River Meuse flows.

- **In 1998**, more than 200 years after the discovery of the first Mosasaurus fossil, palaeontologists discovered the remains of another Mosasaurus in the same location – the St Pietersburg quarry in Maastricht.

▼ Mosasaurus *was a fast swimmer. It had an enormous tail and paddle-shaped limbs, which it probably used as rudders.*

Gliding reptiles

- **One theory** about how reptiles became able to fly is that they evolved from reptiles that were able to glide.

- **Gliding reptiles** were tree-dwellers that jumped from tree to tree and developed a flap of skin that they used like a parachute – to help them soar and to break their fall.

- **Gliding between trees** saves time and energy and avoids the ground between trees, where predators may be lurking.

- *Coelurosauravus* was a tree-dwelling reptile of the Late Permian Period (260–250 mya).

- **The flaps of skin** that *Coelurosauravus* used for gliding stretched over long rods that grew out of the side of its body. Like wings, they could be folded away after use.

- **Palaeontologists** think that *Coelurosauravus* was an ancestor of the modern flying lizard, *Draco volans*, which lives in Southeast Asia.

- *Scleromochlus* was another gliding reptile. It lived in the Late Triassic Period, about 210 mya.

- *Scleromochlus* was about 20 cm long, with long, delicate back legs. It may have had flaps of skin on the sides of its body that would have worked like parachutes – just like those of modern flying squirrels.

- *Sharovipteryx* was another Late Triassic gliding reptile, the remains of which have been found in Central Asia.

- **Like *Scleromochlus*,** *Sharovipteryx* had a lightweight frame and long back legs, but fossils indicate that there was also a flap of skin between its long back legs and its tail.

▼ Coelurosauravus, *which was around 60 cm long, lived in forests in Europe and Madagascar. Palaeontologists initially mistook its gliding rods for fin spines, and thought it was a fish.*

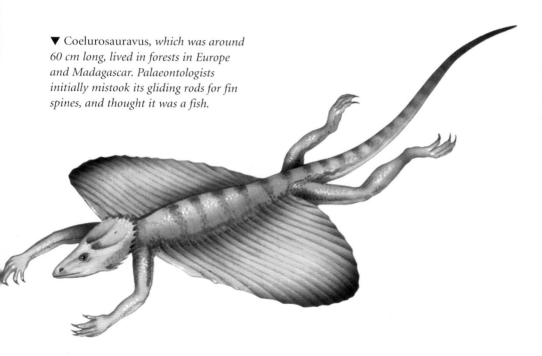

Rhamphorhynchoids

▶ Dimorphodon *had a wingspan of between 1.2 and 2.5 m. Palaeontologists think that it lived and hunted along seashores and rivers.*

- **The earliest pterosaurs** (flying reptiles) were the rhamphorhynchoids. They first appeared in the Late Triassic Period (around 220 mya).

- **Rhamphorhynchoids** had long tails that ended in a diamond-shaped vane, like a rudder.

- **Their tails** gave them stability in flight, which meant they could soar and swoop effectively.

- **One of the first rhamphorhynchoids** – and first flying vertebrates – was *Peteinosaurus*.

- **Well-preserved fossils** of *Peteinosaurus* have been found near Bergamo in Italy.

- **They reveal Peteinosaurus'** sharp, cone-like teeth, and suggest it ate insects, which it caught in the air.

- **In contrast**, another early rhamphorhynchoid, *Eudimorphodon,* had fangs at the front of its mouth and smaller spiked ones behind. This suggests that it ate fish.

- **_Dimorphodon_** was a later rhamphorhynchoid from the Early Jurassic Period (208–180 mya). It had a huge head that looked a bit like a puffin's.

- **_Rhamphorhynchus_** was one of the last rhamphorhynchoids, appearing in the Late Jurassic Period (about 160 mya).

▲ Rhamphorhynchus _had long, sharp jaws that it used to spear fish._

...FASCINATING FACT...
Fossil-hunters have found _Rhamphorhynchus_ fossils alongside those of the early bird _Archaeopteryx_, in Solnhofen, Germany.

133

Pterodactyls

- **Pterodactyls** are a later group of pterosaurs (flying reptiles) than the rhamphorhynchoids.

- **They lived** in the Late Jurassic through to the Late Cretaceous Periods (160–65 mya).

- **Pterodactyls** lacked the long, stabilizing tail of rhamphorhynchoids, but were more effective fliers, able to make quicker turns in the air.

- **They were also** much lighter than rhamphorhynchoids, because their bones were hollow.

- **The pterodactyl** *Pterodactylus* and the rhamphorhynchoid *Rhamphorhynchus* were roughly the same size, but *Pterodactylus* weighed between 1 and 5 kg, while *Rhamphorhynchus* weighed 10 kg.

- **Some of the largest pterodactyls**, such as *Pteranodon,* appeared in the Late Cretaceous Period and had a wingspan of 7 m.

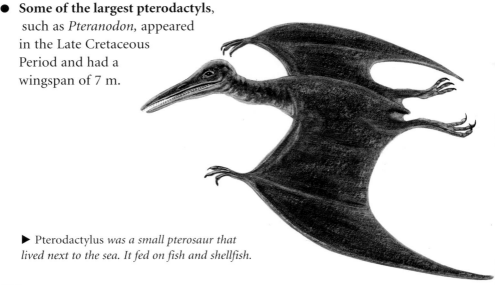

▶ Pterodactylus *was a small pterosaur that lived next to the sea. It fed on fish and shellfish.*

- **Unlike earlier flying reptiles**, *Pteranodon* had no teeth. Instead, it used its long, thin beak to scoop up fish.

- *Pteranodon* also had a pelican-like pouch at the bottom of its mouth – it probably used this to store fish before swallowing them.

- *Pteranodon* weighed about 16 kg. This was heavier than earlier pterodactyls, and suggests it was probably a glider rather than an active flyer.

- *Pteranodon* had a long crest on its head, which may have worked as a rudder during flight.

▼ Pteranodon, *meaning 'wings and no teeth', was once thought to be the largest ever flying reptile – until the discovery of* Quetzalcoatlus *in the 1970s.*

Quetzalcoatlus

- *Quetzalcoatlus* was the largest known flying animal of any kind ever to have lived.

- **It had a wingspan of 15 m** – the size of a small aeroplane!

- **It was also the heaviest** flying reptile, weighing 86 kg. Its bulk suggests that it was not a brilliant flyer, and instead glided as much as possible.

- **Its name** comes from an Aztec word meaning 'feathered serpent'. Quetzalcoatl was the Aztec god of death and resurrection.

- *Quetzalcoatlus* had long, narrow wings, jaws without teeth, and a long, stiff neck.

- **Palaeontologists** were amazed when they discovered the fossilized bones of *Quetzalcoatlus* – they did not think a flying creature could be that large.

- **The discovery** of these bones in inland areas, not coastal regions like those of other flying reptiles, suggests *Quetzalcoatlus* may have soared above deserts, like a vulture.

- **Some palaeontologists** say that *Quetzalcoatlus* was nothing like a vulture because its beak was not designed for ripping at the bodies of dead animals.

- **Another puzzle** for palaeontologists and mathematicians is how *Quetzalcoatlus* could lift itself off the ground to fly.

····FASCINATING FACT····
A student, Douglas Lawson, discovered *Quetzalcoatlus'* bones in the Big Bend National Park, Texas, in 1971.

▼ Quetzalcoatlus *belonged to a family of pterosaurs called the azhdarchids, which had giant wingspans, long necks and toothless beaks. The name 'azhdarchid' comes from the Uzbek word for a dragon.*

Warm-blooded animals

▲ *Some excellently preserved fossils of flying reptiles, such as this* Pterodactyl, *show that they had fur on their bodies. This suggests that they may have been warm-blooded, like modern birds and mammals.*

● **It has been** a long-standing argument among experts whether or not some prehistoric reptiles, such as pterosaurs (flying reptiles) were warm- or cold-blooded.

- **Warm-blooded animals** maintain a constant body temperature and can stay active even when their surroundings are cold.

- **Cold-blooded animals** depend on their surroundings for warmth. They are therefore active during the day but inactive at night, when it is cold.

- **In 1971**, the discovery of a fossil of the pterosaur *Sordes pilosus* provided strong evidence that it was warm-blooded.

- **Fur helps** keep heat in. Warm-blooded mammals have fur because they produce their own heat and try not to lose it.

- **Birds are warm-blooded**, with feathers instead of fur, which do a similar job.

- *Sordes pilosus'* **fur** suggests, therefore, that it was also warm-blooded.

- **Flying requires** a fair amount of brainpower, and brains need a steady temperature to work well.

- **However, flying exposes** the body and the brain to currents of warm and cold air. Therefore, being warm-blooded would have been the only way to maintain the brain's temperature.

. . . **FASCINATING FACT** . . .
Sordes pilosus means 'hairy devil', and impressions in the rock layer around the skeleton show that its body had a furry coat.

Ancestors

- **Experts have many opinions** as to which group (or groups) of reptiles were the ancestors of the dinosaurs.

- **The earliest dinosaurs** appeared in the Middle Triassic Period, about 230–225 mya, so their ancestors must have been around before this.

- **Very early dinosaurs** walked and ran on their strong back limbs, so their ancestors were probably similar.

- **The thecodonts** or 'socket-toothed' group of reptiles may have been the ancestors of the dinosaurs.

- **A thecodont's** teeth grew from roots fixed into pit-like sockets in the jaw bone, as in dinosaurs.

- **Some thecodonts** resembled sturdy lizards. Others evolved into true crocodiles (still around today).

▶ Thecodontosaurus *belonged to a group of reptiles that preceded the dinosaurs. It had a bulky body, long arms and walked on two legs. Like all the first dinosaurs, it was carnivorous.*

. . . FASCINATING FACT . . .
Creatures similar to *Euparkeria* or *Lagosuchus* may have given rise to the first dinosaurs.

- **The ornithosuchian thecodonts** became small, upright creatures with long back legs and long tails.

- **The smaller thecodonts** included *Euparkeria*, at about 60 cm long, and *Lagosuchus*, at about 30 cm long.

- ***Euparkeria* and *Lagosuchus*** were fast-moving creatures that used their sharp claws and teeth to catch insects.

Earliest dinosaurs

- **The first known dinosaurs** appeared about 230–225 mya, in the Middle Triassic Period.

- **The earliest dinosaurs** were small-to-medium meat-eaters with sharp teeth and claws. They ran quickly on their two longer back legs.

- **Fossils of *Herrerasaurus*** date from 228 mya and were found near San Juan in Argentina, South America.

- ***Herrerasaurus* was about 3 m** in total length, and probably weighed some 90 kg.

- **At about the same time and in the same place** as *Herrerasaurus*, there lived a similar-shaped dinosaur named *Eoraptor*, at only 1.5 m long.

- **The name** *Eoraptor* means 'dawn plunderer' or 'early thief'.

◀ Staurikosaurus *was one of the first dinosaurs, a fairly small carnivore measuring about 2 m. It ran fast on two legs, using its long, stiff tail for balance.*

> **...FASCINATING FACT...**
> *Eoraptor* and *Herrerasaurus* hunted small animals
> such as lizards, insects and mammal-like reptiles.

- ***Staurikosaurus* was a meat eater** similar to *Herrerasaurus*. It is known to have lived about the same time, in present-day Brazil, South America.

- ***Procompsognathus*** was another early meat eater. It lived in the Late Triassic Period in Germany.

- ***Pisanosaurus* lived in Argentina** in the Late Triassic Period, and was only 1 m long. It may have been a plant eater similar to *Lesothosaurus*.

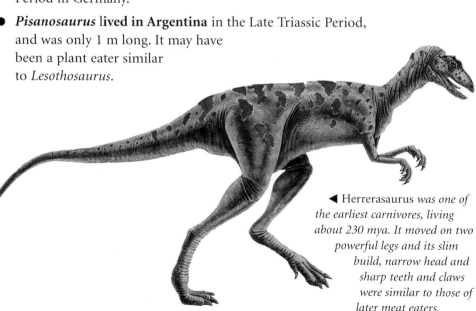

◀ Herrerasaurus *was one of the earliest carnivores, living about 230 mya. It moved on two powerful legs and its slim build, narrow head and sharp teeth and claws were similar to those of later meat eaters.*

Great meat eaters

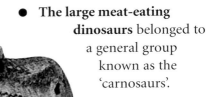

- **The large meat-eating dinosaurs** belonged to a general group known as the 'carnosaurs'.

- **All carnosaurs** were similar in body shape, and resembled the fearsome *Tarbosaurus*.

- ***Tarbosaurus* was very similar** to *Tyrannosaurus*. It lived at the same time, 70–65 mya, but in Asia rather than North America.

- **Some experts believe** that *Tarbosaurus* was an Asian version of the North American *Tyrannosaurus*, and both should have been called *Tyrannosaurus*.

- **The carnosaur** *Albertosaurus* was about 8–9 m long and lived 75–70 mya, in present-day Alberta, Canada.

◀ Albertosaurus, *like the other carnosaurs, was a massive, powerful hunting machine during the Cretaceous Period. It had clawed feet and hands, strong muscular legs, razor sharp teeth and a strong skull to protect it when attacking prey at speed.*

- *Spinosaurus* **was a huge carnosaur** from North Africa, measuring 12 m long and weighing 4–5 tonnes. It had tall, rodlike bones on its back, which may have been covered with skin, like a 'sail'.

- *Daspletosaurus* **was a 9-m long carnosaur** that lived at the end of the Age of Dinosaurs in Alberta, Canada.

- **Largest of all the carnosaurs** was *Giganotosaurus*, the largest meat eater ever to walk the Earth.

- *Giganotosaurus* was up to 16 m long and weighed at least 8 tonnes.

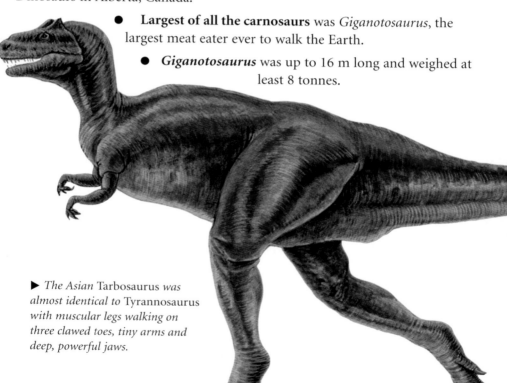

▶ *The Asian* Tarbosaurus *was almost identical to* Tyrannosaurus *with muscular legs walking on three clawed toes, tiny arms and deep, powerful jaws.*

145

Tyrannosaurus

- *Tyrannosaurus* **is not only** one of the most famous of the dinosaurs, but also one about which a great deal is known. Several discoveries have revealed fossilized bones, teeth, whole skeletons and other remains.

- *Tyrannosaurus* **lived at the very end** of the Age of Dinosaurs, about 68–65 mya.

- **The full name** of *Tyrannosaurus* is *Tyrannosaurus rex*, which means 'king of the tyrant reptiles'.

- **The head** of *Tyrannosaurus* was 1.2 m long and had more than 50 dagger-like teeth, some longer than 15 cm.

- *Tyrannosaurus* **fossils** have been found at many sites in North America, including Alberta and Saskatchewan in Canada, and Colorado, Wyoming, Montana and New Mexico in the USA.

- **The arms and hands** of *Tyrannosaurus* were so small that they could not pass food to its mouth, and may have had no use at all.

- **Recent fossil finds** of a group of *Tyrannosaurus*, includes youngsters, suggesting that they may have lived as families in small herds.

- *Tyrannosaurus* **may have been** an active hunter, pounding along at speed after its fleeing prey, or it may have been a skulking scavenger that ambushed old and sickly victims.

> ...FASCINATING FACT...
> *Tyrannosaurus*, when fully grown, was about 12–13 m long and taller than a two-decker bus. It weighed 6–7 tonnes.

● **Until the 1990s**, *Tyrannosaurus* was known as the biggest meat-eating animal ever to walk the Earth, but its size record has been broken by *Giganotosaurus*.

The huge skull of *Tyrannosaurus* was deep from top to bottom, but relatively narrow from side to side. The jaw hinged at the rear of the head, giving a vast gape when the mouth was open.

▼ Tyrannosaurus's *powerful rear legs contrasted greatly with its puny front limbs or 'arms'. As it pounded along, its thick-based tail balanced its horizontal body and head, which was held low. The rear feet were enormous, with each set of three toes supporting some three or four tonnes.*

Curved neck allowed head to face forwards

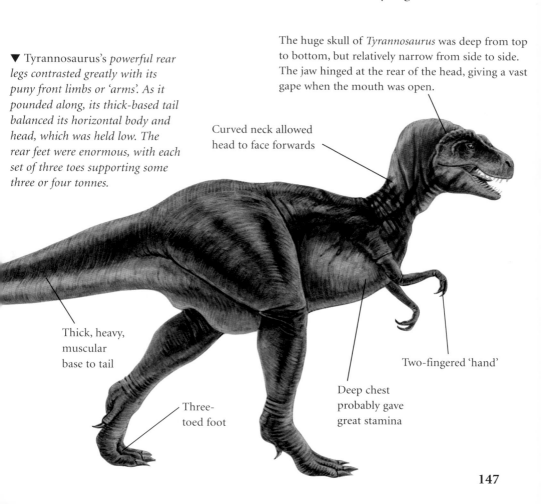

Thick, heavy, muscular base to tail

Three-toed foot

Deep chest probably gave great stamina

Two-fingered 'hand'

147

Allosaurus

▲ *Remains of up to 60* Allosaurus *were found here, at Dinosaur Quarry, Utah, USA. Allosaurus fossils have also been found in Africa, where millions of years ago, there may have been a land bridge to North America.*

- ***Allosaurus* was a huge** meat-eating dinosaur, almost as big as *Tyrannosaurus*.

- ***Allosaurus*** was about 11–12 m in total length.

- **The weight** of *Allosaurus* is variously estimated at 1.5–4 tonnes.

- **The head** of *Allosaurus* was almost 1 m long, but its skull was light, with large gaps or 'windows' that would have been covered by muscle and skin.

- ***Allosaurus* could not only** open its jaws in a huge gape, but it could also flex them so that the whole mouth became wider, for an even bigger bite.

- *Allosaurus* **lived** about 155–135 mya, during the Late Jurassic and Early Cretaceous Periods.

- **Most *Allosaurus* fossils** have been discovered in the states of the American Midwest.

- *Allosaurus* may have hunted the giant sauropod dinosaurs such as *Diplodocus*, *Camarasaurus* and *Brachiosaurus*.

- **Fossils of *Allosaurus*** were identified in Africa, and a smaller or 'dwarf' version was found in Australia.

◀ Allosaurus *almost rivalled* Tyrannosaurus *in size, but lived 70 million years earlier. It was a very common dinosaur and one of the main predators of its period.*

...FASCINATING FACT...
The remains of 60 *Allosaurus* were found in the Cleveland-Lloyd Dinosaur Quarry, Utah, USA.

Coelophysis

- *Coelophysis* **was** a small, agile dinosaur that lived early in the Age of Dinosaurs, about 220 mya.

- **A huge collection of fossils** of *Coelophysis* was found in the late 1940s, at a place now known as Ghost Ranch, New Mexico, USA.

- **Hundreds** of *Coelophysis* were preserved together at Ghost Ranch – possibly a herd that drowned as the result of a sudden flood.

- *Coelophysis* was almost 3 m in length.

- **The very slim, lightweight build** of *Coelophysis* meant that it probably weighed only 25–28 kg.

- *Coelophysis* **belonged to** the group of dinosaurs known as coelurosaurs. It probably ate small animals such as insects, worms and lizards.

- **Long, powerful back legs** allowed *Coelophysis* to run fast.

- **The front limbs** of *Coelophysis* were like arms, each with a hand bearing three large, strong, sharp-clawed fingers for grabbing prey.

- *Coelophysis* **means 'hollow form'**. It was so-named because some of its bones were hollow, like the bones of birds, making it lighter.

- *Coelophysis* had a large number of small, sharp teeth in its long, narrow, birdlike skull.

▲ Coelophysis *was an early therapod living in the Triassic Period, 220 mya. It was about 3 m long with a strong, slim frame for running and clawed hands for grabbing prey.*

151

Carnotaurus

- **The big, powerful, meat-eating** *Carnotaurus* is a member of the carnosaur group of dinosaurs.

- ***Carnotaurus* fossils** come mainly from the Chubut region of Argentina, South America.

- ***Carnotaurus* lived** about 100 mya.

- **A medium-sized dinosaur**, Carnotaurus was about 7.5 m in total length and weighed up to 1 tonne.

- **The skull of** *Carnotaurus* was relatively tall from top to bottom and short from front to back, compared to other carnosaurs like *Allosaurus* and *Tyrannosaurus*, giving it a snub-snouted appearance.

▶ *The fossils of* Carnotaurus *were first discovered in 1985, in Argentina. Like other* carnosaurs, *it had lethally sharp teeth for tearing through the flesh of its prey and powerful legs for hunting it down.*

▶ *The eyebrow 'horns' of* Carnotaurus *are a puzzling feature. They do not seem large or strong enough to be weapons, and in any case, this dinosaur was already a very large and powerful creature. The horns may have grown with maturity, indicating that the owner was adult and able to breed.*

- **The name** *Carnotaurus* means 'meat-eating bull', referring partly to its bull-like face.

- *Carnotaurus* **had two** curious, cone-shaped bony crests or 'horns', one above each eye, where the horns of a modern bull would be.

- **Rows of extra-large scales**, like small lumps, ran along *Carnotaurus* from its head to its tail.

- **Like** *Tyrannosaurus*, *Carnotaurus* had very small front limbs that could not reach its mouth, and may have had no use.

- *Carnotaurus* **probably ate** plant-eating dinosaurs such as *Chubutisaurus*, although its teeth and jaws were not especially big or strong.

Pack-hunters

- **Dinosaurs were reptiles**, but no reptiles today hunt in packs in which members cooperate with each other.

- **Certain types of crocodiles and alligators** come together to feed where prey is abundant, but they do not coordinate their attacks.

- **Fossil evidence** suggests that several kinds of meat-eating dinosaurs hunted in groups or packs.

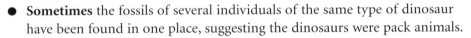

- **Sometimes** the fossils of several individuals of the same type of dinosaur have been found in one place, suggesting the dinosaurs were pack animals.

- **The fossil bones** of some plant-eating dinosaurs have been found with many tooth marks on them, apparently made by different-sized predators, which may have hunted in packs.

- *Tyrannosaurus* may have been a pack-hunter.

- **In southwest Montana, USA,** the remains of three or four *Deinonychus* were found near the fossils of a much larger plant eater named *Tenontosaurus*.

- **A single** *Deinonychus* weighed 60–70 kg, while *Tenontosaurus* weighed 15 times more.

- **One** *Deinonychus* probably would not have attacked a full-grown *Tenontosaurus*, but a group of three or four might have.

◄ *Slender, agile and fast with sharp teeth and grasping claws,* Coelurus *was part of the coelurosaur group, small meat-eaters that hunted lizards, insects, frogs and small mammals. They may also have scavenged on the leftover prey of carnosaurs like* Allosaurus.

. . . **FASCINATING FACT** . . .
Some meat-eaters may have had fairly large brains, enabling them to hunt as a group.

155

Raptors

▶ Velociraptor, *the 'speedy thief', was a typical dromeosaur, with a sharp claw on each foot capable of cutting metre-long gashes into its prey. Its fossils have been found in Central Asia.*

- **'Raptors'** is a nickname for the dromaeosaur group.

- **'Raptor'** is variously said to mean 'plunderer', 'thief' or 'hunter' (birds of prey are also called raptors).

- **Dromaeosaurs** were medium-sized, powerful, agile, meat-eating dinosaurs that lived mainly about 110–65 mya.

- **Most dromaeosaurs** were 1.5–3 m from nose to tail, weighed 20–60 kg, and stood between one and two metres tall.

- *Velociraptor* **lived** 75–70 mya, in what is now the barren scrub and desert of Mongolia in Central Asia.

- **Like other raptors**, *Velociraptor* probably ran fast and could leap great distances on its powerful back legs.

- **The dromaeosaurs** are named after the 1.8-m-long *Dromaeosaurus* from North America – one of the least known of the group, from very few fossil finds.

- **The best-known raptor** is probably *Deinonychus*.

- **The large mouths of dromaeosaurs** opened wide and were equipped with many small, sharp, curved teeth.

...FASCINATING FACT...
On each foot, a dromaeosaur had a large, curved claw that it could swing in an arc to slash through its victim's flesh.

◀ Deinonychus, *in addition to its speed and agility when hunting, was able to leap up onto its prey, balanced by a rigid tail. The name* 'Deinonychus' *means* 'terrible claw'.

Deinonychus

- *Deinonychus* **is one of the best-known** members from the group of meat eaters known as raptors.

- **The Middle Cretaceous Period**, about 115–100 mya, is when *Deinonychus* thrived.

- **Fossils of *Deinonychus*** come from the American Midwest, mainly from Montana and Wyoming.

- *Deinonychus* **was about 3 m long** from nose to tail and weighed 60–70 kg, about the same as an adult human.

- **When remains of** *Deinonychus* were dug up and studied in the 1960s, they exploded the myth that dinosaurs were slow, small-brained and stupid.

- **Powerful, speedy and agile**, *Deinonychus* may have hunted in packs, like today's lions and wolves.

- *Deinonychus* **had large hands** with three powerful fingers, each tipped with a dangerous sharp claw.

- **On each foot**, *Deinonychus* had a massive, scythelike claw that it could flick in an arc to slice open prey.

- **The tail** of *Deinonychus* was stiff and could not be swished.

- *Deinonychus* **and other similar** dromaeosaurs, such as *Velociraptor*, were the basis for the cunning and terrifying raptors of the *Jurassic Park* films.

▶ Deinonychus *were dromaeosaurs (meaning 'swift reptile').*
A combination of sharp teeth and claws and long, powerful legs
for jumping onto prey made Deinonychus *a powerful hunting*
machine. These dinosaurs hunted in packs and so were able to
attack prey much larger than themselves.

Oviraptor

- *Oviraptor* **was an unusual meat eater** from the dinosaur group known as theropods.

- **Fossils of** *Oviraptor* were found in the Omnogov region of the Gobi Desert in Central Asia.

- **From beak to tail-tip**, *Oviraptor* was about 2 m long.

- *Oviraptor* **lived** during the Late Cretaceous Period about 85–75 mya.

- *Oviraptor* **was named** 'egg thief' because the first of its fossils was found lying among the broken eggs of another dinosaur, possibly *Protoceratops*.

▶ Oviraptor's *unusual features included a toothless, parrot-like beak and a hard, bony head crest. The crest may have been used to signify dominant members in a particular group or area.*

- **The mouth of** *Oviraptor* had no teeth. Instead, it had a strong, curved beak, like that of a parrot or eagle.

- **On its forehead**, *Oviraptor* had a tall, rounded piece of bone, like a crest or helmet, sticking up in front of its eyes.

- *Oviraptor's* **bony head crest** resembled that of today's flightless bird, the cassowary.

- *Oviraptor* **may have eaten** eggs, or cracked open shellfish with its powerful beak.

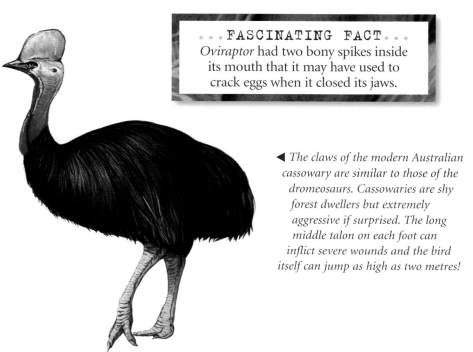

> **. . . . FASCINATING FACT . . . .**
> *Oviraptor* had two bony spikes inside its mouth that it may have used to crack eggs when it closed its jaws.

◀ *The claws of the modern Australian cassowary are similar to those of the dromeosaurs. Cassowaries are shy forest dwellers but extremely aggressive if surprised. The long middle talon on each foot can inflict severe wounds and the bird itself can jump as high as two metres!*

161

Dilophosaurus

◀ Dilophosaurus *had two crests on its head, although the fragile bone structure of these means that it is unlikely they were ever used for fighting rivals. Palaeontologists (fossil experts) think it is possible that the crests were covered in brightly coloured skin as a warning to rivals or for visual display.*

- **Dilophosaurus** was a large meat-eating dinosaur in the group known as the ceratosaurs.

- **About 200 mya**, *Dilophosaurus* roamed the Earth in search of prey.

- **Fossils** of *Dilophosaurus* were found in Arizona, USA, and possibly Yunnan, China.

- **The remains** of *Dilophosaurus* in Arizona, USA, were discovered by Jesse Williams, a Navajo Native American, in 1942.

- **Studying the fossils** of *Dilophosaurus* proved very difficult, and the dinosaur was not given its official name until 1970.

. . . FASCINATING FACT . . .
Dilophosaurus probably weighed about 500 kg
– as much as the biggest polar bears today.

- ***Dilophosaurus* measured** about 6 m from its nose to the end of its very long tail.

- **The name** *Dilophosaurus* means 'two ridged reptile', from the two thin, rounded, bony crests on its head, each shaped like half a dinner plate.

- **The crests** of *Dilophosaurus* were too thin and fragile to be used as weapons for head-butting.

- **Brightly coloured skin** may have covered *Dilophosaurus's* head crests, as a visual display to rivals or enemies.

▶ *The fearsome* Dilophosaurus *was one of the first large meat-eating dinosaurs. It gained the nickname 'terror of the Early Jurassic'.*

Baryonyx

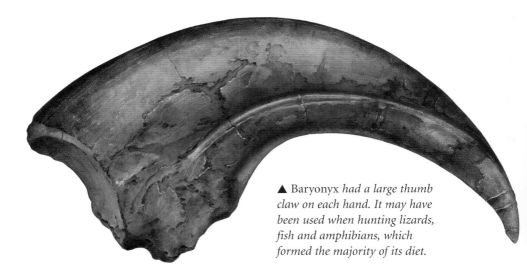

▲ Baryonyx *had a large thumb claw on each hand. It may have been used when hunting lizards, fish and amphibians, which formed the majority of its diet.*

- *Baryonyx* **was a large** meat-eating dinosaur that lived about 120 mya.

- **The first fossil find** of *Baryonyx* was its huge thumb claw, discovered in Surrey, England, in 1983.

- **The total length** of *Baryonyx* was 10–11 m.

- *Baryonyx* **had a slim shape** and long, narrow tail, and probably weighed less than 2 tonnes.

- **The head** of *Baryonyx* was unusual for a meat-eating dinosaur in having a very long, narrow snout, similar to today's slim-snouted crocodiles.

- **The teeth** of *Baryonyx* were long and slim, especially at the front of its mouth.

- **The general similarities** between *Baryonyx* and a crocodile suggest that *Baryonyx* may have been a fish eater.

- ***Baryonyx* may have lurked** in swamps or close to rivers, darting its head forwards on its long, flexible neck to snatch fish.

- **The massive thumb claw** of *Baryonyx* may have been used to hook fish or amphibians from the water.

- **The long thumb claw** of *Baryonyx* measured about 35 cm in length.

▲ *We only know of* Baryonyx *from a single fossil specimen. This was found alongside remains of fish scales, suggesting this dinosaur was a semi-aquatic fish-catcher. It had a straight neck, unlike may theropods and narrow jaws containing 128 serrated teeth.*

165

Ornitholestes

- **Ornitholestes** was a smallish meat-eating dinosaur in the group known as coelurosaurs.

- **The name** *Ornitholestes* means 'bird robber' – experts who studied its fossils in the early 1900s imagined it chasing and killing the earliest birds.

- **Ornitholestes** lived about 150 mya, at the same time as the first birds.

- **Present-day Wyoming, USA**, was the home of *Ornitholestes*, a continent away from the earliest birds in Europe.

- **Only one specimen** of *Ornitholestes* has been found, along with parts of a hand at another site.

- **Ornitholestes** was about 2 m long from nose to tail-tip.

- **Slim and lightweight**, *Ornitholestes* probably weighed only about 12–15 kg.

- **The teeth** of *Ornitholestes* were small and well-spaced, but also slim and sharp, well suited to grabbing small animals for food.

- **Ornitholestes** had very strong arms and hands, and powerful fingers with long claws, ideal for grabbing baby dinosaurs newly hatched from their eggs.

Sharp claws for grasping prey

166

. . . .

...FASCINATING FACT...
According to some experts, *Ornitholestes* may have had a
slight ridge or crest on its nose. Other experts disagree.

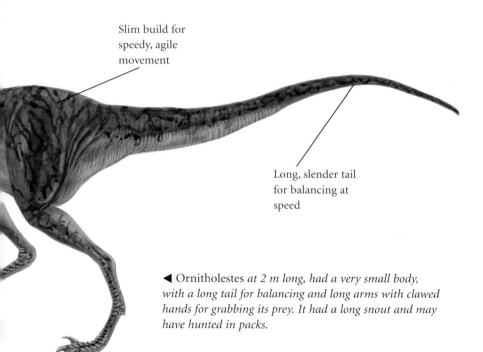

Slim build for
speedy, agile
movement

Long, slender tail
for balancing at
speed

◄ Ornitholestes *at 2 m long, had a very small body,
with a long tail for balancing and long arms with clawed
hands for grabbing its prey. It had a long snout and may
have hunted in packs.*

Dino-birds: 1

Flight feathers suited to agile manoeuvres in the air

Teeth in long, light jaws

Three clawed 'fingers' midway along front of wing

Long tail with tail backbones

▲ Archaeopteryx *could probably glide well, swoop and turn as it pursued flying prey such as dragonflies. However, its long, strong legs suggest that it was also an able walker and runner. So it may have chased victims such as baby lizards and cockroaches on the ground.*

- **The earliest known bird** for which there is good fossil evidence, and which lived during the Age of Dinosaurs, is *Archaeopteryx*.

- *Archaeopteryx* **lived** in Europe during the Late Jurassic Period, about 155–150 mya.

- **At about 60 cm long** from nose to tail-tip, *Archaeopteryx* was about the size of a large crow.

- *Archaeopteryx* **resembled** a small, meat-eating dinosaur in many of its features, such as the teeth in its long, beaklike mouth, and its long, bony tail.

- **In 1951**, a fossilized part-skeleton was identified as belonging to a small dinosaur similar to *Compsognathus*, but in the 1970s it was re-studied and named *Archaeopteryx* – showing how similar the two creatures were.

- **Three clawed fingers** grew halfway along the front of each of *Archaeopteryx*'s wing-shaped front limbs.

- **The flying muscles** of *Archaeopteryx* were anchored to its large breastbone.

- *Archaeopteryx* **may have flown**, but not as skilfully as today's birds.

- *Archaeopteryx* **probably fed** by swooping on prey, running to catch small creatures such as insects and worms, or perhaps even by scavenging carrion.

> **...FASCINATING FACT...**
> *Archaeopteryx* was covered with feathers
> that had the same detailed designs found
> in feathers covering flying birds today.

169

Dino-birds:2

- **Fossils found during the last 20 years** show that some dinosaurs may have been covered with feathers or fur.

- *Sinosauropteryx* was a small, 1-m long meat eater that lived 135 mya in China.

- **Fossils** of *Sinosauropteryx* show that parts of its body were covered not with the usual reptile scales, but with feathers.

- **The overall shape** of *Sinosauropteryx* shows that, despite being feathered, it could not fly.

- **The feathers** of *Sinosauropteryx* may have been for camouflage, for visual display, or to keep it warm – suggesting it was warm-blooded.

- *Avimimus* was a small, light dinosaur. Its fossils come from China and Mongolia, and date from 85–82 mya.

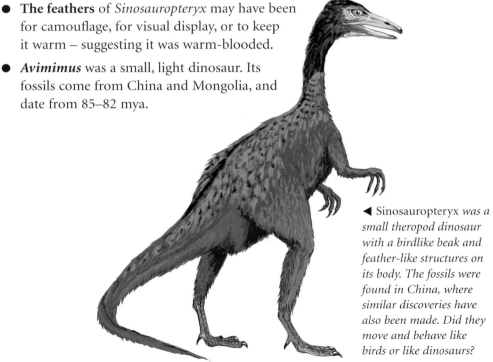

◀ Sinosauropteryx *was a small theropod dinosaur with a birdlike beak and feather-like structures on its body. The fossils were found in China, where similar discoveries have also been made. Did they move and behave like birds or like dinosaurs?*

- **The 1.5 m long** *Avimimus* had a mouth shaped like a bird's beak for pecking at food.

- **The fossil arm bones** of *Avimimus* have small ridges of the same size and shape as the ridges on birds' wing bones, where feathers attach.

- **In modern science,** any animal with feathers is a bird, so some experts say that feathered dinosaurs were not actually dinosaurs or even reptiles, but birds.

- **Some experts say** that birds are not really a separate group of animals, but a subgroup of dinosaurs that lives on today, and they should be regarded as feathered dinosaurs.

▶ Avimimus *may have evolved feathers for warmth or for camouflage.*

171

Ostrich-dinosaurs

- **'Ostrich-dinosaurs'** is the common name of the ornithomimosaurs, because of their resemblance to today's largest bird – the flightless ostrich.

- **Ostrich-dinosaurs** were tall and slim, with two long, powerful back legs for very fast running.

- **The front limbs** of ostrich-dinosaurs were like strong arms, with grasping fingers tipped by sharp claws.

- **The eyes of ostrich-dinosaurs** were large and set high on the head.

- **The toothless mouth** of an ostrich-dinosaur was similar to the long, slim beak of a bird.

- **Ostrich-dinosaurs** lived towards the end of the Cretaceous Period, about 100–65 mya, in North America and Asia.

◀ *At 2 m tall,* Struthiomimus *was a similar height to a modern ostrich. In the legs, the bulk of the muscle was in the hips and upper thighs, as in an ostrich or horse – both rapid runners.*

- **Fossils of the ostrich-dinosaur** *Struthiomimus* from Alberta, Canada, suggest it was almost 4 m in total length and stood about 2 m tall – the same height as a modern ostrich.

- **The ostrich-dinosaur** *Gallimimus* was almost 5 m in length and stood nearly 3 m high.

- **Ostrich-dinosaurs probably ate** seeds, fruits and other plant material, as well as small animals such as worms and lizards, which they may have grasped with their powerful clawed hands.

- **Other ostrich-dinosaurs** included *Dromiceiomimus*, at 3–4 m long, and the slightly bigger *Ornithomimus*.

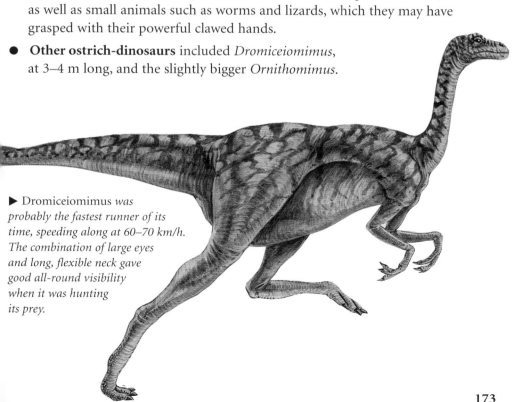

▶ Dromiceiomimus *was probably the fastest runner of its time, speeding along at 60–70 km/h. The combination of large eyes and long, flexible neck gave good all-round visibility when it was hunting its prey.*

173

Eustreptospondylus

- *Eustreptospondylus* **was a large** meat eater that lived in present-day Oxfordshire and Buckinghamshire, in central southern England.

- *Eustreptospondylus* lived about 165 mya.

- **In the 1850s,** a fairly complete skeleton of a young *Eustreptospondylus* was found near Wolvercote, Oxford, but was named as *Megalosaurus*, the only other big meat eater known from the region.

- **In 1964,** British fossil expert Alick Walker showed that the Wolvercote dinosaur was not *Megalosaurus*, and gave it a new name, *Eustreptospondylus*.

- *Eustreptospondylus* means 'well curved', or 'true reversed, backbone'.

- **A full-grown** *Eustreptospondylus* measured about 7 m in total length.

▲ Eustreptospondylus *weighed about the same as a very large lion today, and was doubtless just as deadly. We know about it from a single fossil find, in England, which was originally thought to be of* Megalosaurus, *another carnosaur.*

- *Eustreptospondylus* is estimated to have weighed a massive 200–250 kg.

- **In its enormous mouth**, *Eustreptospondylus* had a great number of small, sharp teeth.

- *Eustreptospondylus* **may have hunted** stegosaurs and also sauropods such as *Cetiosaurus* – both groups that roamed the region at the time.

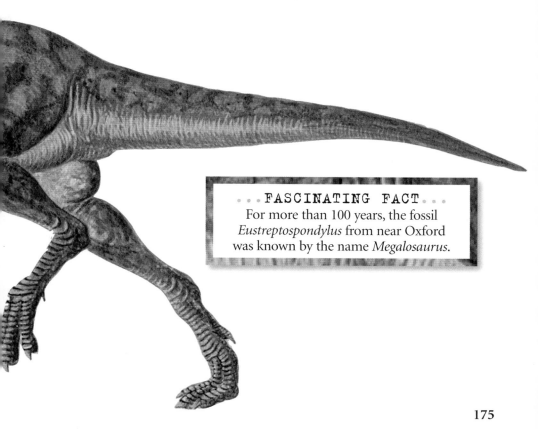

... FASCINATING FACT ...
For more than 100 years, the fossil *Eustreptospondylus* from near Oxford was known by the name *Megalosaurus*.

Smallest dinosaurs

- **One of the smallest dinosaurs** was *Compsognathus*, which lived during the Late Jurassic Period, 155–150 mya.

- **Fossils** of *Compsognathus* come from Europe, especially southern Germany and southeastern France.

- *Compsognathus* was slim, with a long, narrow tail. It probably weighed less than 3 kg.

- **Each hand** of *Compsognathus* had two clawed fingers, and each foot had three long, clawed running toes, with another toe (the first or big toe) placed higher up in the 'ankle' region.

- *Compsognathus* **had small teeth** that were sharp and curved. It probably darted through the undergrowth after insects, spiders, worms and similar small prey.

- **Two other very small dinosaurs** were *Heterodontosaurus* and the 1-m long fabrosaur *Lesothosaurus*.

- **The smallest fossil dinosaur specimens** found to date are of *Mussaurus*, which means 'mouse reptile'.

- *Mussaurus* was a plant-eating prosauropod similar to *Plateosaurus*, which lived in the Late Triassic Period in South America.

- **The fossils of** *Mussaurus* measure just 20 cm long – but these are the fossils of babies, just hatched from their eggs. The babies would have grown into adults measuring 3 m long.

... FASCINATING FACT ...
The little *Compsognathus* was only about 1 m long,
and some specimens were even smaller, at 70 cm long.

▶ Compsognathus *was a carnivorous dinosaur and is relatively rare in terms of fossil finds. At 1 m long and about 3 kg in weight, it was one of the smallest dinosaurs, probably feeding on insects and small reptiles.* Compsognathus *was fast and agile but it is likely that it moved in packs for self-defence.*

Herbivores

▶ During the warm, damp Jurassic Period, there was lush plant life in most areas, covering land that had previously been barren. Massive plant-eaters such as Barosaurus thrived on the high-level fronds, needles and leaves of towering tree ferns, gingkoes and conifers.

Barosaurus,
26 m long and
25–30 tonnes

- **Hundreds of kinds of dinosaur** were herbivores, or plant eaters. As time passed, the plants available for them to eat changed or evolved.

- **Early in the Age of Dinosaurs,** during the Triassic Period, the main plants for dinosaurs to eat were conifer trees, gingkoes, cycads and the smaller seed-ferns, ferns, horsetails and club-mosses.

- **A few cycads** are still found today. They resemble palm trees, with umbrella-like crowns of long green fronds on top of tall, bare, trunk-like stems.

- **In the Triassic Period**, only prosauropod dinosaurs were big enough or had necks long enough to reach tall cycad fronds or gingko leaves.

- **In the Jurassic Period**, tall conifers such as redwoods and 'monkey-puzzle' trees became common.

- **The huge, long-necked sauropods** of the Jurassic Period would have been able to reach high into tall conifer trees to rake off their needles.

- **In the Middle Cretaceous Period**, a new type of plant food appeared – the flowering plants.

- **By the end of the Cretaceous Period** there were many flowering trees and shrubs, such as magnolias, maples and walnuts.

- **No dinosaurs ate grass**, because grasses did not appear on Earth until 30–20 mya, long after the dinosaurs had died out.

...FASCINATING FACT...
Gingkoes are still found today, in the form
of maidenhair trees, with fan-shaped leaves.

179

Prosauropods

- **The prosauropods** were the first really big dinosaurs to appear on Earth. They were plant-eaters that thrived about 230–180 mya.

- **Prosauropods** had small heads, long necks and tails, wide bodies and four sturdy limbs.

- **One of the first prosauropods** was *Plateosaurus*, which lived about 220 mya in present-day France, Germany, Switzerland and other parts of Europe.

- *Plateosaurus* usually walked on all fours, but it may have reared up on its back legs to reach high leaves.

- *Plateosaurus* was up to 8 m in total length, and weighed about 1 tonne.

- **Another early prosauropod** was *Riojasaurus*. Its fossils are 218 mya, and come from Argentina.

- *Riojasaurus* was 10 m long and weighed about 2 tonnes.

- *Anchisaurus* **was one of the smallest prosauropods,** at only 2.5 m long and about 30 kg. It lived in eastern North America about 190 mya.

● **Fossil evidence** suggests that 5-m long *Massospondylus* lived in southern Africa and perhaps North America.

● **The sauropods** followed the prosauropods and were even bigger, but had the same basic body shape, with long necks and tails.

▼ *With their characteristic long necks and tails, the prosauropod group are thought to have preceded (come before) the sauropods. A member of this group,* Riojasaurus *was South America's first big dinosaur.*

181

Plateosaurus

- *Plateosaurus*, a prosauropod, was one of the first really big dinosaurs to appear, some 220 mya.

- **The name** *Plateosaurus* means 'flat reptile'.

- **Groups of** *Plateosaurus* have been found at various sites, including one in Germany and one in France.

- *Plateosaurus* **used** its many small, serrated teeth to crop and chew plant food.

- *Plateosaurus* **had very flexible**, clawed fingers, which it perhaps used to pull branches of food to its mouth.

- *Plateosaurus* **could bend its fingers** 'backwards', allowing it to walk on its hands and fingers, in the same posture as its feet and toes.

▼ *One of the earliest prosauropods,* Plateosaurus *may have reared up to chomp on leaves 2–3 m above the ground.*

- *Plateosaurus's* **thumbs** had especially large, sharp claws, perhaps used as weapons to jab and stab enemies.

- **Fossil experts** once thought that *Plateosaurus* dragged its tail as it walked.

- **Experts today** suggest that *Plateosaurus* carried its tail off the ground, to act as a balance to its head, long neck and the front part of its body.

- *Plateosaurus* **was one of the earliest** dinosaurs to be officially named, in 1837, even before the term 'dinosaur' had been invented.

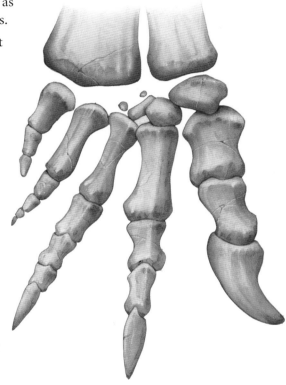

▲ *The front feet of* Plateosaurus *could be hyper-extended. The flexibility of the front feet meant that* Plateosaurus *may have been able to grasp branches when feeding.*

183

Biggest

- **The biggest dinosaurs** were the sauropods such as *Brachiosaurus* and *Argentinosaurus* – but working out how heavy they were when they were alive is very difficult.

- *Brachiosaurus* **is known** from many remains, including almost complete skeletons, so its length can be measured accurately.

- **A dinosaur's weight** is estimated from a scaled-down model of its skeleton 'fleshed out' with muscles, guts and skin on the bones, using similar reptiles such as crocodiles for comparison.

- **The size of a dinosaur** model is measured by immersing it in water to find its volume.

- **The volume of a model dinosaur** is scaled up to find the volume of the real dinosaur when it was alive.

- **The sauropod** *Apatosaurus* is now well known from about 12 skeletons, which between them have almost every bone in its body.

- **Different experts** have 'fleshed out' the skeleton of *Apatosaurus* by different amounts, so estimates of its weight vary from 20 tonnes to more than 50 tonnes.

▲ *It is thought that despite its massive size,* Apatosaurus *would have been able to trot surprisingly quickly on its relatively long legs.*

...FASCINATING FACT...
The weights and volumes of reptiles alive today are used to calculate the probable weight of a dinosaur when it was alive.

A small mouth meant that a large sauropod like *Argentinosaurus* would have had to feed for about 20 hours each day!

Reconstruction of *Argentinosaurus* is based on relatively few of its bones, compared with other bones from similar sauropod dinosaurs

Argentinosaurus may have swallowed pebbles to help digest its food

Human-sized meat eaters present little threat

Massive, heavy tail to swing at attackers

▲ Argentinosaurus *was a South American dinosaur, measuring up to 40 m long and weighing up to 100 tonnes. Despite this, fossil footprints show that some huge sauropods could run nearly as fast as a human!*

● **The length of** *Apatosaurus* is known accurately to have been 23 m.

● **Fossils of a dinosaur called** *Brontosaurus* were found to be identical to those of *Apatosaurus*, and since the name *Apatosaurus* had been given first, this was the name that had to be kept – so, officially, there is no dinosaur called *Brontosaurus*.

Sauropods

- **The sauropods** were the biggest of all the dinosaurs.

- **The huge plant-eating sauropods** lived mainly during the Jurassic Period, 208–144 mya.

- **A typical sauropod** had a tiny head, a very long neck and tail, a huge, bulging body and four massive legs, similar to those of an elephant, but much bigger.

- **Sauropods** included the well-known *Mamenchisaurus, Cetiosaurus, Diplodocus, Brachiosaurus* and *Apatosaurus*.

▼ Apatosaurus *was a huge sauropod, but it may have been able to rear up on its back legs in order to defend itself or its young.*

▼ *For many years, the longest dinosaur known from fairly complete fossil remains was the sauropod* Diplodocus. *However, other dinosaurs, known from fewer fossils, may have been longer. An almost complete fossil skeleton of* Diplodocus, *found around 1900, has been copied many times in plaster, plastic or glass fibre and sent to museums throughout the world.*

- *Rebbachisaurus* **fossils** were found in Morocco, Tunisia and Algeria.

- *Rebbachisaurus* **lived** 120 mya.

- *Cetiosaurus* was about 18 m long and weighed 30 tonnes.

- *Cetiosaurus*, **or 'whale reptile'**, was so-named because French fossil expert Georges Cuvier originally thought that its giant backbones came from a prehistoric whale.

- *Cetiosaurus* **was the first** sauropod to be given an official name, in 1841 – the year before the term 'dinosaur' was invented,

- **The first fossils** of *Cetiosaurus* were discovered in Oxfordshire, England, during the 1830s.

Brachiosaurus

- **Relatively complete** fossil remains exist of *Brachiosaurus*.

- *Brachiosaurus* was a sauropod – a huge plant eater.

- **At 25 m long** from nose to tail, *Brachiosaurus* was one of the biggest of all dinosaurs.

- **Fossils** of *Brachiosaurus* have been found in North America, east and north Africa, and also possibly southern Europe.

- **Estimates of the weight** of *Brachiosaurus* range from about 30 to 75 tonnes.

- *Brachiosaurus* **lived** about 150 mya, and may have survived until 115 mya.

- **The name** *Brachiosaurus* means 'arm reptile' – it was so-named because of its massive front legs.

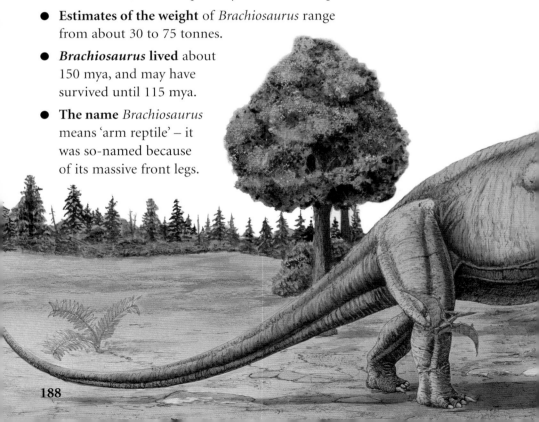

- **With its huge front legs** and long neck, *Brachiosaurus* could reach food more than 13 m from the ground.

- **The teeth** of *Brachiosaurus* were chisel-shaped for snipping leaves from trees.

- ***Brachiosaurus's*** nostrils were high on its head.

◀ Brachiosaurus *had similar body proportions to a giraffe, but it was more than twice as tall and 50 times heavier.*

189

Diplodocus

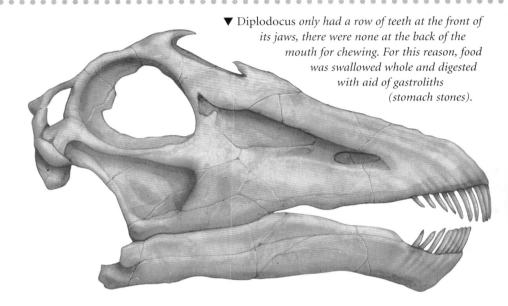

▼ Diplodocus *only had a row of teeth at the front of its jaws, there were none at the back of the mouth for chewing. For this reason, food was swallowed whole and digested with aid of gastroliths (stomach stones).*

- *Diplodocus* **was a huge plant-eating dinosaur** belonging to the group known as the sauropods.

- *Diplodocus* **lived** during the Late Jurassic Period, about 155–145 mya.

- **The first discovery** of *Diplodocus* fossils was in 1877, near Canyon City, Colorado, USA.

- **The main fossils** of *Diplodocus* were found in the Midwest of the USA, in Colorado, Utah and Wyoming.

- **At an incredible 27 m** or more in length, *Diplodocus* is one of the longest known dinosaurs.

...FASCINATING FACT...

Diplodocus's nostrils were so high on its skull
that experts once thought it had a trunk!

- **Although so long,** *Diplodocus* was quite lightly built – it probably weighed 'only' 10–12 tonnes!

- *Diplodocus* probably swung its tiny head on its enormous neck to reach fronds and foliage in the trees.

- **The teeth** of *Diplodocus* were slim rods that formed a comblike fringe only around the front of its mouth.

- *Diplodocus* **may have used** its comblike teeth to strip leaves from twigs and swallow them without chewing.

◄ Diplodocus
*was long but light
for a sauropod, weighing
'only' about 10 tonnes.
Like other sauropods, it used a
combination of sheer size and
a powerful whiplike tail to
defend itself from predators.*

191

Ankylosaurs

- **Ankylosaurs** had a protective armour of bony plates.

- **Unlike the armoured nodosaurs**, ankylosaurs had a large lump of bone at the ends of their tails, which they used as a hammer or club.

- **One of the best-known ankylosaurs**, from the preserved remains of about 40 individuals, is *Euoplocephalus*.

- *Euoplocephalus*, **or 'well-armoured head'**, had bony shields on its head and body, and even had bony eyelids. Blunt spikes ran along its back.

- **The hefty** *Euoplocephalus* was 7 m long and weighed 2 tonnes or more.

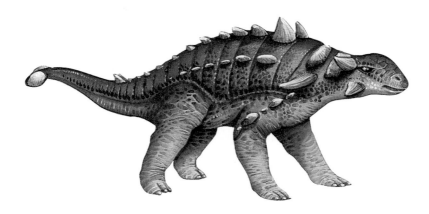

▲ *'Ankylosaur' means 'armoured reptile' and Ankylosaurus most certainly was. Even its skull was protected by bony plates although it had a soft, vulnerable belly which meant that it walked characteristically close to the ground.*

...FASCINATING FACT...

Pinacosaurus was about 6 m long and lived
in Asia 80–75 million years ago.

- *Euoplocephalus* lived about 75–70 mya in Alberta, Canada and Montana, USA.

- **Specimens of** *Euoplocephalus* are usually found singly, so it probably did not live in herds.

- **The ankylosaur** *Pinacosaurus* had bony nodules like chain-mail armour in its skin, and rows of blunt spikes from neck to tail.

- **Ankylosaurs** had small, weak teeth, and probably ate soft, low-growing ferns and horsetails.

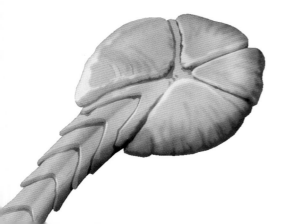

◀ *A powerful tail club was slow-moving* Ankylosaurus's *best weapon. It was made up of plates of fused bone and could be swung at an attacker with great force.*

Triceratops

- **Many fossil remains** of *Triceratops* have been found. It is one of the most studied and best known dinosaurs.

- *Triceratops* **was the largest** of the plant-eating ceratopsians, the 'horn-faced' dinosaurs.

- *Triceratops* **lived at the very end** of the Age of Dinosaurs, about 67–65 mya.

- **Fossils of 50 or so** *Triceratops* have been found in North America, though no complete skeleton has been found.

- *Triceratops* **was about 9 m** long and weighed 5–6 tonnes – as big as the largest elephants of today.

- **As well as a short nose horn** and two long eyebrow horns, *Triceratops* also had a wide, sweeping frill that covered its neck like a curved plate.

- **The neck frill** of *Triceratops* may have been an anchor for the dinosaur's powerful chewing muscles.

- **Acting as a shield,** the bony neck frill of *Triceratops* may have protected it as it faced predators head-on.

- *Triceratops'* **neck frill** may have been brightly coloured, to impress rivals or warn off enemies.

- **The beaklike front** of *Triceratops'* mouth was toothless, but it had sharp teeth for chewing in its cheeks.

◀ Triceratops *had a very short sturdy neck protected by a bony frill. In some ceratopsians however, the frill was simply very tough, bony skin which meant that it was a lot lighter.* Triceratops *moved in herds, giving it some protection from predators and was one of the last dinosaurs at the end of the Cretaceous Period.*

Fabrosaurs

- **Fabrosaurs** were small dinosaurs that lived towards the beginning of the Jurassic Period, about 208–200 mya.

- **The group was named** from *Fabrosaurus*, a dinosaur that was itself named in 1964, from the fossil of a piece of lower jaw bone, found in southern Africa.

  - *Lesothosaurus* **was a fabrosaur**, the fossils of which were found in the Lesotho region of Africa, near the *Fabrosaurus* fossil. It was named in 1978.

▲ *On the outside,* Lesothosaurus *looked similar to small predatory dinosaurs such as* Compsognathus. *But its fossil teeth and jaws show that it was probably a plant eater, and an early member of the ornithischian group.*

- **The lightly built** *Lesothosaurus* was only 1 m long from nose to tail-tip, and would have stood knee-high to an adult human.

- *Lesothosaurus* **had long, slim back legs** and long toes, indicating that it was a fast runner.

- **The teeth and other fossils** of *Lesothosaurus* show that it probably ate low-growing plants such as ferns.

- *Lesothosaurus's* **teeth** were set inwards slightly from the sides of its skull, suggesting it had fleshy cheek pouches for storing or chewing food.

- *Lesothosaurus* **may have** crouched down to rest on its smaller front arms when feeding on the ground.

- *Lesothosaurus* **probably lived in herds**, grazing and browsing, and then racing away at speed from danger.

- **Some experts believe** that *Lesothosaurus* and *Fabrosaurus* were the same, and that the two sets of fossils were given different names.

Mamenchisaurus

- ***Mamenchisaurus* was a massive** plant-eating dinosaur, a sauropod similar in appearance to *Diplodocus*.

- **The weight of** *Mamenchisaurus* has been estimated at 20–35 tonnes.

- ***Mamenchisaurus* lived** during the Late Jurassic Period, from about 160 to 140 mya.

- **The hugely long neck** of *Mamenchisaurus* had up to 19 vertebrae, or neckbones – more than almost any other dinosaur.

- ***Mamenchisaurus*** fossils were found in China.

- **The name** *Mamenchisaurus* is taken from the place where its fossils were discovered – Mamen Stream.

- ***Mamenchisaurus* had the longest neck**, at up to 15 m, of any dinosauryet discovered.

◀ *Over half of* Mamenchisaurus's *length was its enormous neck! However, this was not balanced by a long tail, as in other sauropods like* Diplodocus *or* Brachiosaurus.

- *Mamenchisaurus* **may be a close cousin** of other sauropod dinosaurs found in the region, including *Euhelopus* and *Omeisaurus*.

- *Mamenchisaurus* **may have stretched** its vast neck high into trees to crop leaves, or – less likely – it may have lived in swamps and fed on soft, water-dwelling plants.

...FASCINATING FACT...
Mamenchisaurus was a huge 25 m
from nose to tail tip.

▲ *A skeleton of* Mamenchisaurus's *head and neck. The muscles and the joints between each pair of vertebrae would have been incredibly strong, allowing* Mamenchisaurus *to lift and lower its head and neck easily. In addition, the bones were hollow to reduce the weight of the neck.*

Heterodontosaurus

- *Heterodontosaurus* **was a very small dinosaur** at only 1.2 m in length (about as long as a large dog), and would have stood knee-high to a human.

- *Heterodontosaurus* lived about 205–195 mya, at the beginning of the Jurassic Period.

- **Probably standing partly upright** on its longer back legs, *Heterodontosaurus* would have been a fast runner.

- **Fossils** of *Heterodontosaurus* come from Lesotho in southern Africa and Cape Province in South Africa.

- **Most dinosaurs had teeth of only one shape** in their jaws, but *Heterodontosaurus* had three types of teeth.

▲ Heterodontosaurus *was a bipedal (two-legged), fast-moving, plant-eating dinosaur during the Early Jurassic Period (about 205 mya).*

▶ *The skull of fast-moving* Heterodontosaurus *had three different types of teeth, meaning it could bite and chew its food, yet it was a very small, plant-eating dinosaur. Even the larger meat-eaters, such as* Tyrannosaurus, *only had one type of tooth.*

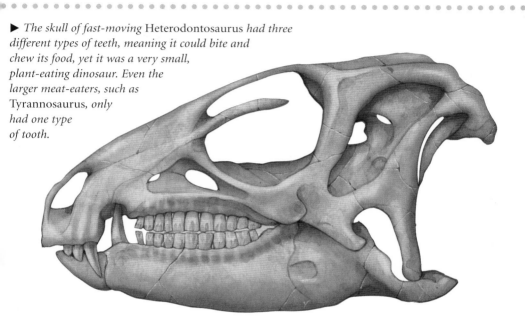

- **The front teeth** of *Heterodontosaurus* were small, sharp and found only in the upper jaw. They bit against the horny, beak-like lower front portion of the mouth.

- **The four middle teeth** of *Heterodontosaurus* were long and curved, similar to the tusks of a wild boar, and were perhaps used for fighting rivals or in self-defence.

- **The back or cheek teeth** of *Heterodontosaurus* were long and had sharp tops for chewing.

- *Heterodontosaurus* **probably ate** low-growing plants such as ferns.

201

Duck-bills

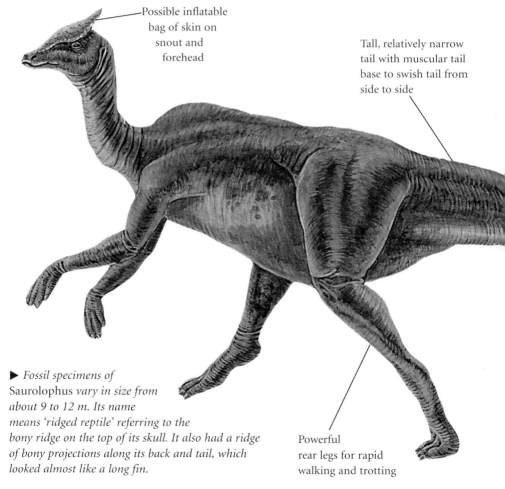

Possible inflatable bag of skin on snout and forehead

Tall, relatively narrow tail with muscular tail base to swish tail from side to side

▶ *Fossil specimens of* Saurolophus *vary in size from about 9 to 12 m. Its name means 'ridged reptile' referring to the bony ridge on the top of its skull. It also had a ridge of bony projections along its back and tail, which looked almost like a long fin.*

Powerful rear legs for rapid walking and trotting

- **'Duck-bills'** is the common name for the group of dinosaurs called the hadrosaurs.

- **Hadrosaurs were big plant eaters** that walked mainly on their two large, powerful rear legs.

- **Hadrosaurs** were one of the last main dinosaur groups to appear on Earth, less than 100 mya.

- **Hadrosaurs were named after** *Hadrosaurus*, the first dinosaur of the group to be discovered as fossils, found in 1858 in New Jersey, USA.

- **Most hadrosaurs had wide mouths** that were flattened and toothless at the front, like a duck's beak.

  - **Huge numbers of cheek teeth,** arranged in rows, filled the back of a hadrosaur's mouth. They were ideal for chewing tough plant food.

    - **The name** *Hadrosaurus* means 'big reptile'.

      - **Some hadrosaurs** had tall, elaborate crests or projections of bone on their heads, notably *Corythosaurus*, *Tsintaosaurus*, *Saurolophus* and *Parasaurolophus*.

- **Hadrosaurs that lacked bony crests** and had low, smooth heads included *Anatosaurus*, *Bactrosaurus*, *Kritosaurus* and *Edmontosaurus*.

> **. . . FASCINATING FACT . . .**
> *Edmontosaurus* may have had a loose bag of skin on its nose that it blew up like a balloon to make a honking or trumpeting noise – perhaps a breeding call.

Pachycephalosaurs

- **The pachycephalosaurs** are named after one of the best-known members of the group, *Pachycephalosaurus*.

- *Pachycephalosaurus* **means** 'thick-headed reptile', due to the domed and hugely thickened bone on the top of its skull – like a cyclist's crash helmet.

- **Pachycephalosaurs** were one of the last dinosaur groups to thrive. They lived 75–65 mya.

- **Pachycephalosaurs were plant eaters** that stood up and ran on their longer back legs.

- *Pachycephalosaurus* was about 4.5 m long from nose to tail, and lived in the American Midwest.

- *Stegoceras*, also from the American Midwest, was 2.5 m long with a goat-sized body.

Extra thick skull bone

◀ *Most of the pachycephalosaur group were quite small and at 8 m* Pachycephalosaurus *was certainly the largest. A solid dome of bone formed the top part of the skull – a protective element when fighting rivals. There were also spikes and nodules of bone decorating the head and face.*

- *Homalocephale*, **another pachycephalosaur**, was about 3 m long and had a flatter skull. It lived in east Asia.

- **Pachycephalosaurs** may have defended themselves by lowering their heads and charging at their enemies.

- **At breeding time**, the males may have engaged in head-butting contests, as some sheep and goats do today.

▲ Stegoceras *was a bipedal (two-legged) dinosaur, but since it moved with its back level, it is unlikely to have been capable of great speed. However, the stance would be useful when involved in head-butting fights with rivals.*

205

Stegosaurs

- **Stegosaurs** were a group of plant-eating dinosaurs that lived mainly during the Late Jurassic Period, 160–140 mya.

- **Stegosaurs are named after** the best-known of their group, *Stegosaurus*.

- **Stegosaurs are often called** 'plated dinosaurs', from the large, flat plates or slabs of bone on their backs.

- **Stegosaurs** probably first appeared in eastern Asia, then spread to other continents, especially North America and Africa.

▼ Kentrosaurus *had an unusual defensive display – a combination of plates and spikes running the length of the body and tail. The 'second brain' that was once thought to fill a space in a stegosaur's hip area is now known to have been a mass of nerves controlling the tail and back legs.*

▼ Stegosaurus *is thought to have had the smallest brain for its body size of all the dinosaurs, but the stegosaur group survived for more than 50 million years! It was a peaceful, slow-moving plant-eater, so did not need the brain power of a fast hunter like Troodon.*

- **The stegosaur** *Kentrosaurus* was about 5 m long and weighed an estimated 1 tonne.

- **The name** *Kentrosaurus* means 'spiky reptile'.

- *Kentrosaurus* lived about 155–150 mya in east Africa.

- **Most stegosaurs had no teeth** at the fronts of their mouths, but had horny beaks, like those of birds, for snipping off leaves.

- **Most stegosaurs chewed** their food with small, ridged cheek teeth.

Stegosaurus

The sails on the back may have been used for temperature control

The 'beak' of *Stegosaurus* had no teeth – food was chewed with the cheek teeth

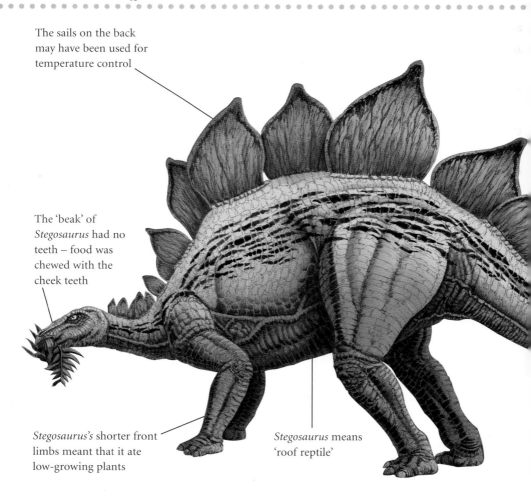

Stegosaurus's shorter front limbs meant that it ate low-growing plants

Stegosaurus means 'roof reptile'

- *Stegosaurus* was the largest of the stegosaur group.

- **Fossils of *Stegosaurus*** were found mainly in present-day Colorado, Utah and Wyoming, USA.

- *Stegosaurus,* **like most of its group**, lived towards the end of the Jurassic Period, about 150 mya.

- **The mighty** *Stegosaurus* was about 8–9 m long from nose to tail-tip and probably weighed more than 2 tonnes.

- **The most striking feature** of *Stegosaurus* was its large, roughly triangular bony plates along its back.

  - **The name** *Stegosaurus* means 'roof reptile'. It was given this name because it was first thought that its 80-cm long bony plates lay flat on its back, overlapping slightly like the tiles on a roof.

    - **It is now thought** that the back plates of *Stegosaurus* stood upright in two long rows.

      - **The back plates** of *Stegosaurus* may have been for body temperature control, allowing the dinosaur to warm up quickly if it stood side-on to the sun's rays.

      - *Stegosaurus's* **back plates** may have been covered with brightly coloured skin, possibly to intimidate enemies – they were too flimsy for protection.

      - *Stegosaurus's* **tail** was armed with four large spikes, probably for swinging at enemies in self defence.

The spiked tail would have delivered a powerful blow

209

Camarasaurus

- *Camarasaurus* **is one of the best known** of all big dinosaurs, because so many almost-complete fossil skeletons have been found.

- *Camarasaurus* was a massive plant-eating sauropod.

- *Camarasaurus* **lived** during the Late Jurassic Period, about 155–150 mya.

- **The famous American fossil-hunter** Edward Drinker Cope gave *Camarasaurus* its name in 1877.

- **The name** *Camarasaurus* means 'chambered reptile', because its backbones, or vertebrae, had large, scoop-shaped spaces in them, making them lighter.

Large nostril and eye sockets

The name sauropod means 'lizard footed'

- **The huge** *Camarasaurus* was about 18 m long

- **Compared to other sauropods**, such as *Diplodocus*, *Camarasaurus* had a relatively short neck and tail, but a very bulky, powerful body and legs.

- **North America, Europe and Africa** were home to *Camarasaurus*.

- **A large, short-snouted, tall head**, like that of *Brachiosaurus*, characterized the appearance of *Camarasaurus*.

- **A fossil skeleton** of a young *Camarasaurus* was uncovered in the 1920s, and had nearly every bone in its body lying in the correct position, as they were in life – an amazingly rare find.

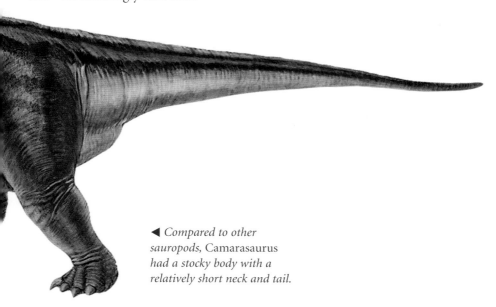

◀ *Compared to other sauropods,* Camarasaurus *had a stocky body with a relatively short neck and tail.*

Ceratopsians

- **Ceratopsians** were large plant eaters that appeared less than 90 mya.

- **Most ceratopsian fossils** come from North America.

- **'Ceratopsian' means 'horn-face',** after the long horns on their snouts, eyebrows or foreheads.

- **Most ceratopsians** had a neck shield or frill that swept sideways and up from behind the head to cover the upper neck and shoulders.

▶ Ceratopsians *were a group of dinosaurs with distinctive neck frills, horned faces and parrot-like beaks. They had very powerful jaws, allowing them to feed on tough plants. It is likely that they moved in herds. A mass grave of ceratopsians unearthed in Canada contained at least 300 skeletons.*

▼ *Chasmosaurus*

▼ *Triceratops*

- **Well-known ceratopsians** included *Triceratops*, *Styracosaurus*, *Centrosaurus*, *Pentaceratops*, *Anchiceratops*, *Chasmosaurus* and *Torosaurus*.

- **The neck frills of some ceratopsians**, such as that of *Chasmosaurus*, had large gaps or 'windows' in the bone.

- **In life**, the windows in the neck frill of a ceratopsian were covered with thick, scaly skin.

- **Ceratopsians** had no teeth in the fronts of their hooked, beaklike mouths.

- **Using rows of powerful cheek teeth**, ceratopsians sheared their plant food.

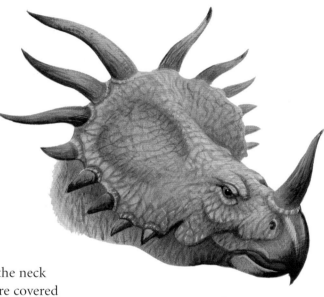

▲ *Styracosaurus*

> ... **FASCINATING FACT** ...
> *Torosaurus* had the longest skull of any land animal ever, at 2.5 m from the front of the snout to the rear of the neck frill.

213

Scelidosaurus

- ***Scelidosaurus* was a medium-sized** armoured dinosaur, perhaps an early member of the group called the ankylosaurs.

- **Fossils of** *Scelidosaurus* have been found in North America, Europe and possibly Asia.

- ***Scelidosaurus*** lived during the Early Jurassic Period, about 200 mya.

- **From nose to tail**, *Scelidosaurus* was about 4 m long.

- ***Scelidosaurus* probably moved about** on four legs, although it could perhaps rear up to gather food.

- **A plant eater**, *Scelidosaurus* snipped off its food with the beaklike front of its mouth, and chewed it with its simple, leaf-shaped teeth.

▲ Scelidosaurus *was a very widespread dinosaur that moved on all-fours and ate plants. It was a forerunner of the bigger, more heavily armoured types.*

214

▶ Scelidosaurus *was covered from head to tail with hard scutes (bony plates in the skin) and nodules. These would have helped to protect it from meat-eating dinosaurs. It was a stocky, heavy-bodied dinosaur which may have meant that it couldn't escape from predators very quickly.*

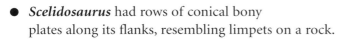

- *Scelidosaurus* is one of the earliest dinosaurs known to have had a set of protective, bony armour plates.

- **A row of about 50 bony plates**, or scutes, stuck up from *Scelidosaurus's* neck, back and tail.

- *Scelidosaurus* had rows of conical bony plates along its flanks, resembling limpets on a rock.

- *Scelidosaurus* **was described in 1859**, and named in 1863, by Richard Owen, who also invented the name 'dinosaur'.

215

Anchisaurus

- *Anchisaurus* **was a prosauropod**, a plant eater with a small head, long neck and long tail.

- **Although officially named as a dinosaur** in 1912, *Anchisaurus* had in fact been discovered almost 100 years earlier.

- *Anchisaurus* **was very small and slim** compared to other prosauropods, with a body about the size of a large dog.

- **Fossils** of *Anchisaurus* date from Early Jurassic times.

- **The remains of** *Anchisaurus* were found in Connecticut and Massachusetts, eastern USA, and in southern Africa.

- **With its small, serrated teeth,** *Anchisaurus* probably bit off the soft leaves of low-growing plants.

▶ Anchisaurus *was about the size of a large pet dog (such as a labrador), but had a long neck and tail.*

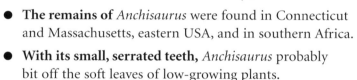

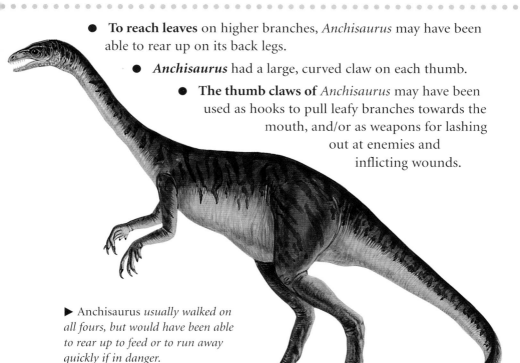

- **To reach leaves** on higher branches, *Anchisaurus* may have been able to rear up on its back legs.

  - *Anchisaurus* had a large, curved claw on each thumb.

    - **The thumb claws of** *Anchisaurus* may have been used as hooks to pull leafy branches towards the mouth, and/or as weapons for lashing out at enemies and inflicting wounds.

▶ Anchisaurus *usually walked on all fours, but would have been able to rear up to feed or to run away quickly if in danger.*

...FASCINATING FACT...
Anchisaurus fossils were discovered in North America in 1818, but at the time they were thought to be human remains!

217

Psittacosaurus

◀ Psittacosaurus *seemed to be an early member of
the dinosaur group known as the ceratopsians or
horn-faces. It had the characteristic birdlike beak,
but had not yet evolved the face horns or neck
shield.* Psittacosaurus *was about the size of a
farmyard pig. Later members of the group
would be enormous, like* Triceratops.

● *Psittacosaurus* **was a plant-eater** in the group known as the ceratopsians, or horn-faced dinosaurs.

● **Living in the Middle Cretaceous Period**, *Psittacosaurus* walked the Earth about 115–10 mya.

● *Psittacosaurus* was named in 1923 from fossils that were found in Mongolia, Central Asia.

● **Fossils** of *Psittacosaurus* have been found at various sites across Asia, including ones in Russia, China and Thailand.

▲ *The beak of a modern-day parrot is similar to that of* Psittacosaurus. *The top jaw overlaps the bottom and can slice through tough plant material.*

● **The rear legs** of *Psittacosaurus* were longer and stronger than its front legs, suggesting that this dinosaur may have reared up to run fast on its rear legs, rather than running on all four legs.

● *Psittacosaurus* measured about 2 m in length.

● **On each foot** *Psittacosaurus* had four toes.

● **The name** *Psittacosaurus* means 'parrot reptile', after the dinosaur's beak-shaped mouth, like that of a parrot.

● **Inside its cheeks,** *Psittacosaurus* had many sharp teeth capable of cutting and slicing through tough plant material.

Massospondylus

- **Massospondylus** was a medium-sized plant eater belonging to the group known as the prosauropods.

  - **Africa and perhaps North America** were home to *Massospondylus*, about 200 mya.

    - **In total**, *Massospondylus* was about 5 m long, with almost half of this length being its tail.

      - **The rear legs** of *Massospondylus* were bigger and stronger than its front legs, so it may have reared up to reach high-up food.

▶ *The tiny head of* Massospondylus *would be kept busy, gathering food to fuel the bulky body. It may have spent 20 hours feeding each day! As with the other sauropods, it digested its food with the help of gastroliths (swallowed stones).*

- **The name** *Massospondylus* means 'huge backbone'.

- **Fossils of more than 80 *Massospondylus*** have been found, making it one of the best-studied dinosaurs.

- ***Massospondylus* had a tiny head** compared to its large body, and it must have spent many hours each day gathering enough food to survive.

- **The front teeth** of *Massospondylus* were surprisingly large and strong for a plant eater, with ridged edges more like meat-eating teeth.

- **The cheek teeth** of *Massospondylus* were too small and weak for chewing large amounts of plant food, so perhaps the dinosaur's food was mashed mainly in its stomach.

- **In the 1980s,** some scientists suggested that *Massospondylus* may have been a meat eater, partly because of the ridged edges on its front teeth.

Tuojiangosaurus

- *Tuojiangosaurus* was a member of the group we know as the plated dinosaurs, or stegosaurs.

- **The first nearly complete dinosaur skeleton** to be found in China was of a *Tuojiangosaurus*, and excellent fossil skeletons are on display in several Chinese museums.

- **The name** *Tuojiangosaurus* means 'Tuo River reptile'.

- *Tuojiangosaurus* lived during the Late Jurassic Period, about 155 mya.

- *Tuojiangosaurus* was 7 m long from nose to tail-tip.

- **The weight of** *Tuojiangosaurus* was probably about one tonne.

- **Like other stegosaurs**, *Tuojiangosaurus* had tall slabs or plates of bone on its back.

- **The back plates of** *Tuojiangosaurus* were roughly triangular and probably stood upright in two rows that ran from the neck to the middle of the tail.

- *Tuojiangosaurus* **plucked low-growing plant food** with the beak-shaped front of its mouth, and partly chewed the plant material with its leaf-shaped, ridge-edged cheek teeth.

> ...**FASCINATING FACT**...
> *Tuojiangosaurus* had four long tail spikes, arranged in two Vs, which it could swing at enemies to keep them at a distance.

▶ Tuojiangosaurus *was a stegosaur, a group of heavily armoured, small-brained herbivores that survived for over 50 million years. Stegosaurs' main defence was their tail. It could deliver a powerful blow with cone-shaped plates on the underside and long wounding spikes at the end.*

Iguanodon

FASCINATING FACT
Iguanodon was one of the very first dinosaurs to be given an official scientific name, in 1825.

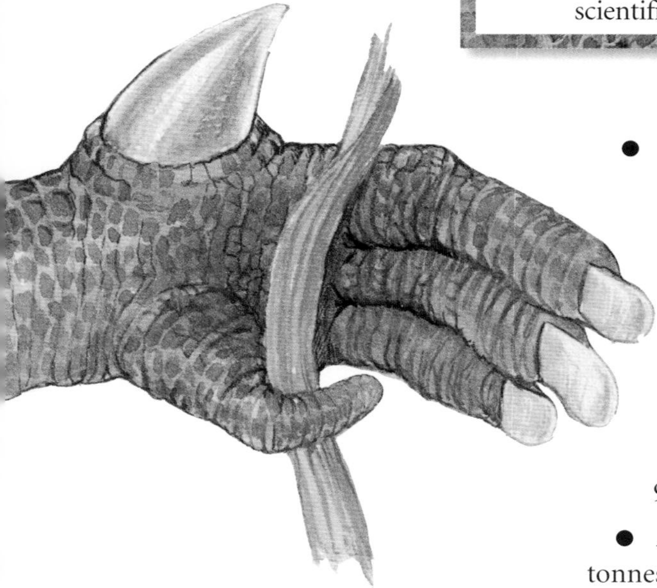

▲ *When a fossil of the thumb spike was first unearthed, palaeontologists thought it belonged on* Iguanodon's *nose!*

- ***Iguanodon* was a large plant eater** in the dinosaur group known as ornithopods.
- **Numerous fossils** of *Iguanodon* have been found in several countries in Europe, including England, Belgium, Germany and Spain.
- ***Iguanodon*** measured about 9 m from nose to tail.
- **A large elephant today**, at 4–5 tonnes, is estimated to weigh about the same as *Iguanodon* did.
- ***Iguanodon* lived** during the Early to Middle Cretaceous Period, 140–110 mya.

▶ *Herbivorous* Iguanodon *may have used its large thumb spike as defence against enemies. It would have delivered a nasty stab wound to the neck or flank.*

- *Iguanodon* **probably walked** and ran on its large, powerful back legs for much of the time, with its body held horizontal.

- **A cone-shaped spike** on *Iguanodon* 's thumb may have been a weapon for jabbing at rivals or enemies.

- **The three central fingers** on *Iguanodon* 's hands had hooflike claws for four-legged walking.

- **The fifth or little finger** of *Iguanodon* was able to bend across the hand for grasping objects, and was perhaps used to pull plants towards the mouth.

◀ Iguanodon *had claws on its feet. But these were rounded and blunt and looked more like hooves.*

225

Nodosaurs

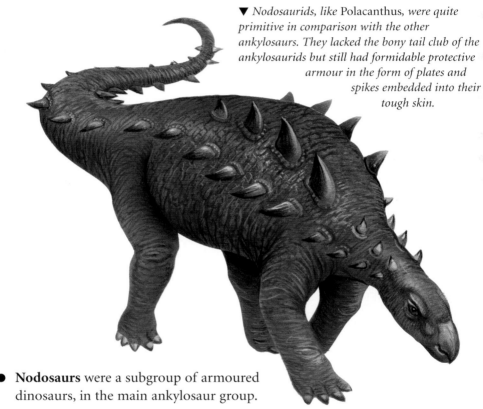

▼ *Nodosaurids, like* Polacanthus, *were quite primitive in comparison with the other ankylosaurs. They lacked the bony tail club of the ankylosaurids but still had formidable protective armour in the form of plates and spikes embedded into their tough skin.*

- **Nodosaurs** were a subgroup of armoured dinosaurs, in the main ankylosaur group.

- **The nodosaur subgroup** included *Edmontonia, Sauropelta, Polacanthus* and *Nodosaurus*.

- **Nodosaurs were slow-moving**, heavy-bodied plant eaters with thick, heavy nodules, lumps and plates of bone in their skin for protection.

- **Most nodosaurs lived** during the Late Jurassic and the Cretaceous Periods, 150–65 mya.

- *Edmontonia* **lived in North America** during the Late Cretaceous Period, 75–70 mya.

- *Edmontonia* **was about seven metres long**, but its bony armour made it very heavy for its size, at 4–5 tonnes.

- **Along its neck, back and tail** *Edmontonia* had rows of flat and spiky plates.

- **The nodosaur** *Polacanthus* was about 4 m long and lived 120–110 mya.

- **Fossils** of *Polacanthus* come from the Isle of Wight, southern England, and perhaps from North America, in South Dakota, USA.

▲ *Nodosaurids were part of the ankylosaur group of dinosaurs. Their bodies were protected with spikes and plates but they did not have a tail club. Like all armoured dinosaurs, they had soft, vulnerable bellies and so moved quite close to the ground.*

. . . . FASCINATING FACT . . . .
Like many nodosaurs, *Edmontonia* and *Polacanthus* probably had long, fierce spikes on their shoulders, used to 'spear' enemies.

227

Segnosaurs

- **Little is known** about the segnosaur group of dinosaurs – the subject of much disagreement among experts.

- **Segnosaurs are named after** almost the only known member of the group, Segnosaurus.

▼ Segnosaurus *is one of those dinosaurs that we just don't know that much about. Scientists have grouped it with the sauropods, but it has some unusual additional features! Instead of having four stocky legs, it may have moved around quite easily on two legs, using its clawed front feet to feed. We do know that it ate plants, but it may have eaten meat as well which no other sauropod did.*

▶ *Another unusual feature of* Segnosaurus *was that it was not typically lizard-hipped.*

- **The name Segnosaurus** means 'slow reptile'.

- **Segnosaurus lived** during the Mid to Late Cretaceous Period, about 90 mya.

- **Fossils of Segnosaurus** were found mainly in the Gobi Desert in Central Asia in the 1970s. The dinosaur was named in 1979 by Mongolian scientist Altangerel Perle.

- **Segnosaurus had a narrow head** and probably a toothless, beaklike front to its mouth.

- **Experts** have variously described Segnosaurus as a predatory meat eater, a swimming or wading fish eater, a rearing-up leaf eater, or even an ant eater.

- **Different experts** have said *Segnosaurus* was a theropod, a prosauropod and an ornithopod.

- **Some scientists have suggested** that Segnosaurus was a huge dinosaur-version of today's anteater that ripped open the nests of termites and ants with its powerful claws.

Sauropelta

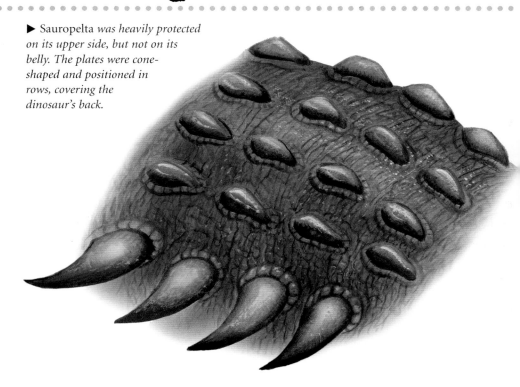

▶ Sauropelta *was heavily protected on its upper side, but not on its belly. The plates were cone-shaped and positioned in rows, covering the dinosaur's back.*

- ***Sauropelta*** was a nodosaur – a type of armoured dinosaur.

- **The name** *Sauropelta* means 'shielded reptile', from the many large, conelike lumps of bone – some almost as big as dinner plates – on its head, neck, back and tail.

- **The larger lumps of bone** on *Sauropelta* were interspersed with smaller, fist-sized bony studs.

- *Sauropelta* **had a row of sharp spikes** along each side of its body, from just behind the eyes to the tail. The spikes decreased in size towards the tail.

- *Sauropelta* **was about 7.5 m long,** including the tail, and its bulky body and heavy, bony armour meant it probably weighed almost 3 tonnes.

- **The armour** of *Sauropelta* was flexible, almost like lumps of metal set into thick leather, so the dinosaur could twist and turn, but was unable to run very fast.

- **Strong, sturdy, pillar-like legs** supported *Sauropelta's* great weight.

- *Sauropelta* probably defended itself by crouching down to protect its softer belly, or swinging its head to jab at an enemy with its long neck spines.

- **Using its beak-like mouth,** *Sauropelta* probably plucked at low-growing plant food.

▶ Sauropelta *was an armoured dinosaur with bony plates on its back and sides and a stiff tail. It was large and stocky, but lacked the defensive advantage of a tail club.*

Monsters

▼ *Only discovered in the 1980s,* Giganotosaurus *was a South American dinosaur. At 15 m long, it may well have been the biggest ever meat-eating dinosaur – bigger than* Tyrannosaurus! *Its short thigh bone may mean that it moved at a similar speed to* Tyrannosaurus *when pursuing prey.*

- **Dinosaurs** can be measured by length and height, but 'biggest' usually means heaviest or bulkiest.

- **Dinosaurs were not the biggest-ever living things** on Earth – some trees are more than 100 times their size.

- **The sauropod dinosaurs** of the Late Jurassic were the biggest animals to walk on Earth, as far as we know.

- **Sauropod dinosaurs** may not have been the biggest animals ever. Today's great whales, and perhaps the massive, flippered sea reptiles called pliosaurs of the Dinosaur Age, rival them in size.

- **For any dinosaur**, enough fossils must be found for a panel of scientists to be sure it is a distinct type, so they can give it a scientific name. They must also be able to estimate its size. With some giant dinosaurs, not enough fossils have been found.

- *Supersaurus* **remains** found in Colorado, USA, suggest a dinosaur similar to Diplodocus, but perhaps even longer, at 35 m.

- *Seismosaurus* **fossils** found in 1991 in the USA may belong to sauropod up to 40 m long.

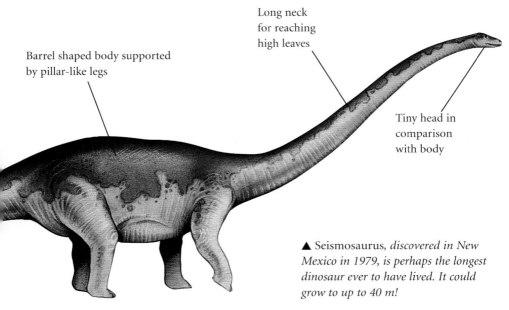

Long neck for reaching high leaves

Barrel shaped body supported by pillar-like legs

Tiny head in comparison with body

▲ Seismosaurus, *discovered in New Mexico in 1979, is perhaps the longest dinosaur ever to have lived. It could grow to up to 40 m!*

233

Myths

▶ Dimorphodon *was one of the early pterosaurs, 190 mya. Attached to the wings were large clawed hands whilst powerful legs indicate that they were used for walking and running.* Dimorphodon *had a large head in comparison to its body, with a deep mouth and sharp teeth for eating small reptiles and fish.*

- **Dinosaurs were the only animals alive** during the Age of Dinosaurs – false, there were many kinds of creatures, from worms, insects and fish to other kinds of reptiles.

- **Dinosaurs flew in the air** – false, although other reptiles called pterosaurs did fly.

- **Dinosaurs lived in the sea** – false, although other reptiles such as ichthyosaurs and plesiosaurs did.

- **Mammals appeared** on Earth after the dinosaurs died out – false. Small mammals lived all through the Age of Dinosaurs.

- **A single kind of dinosaur** survived all through the Age of Dinosaurs – false. A few kinds may have lived for 10, 20 or even 30 million years, but none came close to 160 million years.

- **Dinosaurs were huge** lizards – false. Dinosaurs were reptiles, but not members of the lizard group.

- **Dinosaurs gave birth to babies** – false. As far as we know, all species of dinosaur laid eggs.

- **All dinosaurs** were green – false, probably.

- **Dinosaurs live on today** – false … unless you've found one!

▼ *We really have no ides what colour the dinosaurs were. We can guess by looking at reptiles today, but they could have been any colour!*

⋯ **FASCINATING FACT** ⋯
Dinosaurs and humans fought each other –
false. The last dinosaurs died out more than
60 million years before humans appeared.

235

Male and female

- **In many living reptiles,** females are larger than males.

- **In dinosaur fossils**, the shapes of the hip bones and head crests can indicate if the creatures were male or female.

- **Head crest fossils** of different sizes and proportions belonging to the hadrosaur (duck-billed dinosaur) *Lambeosaurus* have been found.

- **Some** *Lambeosaurus* had short, rounded main crests with small, spikelike spurs pointing up and back.

- **Other** *Lambeosaurus* had a large, angular main crest with a large spur pointing up and back.

- **The head crest differences** in *Lambeosaurus* fossils may indicate that males and females looked different.

- **Remains of the hadrosaur** *Corythosaurus* show two main sizes of head crest, perhaps one belonging to females and the other to males.

- **New studies** in the variations of head crests led to more than eight different species of dinosaurs being reclassified as one species of *Corythosaurus*.

- **In dinosaurs and other animals**, differences between the sexes – either in size or specific features – is known as sexual dimorphism.

...FASCINATING FACT...
In *Parasaurolophus* specimens, some
head crests were twice as long as others
– probably a male-female difference.

◀ Lambeosaurus *was a member of the hadrosaur
group. The hollow crest on its head could have
identified the dominant dinosaur in a
particular area or indicated male and
female members to other members
of a group. It could even have
been used for calling to
each other during the
mating season.*

237

Dinosaur eyes

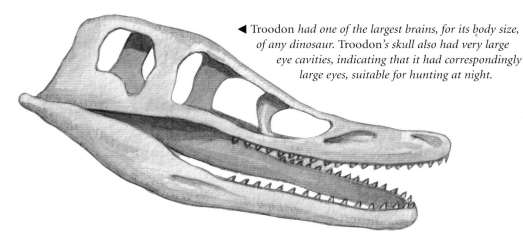

◀ Troodon *had one of the largest brains, for its body size, of any dinosaur. Troodon's skull also had very large eye cavities, indicating that it had correspondingly large eyes, suitable for hunting at night.*

- **No fossils have been found of dinosaur eyes**, because eyes are soft and squishy, and soon rot away after death, or are eaten by scavengers.

- **The main clues** to dinosaur eyes come from the hollows, or orbits, in the skull where the eyes were located.

- **The orbits** in fossil dinosaur skulls show that dinosaur eyes were similar to those of reptiles today.

- **The 6 m long sauropod** *Vulcanodon* had tiny eyes in relation to the size of its head.

- **Small-eyed dinosaurs** probably only had good vision in the daytime.

- **The eyes** of many plant-eating dinosaurs, such as *Vulcanodon*, were on the sides of their heads, giving them all-round vision.

- **The small meat eater** *Troodon* had relatively large eyes, and it could probably see well even in dim light.

. . . .

> ...FASCINATING FACT...
> The plant-eater *Leaellynasaura* had large
> optic lobes, and probably had good eyesight.

- ***Troodon's* eyes** were on the front of its face and pointed forwards, allowing it to see detail and judge distance.

- **Dinosaurs that had large bulges,** called optic lobes, in their brains – detectable by the shapes of their skulls – could probably see very well, perhaps even at night.

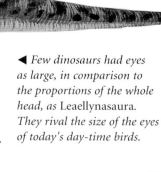

◄ *Few dinosaurs had eyes as large, in comparison to the proportions of the whole head, as* Leaellynasaura. *They rival the size of the eyes of today's day-time birds.*

239

Noses

▲ Ornithomimus *had nasal openings near the tip of its beak, unlike the nostrils of a modern bird.*

- **Dinosaurs breathed** through their mouths and/or noses, like many other creatures today.

- **Fossil dinosaur skulls** show that there were two nose openings, called nares, in the bone.

- **A dinosaur's two nasal openings**, or nares, led to nasal chambers inside the skull, where the smell organs were located.

- **Some meat eaters**, especially carnosaurs such as *Allosaurus* and *Tyrannosaurus*, had very large nasal chambers and probably had an excellent sense of smell.

▶ Tyrannosaurus *had very large nasal cavities which indicates to scientists that it had a very good sense of smell.*

- **In most dinosaurs** the nasal opening were at the front of the snout, just above the upper jaw.

- **In some dinosaurs**, especially sauropods such as *Mamenchisaurus* and *Brachiosaurus*, the nasal openings were higher on the skull, between the eyes.

- **Fossils** show that air passages led from the nasal chambers rearwards into the head for breathing.

- **The nasal openings** in a dinosaur's skull bone led to external openings, or nostrils, in the skin.

- **New evidence** from animals alive today suggests that a dinosaur's nostrils would have been lower down than the nares (the openings in the skull bone), towards the front of the snout.

. . . **FASCINATING FACT** . . .
In hadrosaurs, the nasal passages inside
the bony head crests were over 1-m long.

241

Horns

◄ The structure of a dinosaur horn was made up of two parts: an inner core and an outer protective covering. This is similar to the composition of horns in modern mammals, such as antelope.

...FASCINATING FACT...
Dinosaurs may have used their horns to push over plants or dig up roots for food.

● **A dinosaur's horns** got bigger as the animal grew – they were not shed and replaced each year – just like the antlers of today's deer.

● **Each horn** had a bony core and an outer covering of a horny substance formed mainly from keratin.

● **Horns** were most common among the plant-eating dinosaurs. They were probably used for self-defence and to defend offspring against predators.

● **The biggest horns** belonged to the ceratopsians or 'horn-faced' dinosaurs, such as *Triceratops*.

● **In some ceratopsians**, just the bony core of the horn was about 1 m long, not including the outer sheath.

● **The ceratopsian** *Styracosaurus* or 'spiked reptile' had a series of long horns around the top of its neck frill, and a very long horn on its nose.

- **Horns may have been used** in head-swinging displays to intimidate rivals and make physical fighting less likely.

- **In battle**, male dinosaurs may have locked horns in a trial of strength, as antelopes do today.

- **Armoured dinosaurs** such as the nodosaur *Panoplosaurus* had horn-like spikes along the sides of its body.

▼ *Like other ceratopsians,* Styracosaurus' *frill had a formidable row of horns which formed part of the dinosaur's defence. The frill horns had bony centres which meant that they weighed heavily on the neck.*

Beaks

▲ Some reconstructions of Parasaurolophus *show a 'web' of skin extending from the bony head crest, and curving down to the back of the neck. The skin could have been brightly coloured in life, perhaps part of a visual display for mating, herd dominance or gaining territory.*

- **Several kinds of dinosaurs** had a toothless, beak-shaped front to their mouths.

- **Beaked dinosaurs** included ceratopsians (horn-faces) such as *Triceratops*, ornithopods such as *Iguanodon* and the hadrosaurs (duck-bills), stegosaurs, segnosaurs, ankylosaurs (armoured dinosaurs) and fast-running ostrich-dinosaurs.

- **Most beaked dinosaurs** had chopping or chewing teeth near the backs of their mouths, in their cheeks, but ostrich-dinosaurs had no teeth.

> **...FASCINATING FACT...**
> Some of the largest beaks in relation to body
> size belonged to *Oviraptor* and *Psittacosaurus*.

- **A dinosaur's beak** was made up of the upper (maxilla) and the lower (mandible) jaw bones.

- **Ornithischian (bird-hipped) dinosaurs** had what is called a 'predentary' bone at the front tip of the lower jaw.

- **Ceratopsian (horn-faced) dinosaurs** had a 'rostral' bone at the front tip of the upper jaw.

- **In life**, the bones at the front of a dinosaur's jaw would have been covered with horn, which formed the outer shape of the beak.

- **Dinosaurs almost certainly** used their beaks for pecking, snipping, tearing and slicing their food.

- **Dinosaurs may have** used their beaks to peck fiercely at any attackers.

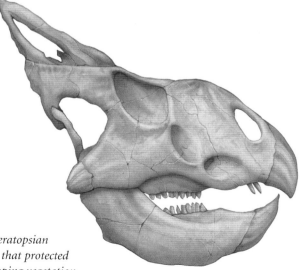

▶ Protoceratops *was the first in the ceratopsian group of dinosaurs. It had a small frill that protected its neck area and a tough beak for cropping vegetation.*

245

Teeth

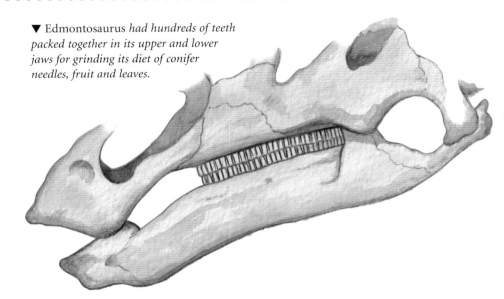

▼ Edmontosaurus *had hundreds of teeth packed together in its upper and lower jaws for grinding its diet of conifer needles, fruit and leaves.*

- **Some of most common fossil remains** of dinosaurs are their teeth – the hardest parts of their bodies.

- **Dinosaur teeth** come in a huge range of sizes and shapes – daggers, knives, shears, pegs, combs, rakes, filelike rasps, crushing batteries and vices.

- **In some dinosaurs**, up to three-quarters of a tooth was fixed into the jaw bone, so only one-quarter showed.

- **The teeth of plant eaters** such as *Iguanodon* had angled tops that rubbed past each other in a grinding motion.

- **Some duck-bill dinosaurs** (hadrosaurs) had more than 1000 teeth, all at the back of the mouth.

▶ *The shape, number and layout of teeth within the jaw bones are clear evidence for what a dinosaur ate. Meat eaters like* Baryonyx *and* Tyrannosaurus *had huge sharp teeth for tearing through the flesh of their prey. Some plant eaters like* Apatosaurus *had no chewing teeth at all!*

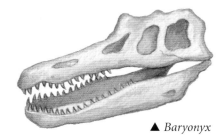

▲ *Baryonyx*

▼ *Apatosaurus*

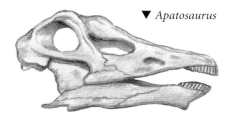

- **Like modern reptiles**, dinosaurs probably grew new teeth to replace old, worn or broken ones.

- **Individual teeth** were replaced at different times.

- **Some of the largest teeth** of any dinosaur belonged to 9 m long *Daspletosaurus*, a tyrannosaur-like meat eater.

- **Some of** *Daspletosaurus's* teeth were up to 18 cm long.

▼ *Tyrannosaurus*

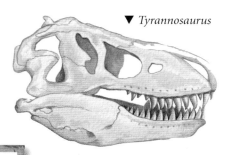

. . . FASCINATING FACT . . .
Troodon, or 'wounding tooth', was named on the evidence of just one or two teeth.

Stomach stones

- **Some dinosaur fossils** are found with unusually smooth, rounded stones, like seashore pebbles, jumbled up among or near them.

- **Smoothed pebbles** occur with dinosaur fossils far more than would be expected by chance alone.

- **Smooth stones** are mainly found with or near the remains of large plant-eating dinosaurs, especially those of prosauropods such as *Massospondylus*, *Plateosaurus* and *Riojasaurus*, sauropods such as *Brachiosaurus* and *Diplodocus*, the parrot-beaked *Psittacosaurus* and the stegosaurs.

- **Some plant-eating dinosaurs** may have used smooth stones to help process their food.

▶ *Dinosaurs in the sauropod group, like* Barosaurus, *did not chew their food before swallowing. Instead, they swallowed stones which ground up the food in a part of the digestive system called the gizzard. This meant that they wasted no time when feeding their huge bodies!*

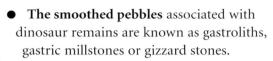

- **The smoothed pebbles** associated with dinosaur remains are known as gastroliths, gastric millstones or gizzard stones.

  - **Gastroliths** were stones that a dinosaur found on the ground and deliberately swallowed into its stomach.

  - **In the dinosaur's stomach**, gastroliths acted as 'millstones', crushing and churning plant food, and breaking it down into a soft pulp for better digestion.

- **As gastroliths churned and rubbed** inside a dinosaur's guts, they became very rounded, smoothed and polished.

- **Gastroliths as small as a pea** and as large as a football have been found.

- **Gastroliths may be the reason why** many big plant eaters, especially sauropods, had no chewing teeth – the mashing was done inside the guts.

▶ *Gastroliths vary in size from smaller than grapes to larger than soccer balls. They have been found adjacent to many dinosaur fossil finds.*

Legs and posture

▶ *The small plant eater* Hypsilophodon *was a bipedal dinosaur, walking and running on its two larger back legs.*

- **All dinosaurs had four limbs**. Unlike certain other reptiles, such as snakes and slow-worms, they did not lose their limbs through evolution.

- **Some dinosaurs**, such as massive, plant-eating sauropods like *Janenschia*, stood and walked on all four legs nearly all the time.

- **The all-fours method** of standing and walking is called 'quadrupedal'.

- **Some dinosaurs**, such as nimble, meat-eating dromaeosaurs like *Deinonychus*, stood and walked on their back limbs only. The front two limbs were used as arms.

- **The back-limbs-only method** of standing and walking is called 'bipedal'.

- **Some dinosaurs**, such as hadrosaurs like *Edmontosaurus*, could move on all four limbs or just on their back legs if they chose to.

- **Today, the only reptiles** that have an almost upright posture are crocodiles and alligators. They can only keep it up for a few seconds though as they gallop along in their 'high walk'.

- **Reptiles** such as lizards and crocodiles have a sprawling posture, in which the upper legs join the body at the sides.

- **Dinosaurs** had an upright posture, with the legs directly below the body.

- **The more efficient upright posture** and gait may be one major reason why dinosaurs were so successful compared to other animals of the time.

▼ Dromaeosaurus *was slim and agile, making it a fast, effective hunter. It ran on two legs, possibly hunting in packs and this combination meant that it could probably prey on much larger animals.*

Hips

- **All dinosaurs are classified** in one of two large groups, according to the design and shape of their hip bones.

- **One of the two large groups of dinosaurs** is the Saurischia, which means 'lizard-hipped'.

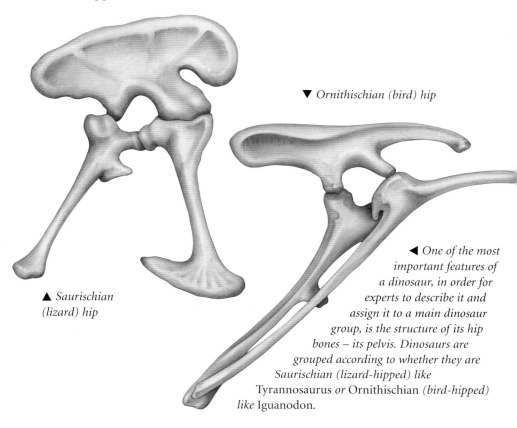

▼ *Ornithischian (bird) hip*

▲ *Saurischian (lizard) hip*

◀ *One of the most important features of a dinosaur, in order for experts to describe it and assign it to a main dinosaur group, is the structure of its hip bones – its pelvis. Dinosaurs are grouped according to whether they are Saurischian (lizard-hipped) like* Tyrannosaurus *or Ornithischian (bird-hipped) like* Iguanodon.

- **In a saurischian dinosaur**, the lower front pair of rod-shaped bones in the pelvis project down and forwards.

- **All meat-eating dinosaurs** belonged to the Saurischia.

- **The biggest dinosaurs**, the plant-eating sauropods, belonged to the Saurischia group.

- **The second of the two groups of dinosaurs** is the Ornithischia, meaning 'bird-hipped'.

- **In an ornithischian dinosaur**, the lower front pair of rod-shaped bones in the pelvis, called the pubis bones, project down and backwards, lying parallel with another pair, the ischium bones.

- **All dinosaurs** in the group Ornithischia, from small *Heterodontosaurus* to huge *Triceratops*, were plant eaters.

- **In addition to hips,** there are other differences between the Saurischia and Ornithischia, such as an 'extra' bone called the predentary at the front tip of the lower jaw in ornithischians.

. . . FASCINATING FACT . . .
The lizard-hipped design of meat-eaters
was better at anchoring leg muscles,
which made them fast runners.

Claws

- **Like reptiles today,** dinosaurs had claws or similar hard structures at the ends of their digits (fingers and toes).

- **Dinosaur claws** were probably made from keratin – the same hard substance that formed their horns, and from which our own fingernails and toenails are made.

- **Claw shapes and sizes** relative to body size varied greatly between dinosaurs.

- **In many meat-eating dinosaurs** that ran on two back legs, the claws on the fingers were long and sharp, similar to a cat's claws.

- **A small, meat-eating dinosaur** such as *Troodon* probably used its finger claws for grabbing small mammals and lizards, and for scrabbling in the soil for insects and worms.

- **Larger meat-eating dinosaurs** such as *Allosaurus* may have used their hand claws to hold and slash their prey.

- **Huge plant-eating sauropods** such as *Diplodocus* had claws on its elephant-like feet that resembled nails or hooves.

- **Many dinosaurs** had five clawed digits on their feet, but some, such as *Tyrannosaurus*, had only three toes on each foot to support their weight.

- **Some of the largest dinosaur claws** belonged to *Deinocheirus* – its massive finger claws were more than 35 cm long.

- ***Deinocheirus* was probably** a gigantic ostrich-dinosaur that lived in the Late Cretaceous Period in Mongolia. Only parts of its fossil hands and arms have been found, so the rest of it remains a mystery.

▶ Troodon *may have been the best-equipped dinosaur hunter ever. It had a bigger brain than most and its large eyes may have been useful for hunting at night.* Troodon's *long, lethal claws would have enabled it to grab and hold prey while running at speed.*

Long, sharp
claws and teeth

Large eyes and brain cavity

Skin

- **Several fossils of dinosaur skin** have been found, revealing that dinosaurs had scales, like today's reptiles.

- **As in crocodiles**, the scales of a dinosaur were embedded in its thick, tough, leathery hide, rather than lying on top of its skin and overlapping, as in snakes.

- **When the first fossils** of dinosaur skin were found in the mid 1800s, scientists thought they were from giant prehistoric crocodiles.

- **Fossil skin** of the horned dinosaur *Chasmosaurus* has been found.

- ***Chasmosaurus* had larger bumps or lumps**, called tubercles, scattered among its normal-sized scales.

▼ *Specific dinosaur markings like those seen on this reconstruction of* Corythosaurus *can only be guessed at. Scientists use information from the skin colours and textures of living reptiles such as lizards to predict what dinosaur colours and markings might have looked like.*

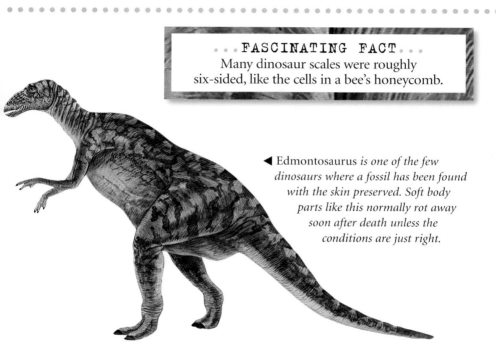

◄ Edmontosaurus *is one of the few
dinosaurs where a fossil has been found
with the skin preserved. Soft body
parts like this normally rot away
soon after death unless the
conditions are just right.*

● **Samples of fossil skin** belonging to the duck-bill hadrosaur *Edmontosaurus*
have been found.

● *Edmontosaurus* **was covered** in thousands of small scales, like little pebbles,
with larger lumps or tubercles spaced among them.

● **Various specimens** of fossil skin show that the scales of *Iguanodon*-type
dinosaurs were larger than those of same-sized, similar duck-bill dinosaurs.

● **Scaly skin** protected a dinosaur against the teeth and claws of enemies,
accidental scrapes, and the bites of small pests such as mosquitoes and fleas.

257

Armour

- **Many kinds of dinosaurs** had protective 'armour'.

- **Some armour** took the form of bony plates, or osteoderms, embedded in the skin.

- **A dinosaur with armour** might weigh twice as much as a same-sized dinosaur without armour.

- **Armoured dinosaurs** are divided into two main groups – the ankylosaurs and the nodosaurs.

- **The large sauropod** *Saltasaurus* had a kind of armour.

- *Saltasaurus* **had hundreds** of small, bony lumps, each as big as a pea, packed together in the skin of its back.

- **On its back**, *Saltasaurus* also had about 50 larger pieces of bone the size of a human hand.

- *Saltasaurus* **is named after** the Salta region of Argentina, where its fossils were found.

- **Uruguay** provided another site for *Saltasaurus* fossils.

- *Saltasaurus* **was 12 m long** and weighed about 3–4 tonnes.

▶ Ankylosaurus's *tail club was nearly 1 m across and could deliver a crippling blow to an unsuspecting predator. In addition to this, the back and head were protected by large bony lumps and plates.*

A predator like *Spinosaurus* would need to attack *Ankylosaurus* very carefully!

Ankylosaurus's hefty tail club could deliver a painful blow

Head crests

▲ Parasaurolophus *may have used the hollow tubes inside its long head crest to make sounds. The tubes ran from the nose to the end of the crest. These sounds may have been used to identify themselves or as warnings of danger.*

- **Many dinosaurs** had lumps, bumps, plates, bulges, ridges or other shapes of bone on their heads, called head crests.

- **Head crests** may have been covered with brightly coloured skin in life, for visual display.

- **Meat eaters with head crests** included *Carnotaurus* and *Dilophosaurus*.

- **The dinosaurs with the largest** and most complicated head crests were the hadrosaurs.

- **The largest dinosaur head crest** was probably a long, hollow, tubular shape of bone belonging to the hadrosaur *Parasaurolophus*.

- **The head crests of hadrosaurs** may have been involved in making sounds.

- **Some years ago** the hadrosaur *Tsintaosaurus* was thought to have a very unusual head crest – a hollow tube sticking straight up between the eyes, like a unicorn's horn.

- **The so-called head crest** of *Tsintaosaurus* is now thought to be the fossil part of another animal, and not part of *Tsintaosaurus* at all.

- *Tsintaosaurus* is now usually known as *Tanius*, a hadrosaur with a small crest or no crest at all!

FASCINATING FACT
The head crests of some large
Parasaurolophus, perhaps full-grown males,
reached an incredible 1.8 m in length.

Sails

- **Long, bony extensions**, like rods or spines, stuck up from the backs of some dinosaurs.

- **In life**, a dinosaur's bony extensions may have held up a large area of skin, commonly called a back sail.

- **Dinosaurs with back sails** included the huge meat eater *Spinosaurus* and the large plant eater *Ouranosaurus*.

▶ *The predator* Spinosaurus *was almost as large as* Tyrannosaurus. *Its sail would have been almost 2 m tall.*

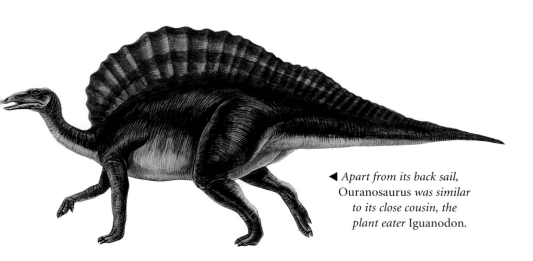

◀ *Apart from its back sail,*
Ouranosaurus *was similar
to its close cousin, the
plant eater* Iguanodon.

- *Spinosaurus* **and** *Ouranosaurus* **both lived 100 mya.**

- **Fossils of** *Spinosaurus* and *Ouranosaurus* were found in North Africa.

- **The skin** on a dinosaur's back sail may have been brightly coloured, or may even have changed colour, like the skin of a chameleon lizard today.

- **A dinosaur's back sail** may have helped to control its body temperature.

- **Standing sideways** to the sun, a back sail would absorb the sun's heat and allow the dinosaur to warm up quickly, ready for action.

- **Standing in the shade**, a back sail would lose warmth and help the dinosaur to avoid overheating.

- **The bony back rods** of *Spinosaurus* were up to 1.6 m tall.

Dinosaur feet

▶ *Even though they were almost certainly slow-moving beasts, the splay-toed feet of sauropods were cushioned, much like the feet of elephants today.*

● **Dinosaur feet differed**, depending on the animal's body design, weight and general lifestyle.

● **A typical dinosaur's front feet** had metacarpal bones in the lower wrist or upper hand, and two or three phalanges bones in each (finger or toe), tipped by claws.

● **The rear feet** of a typical dinosaur had metatarsal (instead of metacarpal) bones in the lower ankle.

● **Some dinosaurs had five toes** per foot, like most other reptiles (and most birds and mammals).

● **Sauropods** probably had feet with tough, rounded bases supported by a wedge of fibrous, cushion-like tissue.

> **FASCINATING FACT**
> The dinosaur group that includes all the meat-eaters, both large and small, is named the theropods, or 'beast feet'.

264

- **Most sauropods** had claws on their first three toes, and smaller, blunter 'hooves' on the other two toes.

- **Ostrich-dinosaurs** such as *Gallimimus* had very long feet and long, slim toes for fast running.

- **Many fast-running dinosaurs** had fewer toes, to reduce weight – *Gallimimus* had three toes per back foot.

- **The dinosaur group** that includes *Iguanodon*, duck-billed dinosaurs, *Heterodontosaurus* and many other plant eaters is named the ornithopods, or 'bird feet'.

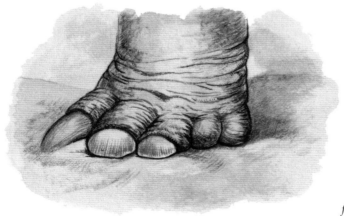

◀ Apatosaurus *was a massive beast, but could trot surprisingly quickly on its relatively long legs. It had a sharp, 17 cm claw on each front foot which could have been to protect it from enemies or to help it to balance its huge frame.*

Footprints

- **Thousands of fossilized dinosaur** footprints have been found. They are located all over the world.

- **Some dinosaurs left footprints** when they walked on the soft mud or sand of riverbanks. Then the mud baked hard in the sun, and was covered by more sand or mud, which helped preserve the footprints as fossils.

- **Some fossil footprints** were made when dinosaur feet left impressions in soft mud or sand that was then covered by volcanic ash, which set hard.

- **Many footprints** have been found together in lines, called 'trackways'. These suggest that some dinosaurs lived in groups, or used the same routes regularly.

- **The distance between same-sized footprints** indicates whether a dinosaur was walking, trotting or running.

▶ *This footprint shows that* Tyrannosaurus *walked on the tips of its toes as opposed to on flat feet like most large dinosaurs. Each foot would have supported about 3–4 tonnes in weight.*

▶ *Many fossil footprints of similar shapes but different sizes, some overlapping, show a herd of mixed size and varying age passed this way. The relative positions of footprints indicate how the dinosaur was standing or moving.*

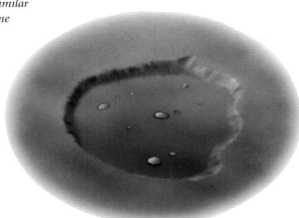

- **Footprints of big meat eaters** such as *Tyrannosaurus* show three toes with claws, on a forward-facing foot.

- **In big plant eaters** such as *Iguanodon*, each footprint shows three separate toes, but less or no claw impressions, and the feet point slightly inwards.

- **In giant plant-eating sauropods**, each footprint is rounded and has indentations of nail-like 'hooves'.

- **Some sauropod footprints** are more than 1 m across.

FASCINATING FACT
Hadrosaur footprints 135 cm long and 80 cm wide were found near Salt Lake City, Utah, USA.

Tails

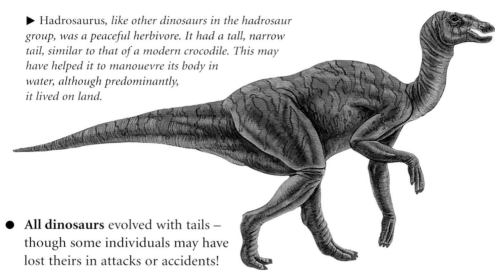

▶ Hadrosaurus, *like other dinosaurs in the hadrosaur group, was a peaceful herbivore. It had a tall, narrow tail, similar to that of a modern crocodile. This may have helped it to manouevre its body in water, although predominantly, it lived on land.*

- **All dinosaurs** evolved with tails – though some individuals may have lost theirs in attacks or accidents!

- **The length of the tail** relative to the body, and its shape, thickness and special features, give many clues as to how the dinosaur used it.

- **The longest tails,** at more than 17 m, belonged to the giant plant-eating sauropods such as *Diplodocus*.

- **Some sauropods** had a linked chain of more than 80 separate bones inside the tail – more than twice the usual number.

- **A sauropod** may have used its tail as a whip to flick at enemies.

- **Many meat-eating dinosaurs** that stood and ran on their back legs had thick-based tails to counterbalance the weight of their bodies and heads.

- **Small, fast, agile meat eaters**, such as *Compsognathus*, used their tails for balance when leaping and darting about.

- **The meat eater** *Ornitholestes* had a tail that was more than half of its 2 m length, and was used as a counterbalance-rudder to help it turn corners at speed.

- **The armoured dinosaurs** known as ankylosaurs had two huge lumps of bone at the ends of their tails, which they swung at their enemies like a club.

- **The tails of the duck-billed dinosaurs** (hadrosaurs) may have been swished from side to side in the water as an aid to swimming.

▶ Compsognathus *had a long stiff tail that helped it to balance and turn quickly when it was running fast.*

Colours

- **No one knows** for certain what colours dinosaurs were.

- **There are several good fossil specimens** of dinosaur skin, but all of them are stone coloured, because fossils are living things that have turned to stone.

- **Some experts believe** that dinosaurs were similar in colour to crocodiles – dull greens and browns.

- **Dinosaurs** that were dull greens and browns would have been well camouflaged among trees, rocks and earth.

- **According to some experts**, certain dinosaurs may have been bright yellow, red or blue, and could even have been striped or patched, like some of today's lizards and snakes.

- **Some dinosaurs** may have been brightly coloured to frighten off predators or to intimidate rivals at breeding time.

- **The tall 'sails'** of skin on the backs of the plant eater *Ouranosaurus* and the meat eater *Spinosaurus* may have been for visual display, as well as for (or instead of) temperature control.

- **The large, bony back plates** on stegosaurs may have been used for colourful displays to rivals.

- **The large neck frills** of horned dinosaurs such as *Triceratops* were possibly very colourful and used for display.

- **Recent finds** of dinosaur skin and scales with microscopic ridges and patterns on their surface may show how the scales reflected light, and so what colour they would have appeared.

▶ *Colourful images like this one of Giganotosaurus are no more than fanciful guesses – scientists just don't know what colour dinosaurs were because there is no evidence. Certain body parts, like sails and head crests may have been brightly coloured to attract mates or scare rivals.*

Brains

- **There is a broad link** between the size of an animal's brain compared to the size of its body, and the level of intelligence it shows.

- **Some fossil dinosaur skulls** have preserved the hollow where the brain once was, revealing the approximate size and shape of the brain.

- **In some cases** a lump of rock formed inside a fossil skull, taking on the size and shape of the brain.

- **The tiny brain** of *Stegosaurus* weighed about 70–80 g, while the whole dinosaur weighed up to 2 tonnes.

- **The brain** of *Stegosaurus* was only 1/25,000th of the weight of its whole body (in a human it is 1/50th).

▼ *Scientists think that it was the small, meat-eating theropods who had the largest brains and therefore, the most intelligence. Deinonychus, a pack hunter, was a member of this dinosaur group.*

▼ Stegosaurus *had the smallest known brain for its body size of any dinosaur – it was about the size of a golf ball!*

▼ *A peaceful plant eater,* Stegosaurus *would have had little use for the intelligence of a stealthy hunter like* Troodon.

- *Brachiosaurus's* **brain** was perhaps only 1/100,000th of the weight of its whole body.

- **The brain of the small meat eater** *Troodon* was about 1/100th the weight of its whole body.

- **The brain-body size comparison** for most dinosaurs is much the same as the brain-body size for living reptiles.

- **Small and medium sized meat eaters** such as *Troodon* may have been as 'intelligent' as parrots or rats.

- **It was once thought** that *Stegosaurus* had a 'second brain' in the base of its tail! Now this lump is thought to have been a nerve junction.

Warm or cold blood?

▶ *In very well-preserved fossils, the detailed microscopic structure inside bones can give clues to whether dinosaurs were warm- or cold-blooded. Also, lizards like this Australian frilled lizard may give us vital clues to dinosaur biology.*

- **If dinosaurs were cold-blooded** and obtained heat only from their surroundings, like reptiles today, they would have been slow or inactive in cold conditions.

- **If dinosaurs were warm-blooded**, like birds and mammals today, they would have been able to stay warm and active in cold conditions.

- **Some time ago** experts believed that all dinosaurs were cold-blooded, but today there is much disagreement.

- **One type of evidence** for warm-bloodedness comes from the detailed structure of the insides of very well-preserved fossil bones.

- **The inside structure** of some fossil dinosaur bones is more like that of warm-blooded creatures than reptiles.

- **Certain small, meat-eating dinosaurs** may have evolved into birds, and since birds are warm-blooded, these dinosaurs may have been, too.

- **In a 'snapshot' count** of dinosaur fossils, the number of predators compared to prey is more like that in mammals than in reptiles.

- **Some dinosaurs** were thought to live in herds and raise families, as many birds and mammals do today. In reptiles, such behaviour is rare.

- **Most dinosaurs stood upright** on straight legs, a posture common to warm-blooded creatures, but not to other, cold-blooded reptiles.

- **If dinosaurs had been warm-blooded**, they would probably have needed to eat at least 10 times more food than if they were cold-blooded, to 'burn' food energy and make heat.

◄ *Crocodiles, which were around even in the very earliest dinosaur period (the Triassic) are cold-blooded.*

Nests and eggs

- **There are hundreds of discoveries** of fossil dinosaur eggs and nests, found with the parent dinosaurs.

- **Eggs and nests** are known of the pig-sized plant eater *Protoceratops*, an early kind of horned dinosaur.

- **Many *Protoceratops'* nests** were found in a small area, showing that these dinosaurs bred in colonies.

- ***Protoceratops'* nests** were shallow, bowl-shaped pits about 1 m across, scraped in the dry, sandy earth and surrounded by low walls.

- **At the *Protoceratops* site**, it was discovered that new nests had been made on top of old ones, showing that the colony was used again year after year.

- **The female *Protoceratops*** laid a clutch of 20 or so tough-shelled, sausage-shaped eggs.

- ***Protoceratops'* eggs** were probably covered with earth and incubated by the heat of the sun.

- **Nests and eggs** of the small plant eater *Orodromeus* have been found in Montana, USA.

- **In each nest** about 20 *Orodromeus* eggs were arranged neatly in a spiral, starting with one in the centre and working outwards.

- ***Protoceratops* arranged** its eggs neatly in its nest, in a circle or spiral shape resembling the spokes of a wheel.

▶ *The name* Maiasaura *means 'good mother lizard'.*
Palaeontologists think that Maiasaura *cared for its young until they were old enough to look after themselves. It is known that they bred in the same areas each year and may have formed groups to do so, creating a kind of dinosaur nursery!*

Growth and age

▲ Tyrannosaurus *may have taken between 20 and 50 years to reach adult size. This would depend largely on how much food was available, as in reptiles such as crocodiles today.*

- **No one knows for sure** how fast dinosaurs grew, how long they took to reach full size, or how long they lived.

- **Most estimates** of dinosaur growth rates and ages come from comparisons with today's reptiles.

- **Some reptiles today** continue to grow throughout their lives, although their growth rate slows with age.

- **Dinosaurs** may have grown fast as youngsters and slower as adults, never quite stopping until they died.

- **Estimates for the age of a full-grown meat eater** such as *Tyrannosaurus* range from 20 to more than 50 years.

- **Full-grown, small meat eaters** such as *Compsognathus* may have lived to between 3 and 10 years old.

- **A giant sauropod** probably lived to be about 50 years old, or even over 100 years old.

- **Like many reptiles today**, a dinosaur's growth rate probably depended largely on its food supply.

- **Dinosaurs** probably ate a lot and grew fast when food was plentiful, and slowed down when food was scarce.

- **During its lifetime**, a big sauropod such as *Brachiosaurus* would have increased its weight 2000 times (compared to 20 times in a human).

Babies

- **As far as we know,** female dinosaurs laid eggs, from which their babies hatched.

- **The time between** eggs being laid and babies hatching out is called the incubation period.

- **Incubation periods** for dinosaur eggs probably varied by weeks or months depending on the temperature, as in today's reptiles.

- **Many fossils** of adult *Maiasaura* (a duck-bill dinosaur, or hadrosaur) have been found, together with nests, eggs and hatchlings (just-hatched babies).

- **Fossils of** *Maiasaura* come mainly from Montana, USA.

◀ *Various clues from fossil evidence show that* Maiasaura *may have brought food back to newly hatched young in the nest. Fossil finds show that leg bones of new hatchlings were not strong enough for them to walk about and feed themselves.*

▲ *The first dinosaur eggs ever discovered were from* Protoceratops. *Palaeontologists were able to see that there were tiny holes in the shells to allow air to pass through to the baby dinosaur.*

- **The name** *Maiasaura* means 'good mother reptile'.
- **The teeth of** *Maiasaura* babies in the nest are slightly worn, showing that they had eaten food.
- **The leg bones and joints** of the *Maiasaura* babies were not quite fully formed, showing that they were not yet able to move about to gather their own food.
- **Evidence** from *Maiasaura* and other nesting sites shows that dinosaurs may have been caring parents, protecting and feeding their young.

Coprolites: dino-dung

- **Coprolites** are the fossilized droppings, or dung, of animals from long ago, such as dinosaurs.

- **Dinosaur coprolites** are not soft and smelly – like other fossils, they have become solid rock.

- **Many thousands** of dinosaur coprolites have been found at fossil sites all over the world.

- **Cracking or cutting open** coprolites sometimes reveals what the dinosaur had recently eaten.

- **Coprolites** produced by large meat eaters such as *Tyrannosaurus* contain bone from their prey.

- **The microscopic structure** of the bones found in coprolites shows the age of the prey when it was eaten. Most victims were very young or old, as these were the easiest creatures for a predator to kill.

▲ *Fossilized droppings have been turned to rock, so they are no longer squishy or smelly. Their contents give many clues to dinosaur diets.*

◄ *Fragments of bone have been found in the coprolites of meat-eating dinosaurs like these* Tyrannosaurus. *Scientists can also find out what plants were growing in a particular period or area by studying the coprolites of herbivorous dinosaurs.*

- **Coprolites produced by small meat eaters** such as *Compsognathus* may contain the hard bits of insects, such as the legs and wing-cases of beetles.

- **Huge piles of coprolites** found in Montana, USA, were probably produced by the large plant-eater *Maiasaura*.

- *Maiasaura* **coprolites** contain the remains of cones, buds and the needle-like leaves of conifer trees, showing that these dinosaurs had a tough diet.

... FASCINATING FACT ...
One of the largest dinosaur coprolites found measures 44 cm long and was probably produced by *Tyrannosaurus*.

283

Migration

- **Almost no land reptiles today** go on regular, long-distance journeys, called migrations.

- **Over the past 30 years**, scientists have acquired evidence that some dinosaurs regularly migrated.

- **Evidence for migrating dinosaurs** comes from the positions of the continents at the time. In certain regions, cool winters would have prevented the growth of enough plants for dinosaurs to eat.

- **Fossil evidence suggests** that some plants stopped growing during very hot or dry times, so it is possible that some dinosaurs would have had to migrate to find food.

- **The footprints or tracks** of many dinosaurs travelling in herds is possible evidence that some dinosaurs migrated.

- **Dinosaurs that may have migrated** include *Centrosaurus* and *Pachyrhinosaurus*, sauropods such as *Diplodocus*, and ornithopods such as *Iguanodon* and *Muttaburrasaurus*.

◀ *Few modern reptiles migrate seasonally.* Centrosaurus, *a dinosaur from the Cretaceous Period, made a migration (indicated here by the arrow) from North America to the sub-Arctic region for the short summer when plant growth was lush.*

▲ *Fossils of* Pachyrhinosaurus *have been found in parts of Alaska that were inside the Arctic Circle at the end of the Cretaceous Period. Since they did not live here permanently, it is reasonable to suppose that they migrated here.*

● **One huge fossil site** in Alberta, Canada, contains the fossils of about 1000 *Pachyrhinosaurus* – perhaps a migrating herd that got caught in a flood.

● **In North America**, huge herds of *Centrosaurus* migrated north for the brief sub-Arctic summer, when plants were abundant, providing plentiful food.

● **In autumn**, *Centrosaurus* herds would have travelled south again to overwinter in the forests.

285

Hibernation

▲ *This is Antarctica as it is today, but throughout the Dinosaur Age, there were no ice caps at the poles at all! However, Australia (where a number of dinosaur fossils have been discovered) was quite close to where Antarctica is now. This means that even with a mild climate, dinosaurs would have faced difficulties in the long winter days.*

- **Dinosaurs may have gone into an inactive state** called hibernation during long periods of cold conditions, as many reptiles do today.

- **Dinosaurs such as the small plant eater** *Leaellynasaura*, found at 'Dinosaur Cove', Australia, may have had to hibernate due to the yearly cycle of seasons in the area.

- **Dinosaur Cove, Australia**, was nearer the South Pole when dinosaurs lived there, 120–100 mya.

- **The climate** was relatively warm 120–100 mya, with no ice at the North or South Poles.

- **Dinosaurs at Dinosaur Cove, Australia**, would have had to cope with long hours of darkness during winter, when few plants grew.

- **Australia's Dinosaur Cove dinosaurs** may have hibernated for a few months each year to survive the cool, dark conditions.

- **The eyes and brain shape** of *Leaellynasaura* from Dinosaur Cove, Australia, suggest that this dinosaur had good eyesight.

- ***Leaellynasaura* may have needed** good eyesight to see in the winter darkness, or in the dim forests.

- **Dinosaur fossils** have been found in the Arctic region near the North Pole.

- **Arctic dinosaurs** either hibernated during winter, or migrated south to warmer regions.

◀ Leaellynasaura *may have hibernated through the polar winter, although we cannot be sure.*

.·.·.FASCINATING FACT.·.·.
Leaellynasaura may have slept through the cold season, perhaps protected in a cave or burrow.

287

Speed

◄ Ornithomimus *was one of the fastest dinosaurs of all! Moving in packs, it would have been able to outrun most predators. The legs were long, slim and powerful and the stiff tail would have provided balance when running at speed.*

- **The fastest-running dinosaurs** had long, slim, muscular legs and small, lightweight bodies.

- **'Ostrich-dinosaurs'** were probably the speediest dinosaurs, perhaps attaining the same top speed as today's ostrich – 70 km/h.

- **The main leg muscles** of the ostrich-dinosaur *Struthiomimus* were in its hips and thighs.

- **The hip and leg design** of ostrich-dinosaurs meant that they could swing their limbs to and fro quickly, like those of a modern racehorse.

- **Large, powerful, plant-eating dinosaurs** such as the 'duck-bill' *Edmontosaurus* may have pounded along on their huge back legs at 40 km/h.

- **Plant eaters** such as *Iguanodon* and *Muttaburrasaurus* may have trotted along at 10–12 km/h for many hours.

- **Some experts think** that the great meat eater *Tyrannosaurus* may have been able to run at 50 km/h.

- **Other experts think** *Tyrannosaurus* was a relatively slow runner at 30 km/h (almost human sprinting speed).

- **The slowest dinosaurs** were giant sauropods such as *Brachiosaurus*, which probably plodded at 4–6 km/h (about human walking speed).

- **Today's fastest runner,** the cheetah, would beat any dinosaur with its maximum burst of speed of more than 100 km/h.

▶ Brachiosaurus *probably moved around at a walk. Its sheer size would have made speed virtually impossible and its size provided protection from predators.*

289

Herds

- **When the fossils of many individuals** of the same type are found together, there are various possible causes.

- **One reason why** individuals of the same dinosaur type are found preserved together is because their bodies were swept to the same place by a flood.

- **A group of individuals** of the same type may have died in the same place if they had lived there as a group.

- **There is much evidence** that various dinosaur types lived in groups or herds, examples being *Diplodocus*, *Triceratops* and *Iguanodon*.

- **Some fossil groups** include dinosaurs of different ages, from newly hatched babies to youngsters and adults.

▶ *Dinosaurs such as the ceratopsian* Centrosaurus *moved about in herds. This may have been partly for protection against predators.*

- **Fossil footprints** suggest some dinosaurs lived in herds.

- **Footprints** of a plant-eating dinosaur were found with the prints of a meat eater to one side of them – perhaps evidence of a hunter pursuing its victim.

- **Sometimes** the footprints of many dinosaurs of the same type are found together, suggesting a herd.

- **Sometimes larger footprints** are found to the sides of smaller ones, possibly indicating that adults guarded their young between them.

▲ A mixed-age herd would have left similar footprints of different sizes.

. . . FASCINATING FACT . . .
At Peace River Canyon, British Columbia, Canada, some 1700 footprints were found.

291

Sounds

- **Few reptiles today make sounds,** except for a simple combination of hisses, grunts and coughs.

- **Fossils suggest that dinosaurs** could have made a variety of sounds in several different ways.

- **The bony, hollow head crests** of duck-bills (hadrosaurs) may have been used for making sounds.

- **The head crests of some hadrosaurs** contained tubes called respiratory airways, used for breathing.

- **Air** blown forcefully through a hadrosaur's head crest passages could have made the whole crest vibrate.

- **A hadrosaur's vibrating head crest** may have made a loud sound like a honk, roar or bellow – similar to an elephant trumpeting with its trunk.

- **Fossil skulls** of some hadrosaurs, such as *Edmontosaurus* and *Kritosaurus*, suggest that there was a loose flap of skin, like a floppy bag, between the nostrils and the eyes.

- *Kritosaurus* may have inflated its loose nasal flap of skin like a balloon to make a honking or bellowing sound, as some seals do today.

- **Dinosaurs may have made sounds** to keep in touch with other members of their herd, to frighten away enemies, to intimidate rivals and to impress potential mates at breeding time.

> ...**FASCINATING FACT**...
> By blowing through models of hadrosaur head crests, a wide range of sounds can be made – a bit like those of brass and wind instruments!

Tyrannosaurus
may have been
startled by the
noise of its prey

◀ *In a battle between predator
and prey,* Tyrannosaurus *would
have been startled or even
warned off by the trumpeting
of* Parasaurolophus. *The
effect of sudden noise on
the predator may have
given the plant-eating
hadrosaur time to
escape. Its noise may
have also summoned
members of its herd
for massed defence
against the huge
meat-eater.*

Long, hollow crest
may have resonated
to make a loud call

Powerful rear legs
used for kicking
in self defence

Tail used for
lashing out

North America

▶ Coelophysis *was discovered located in New Mexico, USA, in about 1881. In the late 1940s, another expedition found dozens of skeletons in a mass dinosaur grave.*

- **The majority** of dinosaur fossils have been found in North America.

- **Most dinosaur fossils** in North America come from the dry, rocky 'badlands' of the Midwest region, which includes Alberta in Canada, and the US states of Montana, Wyoming, Utah, Colorado and Arizona.

- **Fossils of the most famous dinosaurs** come from North America, including *Allosaurus, Tyrannosaurus, Diplodocus, Triceratops* and *Stegosaurus*.

- **Several fossil-rich sites** in North America are now national parks.

- **The US Dinosaur National Monument**, on the border of Utah and Colorado, was established in 1915.

- **The Cleveland-Lloyd Dinosaur Quarry** in Utah contains fossils of stegosaurs, ankylosaurs, sauropods and meat eaters such as *Allosaurus*.

- **Along the Red Deer River** in Alberta, a large area with thousands of fossils has been designated the Dinosaur Provincial Park.

- **Fossils found in Alberta** include those of the meat eater *Albertosaurus*, armoured *Euoplocephalus* and the duck-bill *Lambeosaurus*.

- **The Dinosaur Provincial Park** in Alberta is a United Nations World Heritage Site – the same status as the pyramids of ancient Egypt.

- **A huge, 20 m long plant eater** was named *Alamosaurus* after the famous Battle of the Alamo in Texas in 1836.

Colville (Alaska)

Dinosaur Provincial
Park (Canada)

Peace River
(Canada)

Bay of Fundy
(Canada)

Mt Tom (USA)

Drumheller (Canada)

Hell Creek (USA)

Choteau (USA)

Billings (USA)

Lance Creek (USA)

Cleveland–Lloyd
Dinosaur Quarry

Como Ridge (USA)

Haddonfield
(USA)

Dinosaur Nat. Monument

Garden Park (USA)

Paluxy River
(USA)

Moreno Hills (USA)

San Juan River (USA)

Coahuila State
(Mexico)

Ghost Ranch (USA)

▲ *Some of the main dinosaur fossil sites in North America.*

South America

- **Many of the most important discoveries** of dinosaur fossils in the last 30 years were made in South America.

- **Dinosaur fossils have been found** from the north to the south of the continent, in the countries of Colombia, Peru, Chile, Brazil, Uruguay and Argentina.

- **Most dinosaur fossils in South America** have been found on the high grassland, scrub and semi-desert of southern Brazil and Argentina.

- **Some of the earliest known dinosaurs**, such as *Herrerasaurus* and *Eoraptor*, lived more than 225 mya in Argentina.

- **Some of the last dinosaurs**, such as the sauropods *Saltasaurus* and *Titanosaurus*, lived in Argentina.

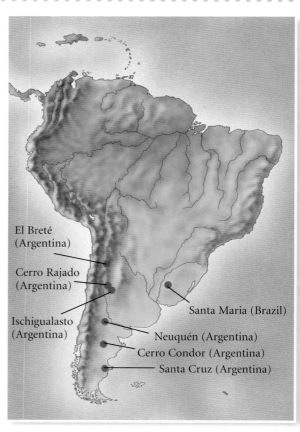

El Breté (Argentina)

Cerro Rajado (Argentina)

Santa Maria (Brazil)

Ischigualasto (Argentina)

Neuquén (Argentina)

Cerro Condor (Argentina)

Santa Cruz (Argentina)

▲ *Dinosaur fossils found in South America since the 1970s have revealed unique kinds of dinosaur. These include the biggest predatory dinosaurs, some of the earliest members of the dinosaur group, and possibly the largest of all dinosaurs.*

◀ *At the dawn of the Dinosaur Age, meat eaters such as* Herrerasaurus *were about in South America – some of the last dinosaurs lived there too.*

- **Fossils of the meat-eating predator** *Piatnitzkyosaurus* come from Cerro Condo in southern Argentina.

- ***Piatnitzkyosaurus* was similar** to the great predator *Allosaurus* of North America, but at 4–5 m long was less than half its size.

- **Like many dinosaurs in Argentina**, *Piatnitzkyosaurus* lived during the Middle Jurassic Period.

- **Remains of about ten huge** *Patagosaurus* sauropods were found in the fossil-rich region of Chubut, Argentina, from 1977.

297

Europe

- **The first dinosaur fossils** ever discovered and given official names were found in England.

- **One of the first almost complete dinosaur skeletons** found was that of the big plant eater *Iguanodon*, in 1871, in southern England.

- **Some of the most numerous early fossils found** were those of *Iguanodon*, discovered in a coal mine in the Belgian village of Bernissart in 1878.

- **About 155–150 mya,** Solnhofen in southern Germany was a mosaic of lush islands and shallow lagoons – ideal for many kinds of life.

▲ *During the Jurassic Period, 248–208 mya, much of Europe would have looked like this. There was a much warmer, damper, more tropical climate, where ferns, ginkgoes, horsetails and cycads flourished alongside forests of conifers and tree-ferns.*

- **In sandstone** in the Solnhofen region of Germany, fossils of amazing detail preserved the tiny *Compsognathus* and the first known bird, *Archaeopteryx*.

- **Fossils of tiny *Compsognathus*** were found near Nice in southern France.

- **Many fossils** of the plant-eating prosauropod *Plateosaurus* were recovered from Trossingen, Germany, in 1911–12, 1921–23 and 1932.

- **Some of the largest fossil dinosaur eggs**, measuring 30 cm long (five times longer than a hen's egg), were thought to have been laid by the sauropod *Hypselosaurus* near Aix-en-Provence in southern France.

- **The Isle of Wight** off southern England has provided so many dinosaur fossils that it is sometimes known as 'Dinosaur Island'.

- **Fossils of *Hypsilophodon*** have been found in eastern Spain, and those of *Camptosaurus* on the coast of Portugal.

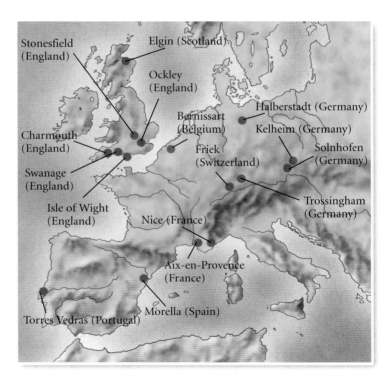

Stonesfield (England)
Elgin (Scotland)
Ockley (England)
Bernissart (Belgium)
Halberstadt (Germany)
Kelheim (Germany)
Charmouth (England)
Friek (Switzerland)
Solnhofen (Germany)
Swanage (England)
Isle of Wight (England)
Nice (France)
Trossingham (Germany)
Aix-en-Provence (France)
Morella (Spain)
Torres Vedras (Portugal)

▲ *Dinosaur fossils are often found in Europe.*

299

Africa

- **The first major discoveries** of dinosaur fossils in Africa were made from 1907, at Tendaguru in present-day Tanzania, east Africa.

- **Discoveries at Tendaguru** in east Africa included the giant sauropod *Brachiosaurus*, the smaller *Dicraeosaurus*, and the stegosaurlike Kentrosaurus.

- **Remains** of the massive sauropod *Cetiosaurus* were uncovered in Morocco, north Africa.

- *Camarasaurus*, **a 20-tonne plant eater**, is known from fossils found in Niger, as well as from European and North American fossils.

- **Fossils** of the huge, sail-backed meat eater *Spinosaurus* come from Morocco and Egypt.

- **The sail-backed plant eater** *Ouranosaurus* is known from remains found in Niger.

- **Many sauropod fossils** were uncovered at sites in Zimbabwe, including *Barosaurus* and *Vulcanodon*.

- **Remains** of the medium-sized plant-eating prosauropod *Massospondylus* were extracted from several sites in southern Africa.

- **Fossils** thought to belong to the small prosauropod *Anchisaurus* were found in southern Africa, the only site for this dinosaur outside North America.

- **During the 1908–12 fossil-hunting expedition** to Tendaguru, more than 250 tonnes of fossil bones and rocks were carried by people for 65 km to the nearest port, for transport to Germany.

▶ *In Africa, as elsewhere, fossils are easier to find in places with bare, rocky soils.*

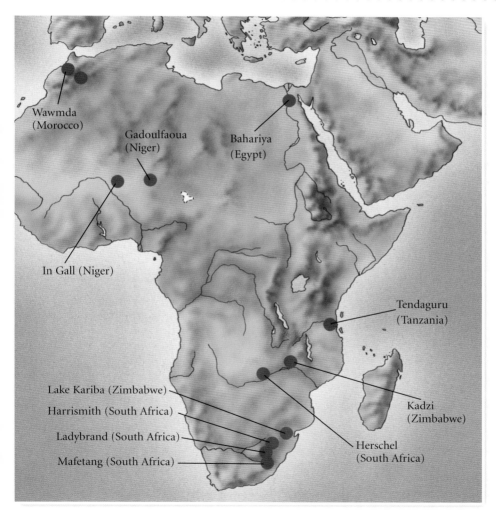

Wawmda
(Morocco)

Gadoulfaoua
(Niger)

Bahariya
(Egypt)

In Gall (Niger)

Tendaguru
(Tanzania)

Lake Kariba (Zimbabwe)

Harrismith (South Africa)

Ladybrand (South Africa)

Mafetang (South Africa)

Kadzi
(Zimbabwe)

Herschel
(South Africa)

Gobi Desert

- **The Gobi** covers much of southern Mongolia and parts of northern China. During the Age of Dinosaurs, it was a land of scrub and scattered trees.

- **The first fossil-hunting expeditions** to the Gobi Desert took place in 1922–25, organized by the American Museum of Natural History.

- **The 1922–25 Gobi expeditions** set out to look for fossils of very early humans, but instead found some amazing dinosaur remains.

- **The first fossil dinosaur eggs** were found by the 1922–25 expeditions.

- *Velociraptor*, *Avimimus* and *Pinacosaurus* were discovered in the Gobi.

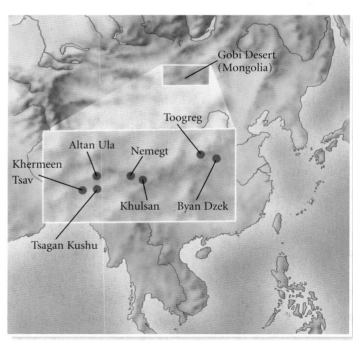

▶ *The Gobi's fossil sites are far from any towns.*

▲ *The temperature in the Gobi Desert can be severe, with fluctuations of 80°C between winter and summer. The climate is harsh and dry, but many interesting fossil finds have been made there.*

- **Russian fossil-hunting trips** into the Gobi Desert in 1946 and 1948–49 discovered new types of armoured dinosaurs, duck-billed dinosaurs, and the huge meat eater *Tarbosaurus*.

- **More expeditions to the Gobi** in the 1960s–70s, especially to the fossil-rich area of the Nemegt Basin, found the giant sauropod *Opisthocoelicaudia* and the 'helmet-headed' *Prenocephale*.

- **Other dinosaurs** found in the Gobi include the ostrich-dinosaur *Gallimimus* and the strong-beaked 'egg thief' *Oviraptor*.

- **The inhospitable Gobi** can be -40°C in winter and 40°C in summer.

- **Despite the harsh conditions**, the Gobi Desert is one of the most exciting areas in the world for finding dinosaur fossils.

Asia

- **Hundreds of kinds of dinosaurs** have been discovered on the continent of Asia.

- **In Asia**, most of the dinosaur fossils that have been found so far were located in the Gobi Desert, in Central Asia, and in present-day China. Some were also found in present-day India.

- **Remains of the huge plant-eating sauropod** *Titanosaurus* were uncovered near Umrer, in central India.

- *Titanosaurus* was about 12 m long and weighed 5–10 tonnes.

- *Titanosaurus* **lived about 70 mya**, and was very similar in shape to its close cousin of the same time, *Saltasaurus*, from South America.

▼ Tuojiangosaurus *is sometimes portrayed as having its legs bent out to the sides, like a lizard, but palaeontologists now think that they were much straighter, like those of other dinosaurs. Theories about dinosaurs are constantly being updated and revised – that's what makes them so exciting!*

▶ *Dinosaur fossil finds span this vast continent.*

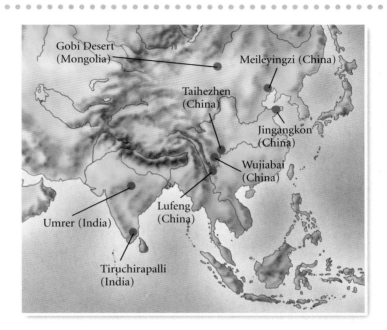

- **Fossils** of the sauropod *Barapasaurus* were found in India. They date from the Early Jurassic Period, about 180 mya.

- *Barapasaurus* was 18 m long and probably weighed more than 20 tonnes.

- **Fossils** of the dinosaur *Dravidosaurus*, from the stegosaur group, were found near Tiruchirapalli in southern India.

- *Dravidosaurus* was about 3 m in total length. It lived much later than other stegosaurs, in the Late Cretaceous Period about 70 mya.

- *Dravidosaurus* **had bony plates** sticking up from its back, like *Stegosaurus*.

305

China

- **For centuries**, dinosaur fossils in China were identified as belonging to folklore creatures such as dragons.

- **The first dinosaur fossils** studied scientifically in China were uncovered in the 1930s.

- **Because of China's political isolation in the past**, many dinosaur fossils found there remained unknown to scientists in other countries.

- **From the 1980s**, dinosaur discoveries in almost every province of China have amazed scientists from around the globe.

▼ Caudipteryx *was an unusual dinosaur that lived in what is now China. Like all scaly or feathery reconstructions, the colours of this bird-reptile are the result of intelligent guesswork.*

. . . FASCINATING FACT . . .
Of all the world's countries, probably only the USA has more fossil dinosaurs than China.

- **A few exciting dinosaur finds** in China have been fakes, such as part of a bird skeleton that was joined to the part-skeleton of a dinosaur along a natural-looking crack in the rock.

- **Some better-known Chinese finds** of dinosaurs include *Mamenchisaurus*, *Psittacosaurus*, *Tuojiangosaurus* and *Avimimus*.

- **Remains of the prosauropod** *Lufengosaurus* were uncovered in China's southern province of Yunnan, in 1941.

- **China's** *Lufengosaurus* lived during the Early Jurassic Period, and measured about 6–7 m long.

- **Many recently found fossils** in China are of feathered dinosaurs.

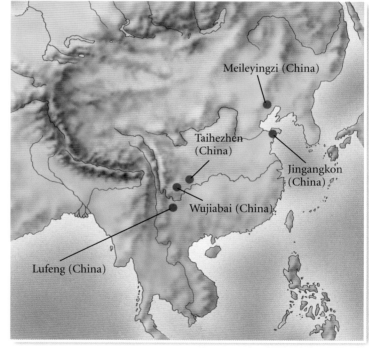

Meileyingzi (China)

Taihezhen (China)

Jingangkon (China)

Wujiabai (China)

Lufeng (China)

▲ *Recent fossil finds in China are causing scientists to change many long-held ideas.*

Australia

▶ *Many exciting fossils have been found in Australia over the past 40 years, with most unique to this region, the smallest of all the continents.*

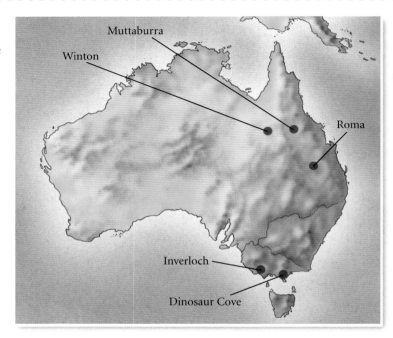

Muttaburra

Winton

Roma

Inverloch

Dinosaur Cove

- **In the past 40 years**, some of the most exciting discoveries of dinosaur fossils have come from Australia.

- **Remains of the large plant eater** *Muttaburrasaurus* were found near Muttaburra, Queensland.

- *Muttaburrasaurus* was about 7 m long and similar in some ways to the well-known plant eater *Iguanodon*.

- **Fossils of *Rhoetosaurus***, a giant plant eater, were found in 1924 in southern Queensland.

- **The sauropod *Rhoetosaurus*** was 17 m long and lived 170 mya.

- **Near Winton, Queensland**, more than 3300 footprints show where about 130 dinosaurs once passed by.

> ... FASCINATING FACT ...
> Dinosaur Cove is difficult to reach, and many of the fossils are in hard rocks in the middle of sheer cliffs with pounding waves far beneath.

- **One of the major new fossil sites** in Australia is 'Dinosaur Cove', on the coast near Melbourne, Victoria.

  - **Fossil-rich rocks** at 'Dinosaur Cove' are part of the Otway-Strzelecki mountain ranges, and are 120–100 mya.

    - **Remains found at 'Dinosaur Cove'** include *Leaellynasaura* and a smaller version of the huge meat eater *Allosaurus*.

◄ Muttaburasaurus *lived 110 million years ago in what is now New South Wales, Australia. It was bipedal (it walked on two legs), a cousin of* Iguanodon, *and weighed about 4 tonnes.*

309

Age of Dinosaurs

- **The Age of Dinosaurs** corresponds to the time period that geologists call the Mesozoic Era, from about 248–65 mya.

- **The Mesozoic Era** is divided into three shorter time spans – the Triassic, Jurassic and Cretaceous Periods.

- **During the Triassic Period,** 248– 208 mya, the dinosaurs began to evolve.

- **During the Jurassic Period** – about 208–144 mya – the dinosaurs reached their greatest size.

- **The Cretaceous Period** is when dinosaurs were at their most varied – about 144–65 mya.

- **In the Triassic Period**, all the continents were joined together in one supercontinent – Pangaea.

- **In the Jurassic Period**, the supercontinent of Pangaea separated into two huge land masses – Laurasia in the north and Gondwanaland in the south.

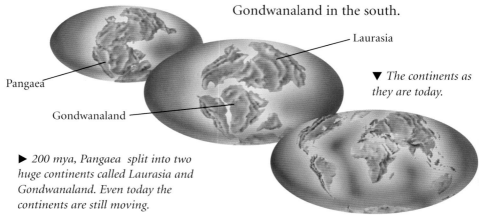

Pangaea

Laurasia

Gondwanaland

▼ *The continents as they are today.*

▶ *200 mya, Pangaea split into two huge continents called Laurasia and Gondwanaland. Even today the continents are still moving.*

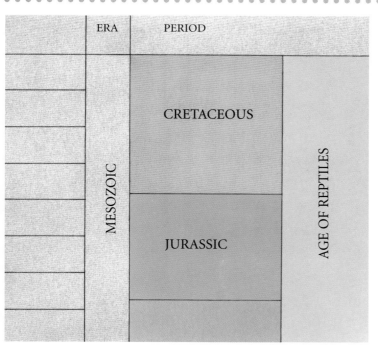

ERA	PERIOD
MESOZOIC	CRETACEOUS
	JURASSIC

AGE OF REPTILES

◄ *Dinosaurs ruled the land for 160 million years – longer than any other animal group.*

- **In the Cretaceous Period,** Laurasia and Gondwanaland split, and the continents as we know them began to form.

- **In the Mesozoic Era,** the major land masses gradually moved across the globe in a process known as 'continental drift'.

- **The joining and separating** of the continents affected which kinds of dinosaurs lived where. During the Triassic Period, the earliest mammals and the first dinosaurs appeared.

Names: 1

- **Every dinosaur has a scientific name**, usually made up from Latin or Greek, and written in italics.

- **Many dinosaur names** end in -saurus, which some say means 'reptile' and others say means 'lizard' – even though dinosaurs were not lizards.

- **Dinosaur names** often refer to a feature that no other dinosaur had. *Baryonyx*, for example, means 'heavy claw', a name taken from the massive claw on its thumb.

- **The medium-sized meat eater** *Herrerasaurus* from Argentina was named after Victorino Herrera, the farmer who first noticed its fossils.

- **Many dinosaur names are real tongue-twisters**, such as *Opisthocoelicaudia*, pronounced 'owe-pis-thowe-see-lee-cord-ee-ah'.

- ***Opisthocoelicaudia*** means 'posterior tail cavity', and refers to the joints between the backbones in the tail.

▼ *The naming of* Troodon *was originally based on the finding of a single curved, serrated 'wounding' tooth.*

▲ *Some well-known predators from the Age of Dinosaurs!*

312

- **Some dinosaurs** were named after the place where their fossils were found. Minmi was located near Minmi Crossing in Queensland, Australia.

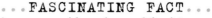

...**FASCINATING FACT**...
Triceratops, or 'three-horned face', is one of the best known dinosaur scientific names.

- **Some dinosaur groups** are named after the first-discovered or major one of its kind, such as the tyrannosaurs or stegosaurs.

- **The fast-running ostrich-dinosaurs' name,** ornithomimosaurs, means 'bird-mimic reptiles'.

MEAT—EATERS:

Troodon *Meaning:* wounding tooth *Pronounced:* TROH-oh-don/Late Cretaceous	*Tyrannosaurus* *Meaning:* tyrant lizard *Pronounced:* tie-RAN-oh-sore-us/Late Cretaceous	*Ornitholestes* *Meaning:* bird robber *Pronounced:* Or-nith-oh- LES –teez/Late Jurassic
Oviraptor *Meaning:* egg thief *Pronounced:* OH-vee-RAP-tor/Late Cretaceous	*Dilophosaurus* *Meaning:* two-ridged lizard *Pronounced:* die-LOAF-oh-sore-us/Early Jurassic	*Coelurus* *Meaning:* hollow tail *Pronounced:* seel-YEW-rus/Late Jurassic
Baryonyx *Meaning:* heavy claw *Pronounced:* bah-ree-ON-icks/Late Jurassic	*Coelophysis* *Meaning:* hollow form *Pronounced:* seel-OH-fie-sis/Late Triassic	*Tarbosaurus* *Meaning:* alarming lizard *Pronounced:* TAR-bow-SORE-us/Late Cretaceous
Deinonychus *Meaning:* terrible claw *Pronounced:* die-NON-i-kuss/Early Cretaceous	*Velociraptor* *Meaning:* quick plunderer *Pronounced:* vel-OSS-ee-rap-tor/Late Cretaceous	*Struthiomimus* *Meaning:* ostrich mimic *Pronounced:* STRUTH-ee-oh-MEEM-us/Late Cretaceous

Names: 2

- **More than 100 kinds of dinosaurs** have been named after the people who first discovered their fossils, dug them up, or reconstructed the dinosaur.

- **The very large duck-bill** (**hadrosaur**) *Lambeosaurus* was named after Canadian fossil expert Lawrence Lambe.

- **Lawrence Lambe** worked mainly during the early 1900s, and named one of his finds *Stephanosaurus*.

- **In the 1920s,** *Stephanosaurus* was re-studied and renamed, along with *Didanodon*, as *Lambeosaurus*, in honour of Lambe's great work.

- **The full name** of the 'heavy-claw' meat eater *Baryonyx* is *Baryonyx walkeri*, after Bill Walker, the discoverer of its massive claw.

- **Part-time fossil-hunter** Bill Walker found the claw of *Baryonyx* in a clay pit quarry in Surrey, England.

...FASCINATING FACT...
Australian *Leaellynasaura* was named after Lea Ellyn, the daughter of its discoverers.

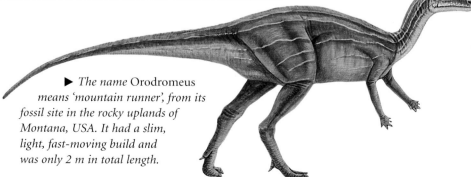

▶ *The name* Orodromeus *means 'mountain runner', from its fossil site in the rocky uplands of Montana, USA. It had a slim, light, fast-moving build and was only 2 m in total length.*

HERBIVORES:

Plateosaurus *Meaning:* flat lizard *Pronounced:* plat-ee-oh-sore-us/Late Triassic	**Iguanodon** *Meaning:* iguana tooth *Pronounced:* ig-WHA-noh-don/Early Cretaceous	**Segnosaurus** *Meaning:* slow lizard *Pronounced:* SEG-no-SORE-us/Late Cretaceous
Brachiosaurus *Meaning:* arm lizard *Pronounced:* BRAK-ee-oh-sore-us/Late Jurassic	**Psittacosaurus** *Meaning:* parrot lizard *Pronounced:* SIT-ak-oh-sore-us/Early Cretaceous	**Seismosaurus** *Meaning:* earth-shaking lizard *Pronounced:* SIZE-moh-SORE-us/Late Jurassic
Heterodontosaurus *Meaning:* different-teeth lizard *Pronounced:* HET-er-oh-DON'T-oh-sore-us/Early Jurassic	**Ankylosaurus** *Meaning:* stiff lizard *Pronounced:* an-KIE-loh-sore-us/Late Cretaceous	**Orodromeus** *Meaning:* mountain runner *Pronounced:* or-oh-DROM-ee-us/Late Cretaceous
Camarasaurus *Meaning:* chambered lizard *Pronounced:* KAM-ar-a-sore-us/Late Jurassic	**Pachycephalosaurus** *Meaning:* thick-headed lizard *Pronounced:* pack-i-KEF-al-oh-sore-russ/Late Cretaceous	**Saltasaurus** *Meaning:* Salta reptile *Pronounced:* Salt-AH-sore-us/Late Cretaceous

▲ *These are just a few of the plant-eating dinosaurs that existed during the Age of Dinosaurs.*

- **Some dinosaur names** are quite technical, such as *Diplodocus*, which means 'double beam' – it was named for its tail bones, which have two long projections like a pair of skis.

- **The 4-m long plant eater** *Othnielia*, related to *Hypsilophodon*, was named after the American fossil-hunter Othniel Charles Marsh.

- *Parksosaurus*, a 2.5 m long plant eater related to *Hypsilophodon*, was named in honour of Canadian dinosaur expert William Parks.

Archosaurs

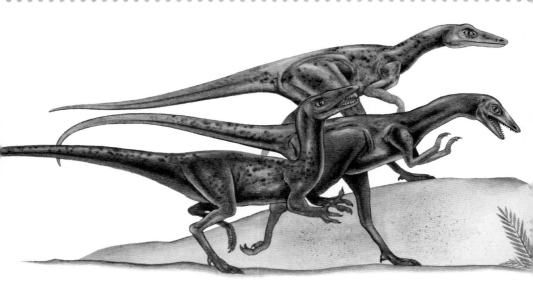

▲ *The archosaur* Ornithosuchus *outwardly resembled some of the Jurassic and Cretaceous meat eaters. However, it was probably not a dinosaur but a close cousin.*

- **Archosaurs** were a very large group of reptiles that included the dinosaurs as one of their subgroups.

- **Other archosaur subgroups** included thecodonts, flying reptiles called pterosaurs, and crocodiles.

- **The thecodonts** included a smaller reptile group, the ornithosuchians – possibly the dinosaurs' ancestors.

- **One of the most dinosaur-like of the archosaurs** was the thecodont *Ornithosuchus*.

▶ Rhamphorhynchus *measured about 1 m across its wingtips. Its fossils date from the same time, the Late Jurassic Period, and the same area, Southern Germany, as the fossils of the earliest known bird,* Archaeopteryx.

- **The 4-m long** *Ornithosuchus* stood almost upright.

- *Ornithosuchus* **fossils** were found in Scotland.

- **Sharp-toothed** *Ornithosuchus* was probably a powerful predator.

- **Features** in *Ornithosuchus* 's backbone, hips and feet indicate that it was almost certainly not a dinosaur.

- **The archosaur** *Longisquama* was a lizard-like reptile only 15 cm long, with tall scales forming a V-shaped row along its back.

- **Archosaur means 'ruling reptile'**, and archosaurs did indeed rule the land, swamps and skies for over 170 million years.

317

Cousins: land

- **Land animals** during the Age of Dinosaurs included insects, spiders, other reptiles, birds and mammals.

- **Dinosaurs** had many large, fierce, reptile enemies.

- **One of the biggest** non-dinosaur land reptiles was *Deinosuchus* (or *Phobosuchus*), a type of crocodile.

- ***Deinosuchus*** lived in the Late Cretaceous Period, in present-day Texas, USA.

- **The fossil skull** of *Deinosuchus* measures about 2 m long, much bigger than any crocodile of today.

- **The first mammals** appeared on Earth at about the same time as the early dinosaurs.

▲ Oligokyphus *resembled a weasel and had a fully upright, four-legged posture. It had no canine teeth, but a pair of enlarged incisors like a beaver.*

▲ Branchiosaurus *was a very early amphibian from the early Carboniferous to the early Permian Period (300 mya). Like all amphibians, it lived near water in which it laid its eggs.*

- **Various kinds of mammals** survived all through the Age of Dinosaurs, although none grew larger than a pet cat.

- **One of the first mammals** known from fossils is *Megazostrodon*, which resembled a shrew of today.

- *Megazostrodon* **was just 12 cm long** and its fossils, from 220–210 mya, come from southern Africa.

- **If *Deinosuchus's* body** was in proportion to its skull, it would have been 15 m long!

Cousins: sea

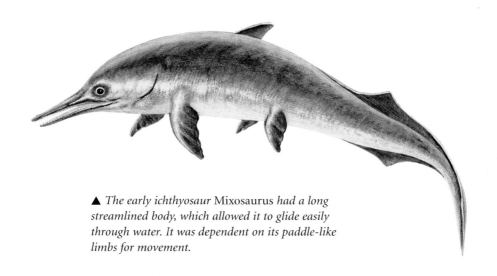

▲ *The early ichthyosaur* Mixosaurus *had a long streamlined body, which allowed it to glide easily through water. It was dependent on its paddle-like limbs for movement.*

- **Placodont reptiles** lived mainly during the Triassic Period. They were shaped like large salamanders or turtles, and probably ate shellfish.

- **The placodont** *Placodus* was about 2 m long and looked like a large, scaly newt.

- **The nothosaurs** were fish-eating reptiles of the Triassic Period. They had small heads, long necks and tails, and four flipper-shaped limbs.

- **Fossils** of the 3 m long nothosaur *Nothosaurus* have been found across Europe, Asia and Africa.

- **The dolphin-like ichthyosaur reptiles** had back fins, two-lobed tails and flipper-shaped limbs.

- **Many kinds of ichthyosaurs** thrived in the seas during the Triassic and Jurassic Periods, although they had faded away by the middle of the Cretaceous Period.

- **One of the biggest ichthyosaurs** was *Shonisaurus*, which measured up to 15 m long.

- **The plesiosaurs** were fish-eating reptiles of the Mesozoic Era, with small heads, plump bodies, four flipper-shaped limbs and short, tapering tails.

- **The plesiosaur** *Elasmosaurus* was up to 14 m long, with more than half of this length being its extraordinarily long, snakelike neck.

▶ Peloneustes *had a streamlined shape, which enabled it to swim rapidly after its fast-moving prey, such as squid, cuttlefish and ammonites.*

. . . FASCINATING FACT . . .
One of the biggest meat-eaters ever was the short-necked plesiosaur *Liopleurodon*, at 20 m long and 50 tonnes in weight.

321

Cousins: air

- **Many flying creatures** lived during the Age of Dinosaurs, especially insects such as flies and dragonflies, and also birds.

- **The main flying reptiles** during the Age of Dinosaurs were the pterosaurs, or 'winged reptiles'.

- **Hundreds of different kinds** of pterosaurs came and went through almost the entire Age of Dinosaurs, about 220–65 mya.

- **The arms of a pterosaur** resembled wings – a light, thin, stretchy wing membrane was held out mainly by the finger bones, especially the fourth finger.

- **Pterosaurs** are sometimes called pterodactyls, but *Pterodactylus* was just one kind of pterosaur.

- *Pterodactylus* **had a wing span** of between one and two metres. It lived 150–140 mya in southern Germany.

- **Some pterosaurs**, such as *Pterodactylus*, had very short tails, or no tail at all.

- **The pterosaur** *Rhamphorhynchus* had a long, trailing tail with a widened, paddle-shaped end.

- **Fossils** suggest that some pterosaurs, such as Sordes, had fur, and may have been warm-blooded, agile fliers rather than slow, clumsy gliders.

> ... **FASCINATING FACT** ...
> The biggest pterosaur, and the largest flying animal ever,
> was Quetzalcoatlus. Its 'beak' was longer than the height
> of an adult human, and its wingspan was almost 12 m!

▲ Pteranodon *had a long projection on the back of its head.*

Extinction

▶ *We can only guess at the havoc when a massive meteorite hit Earth, 65 mya. Whether this was the main cause of the mass extinction, or the 'last straw' following other problems, is not clear. What we do know is that all dinosaurs perished along with ichthyosaurs, plesiosaurs (sea-dwelling beasts) and pterosaurs (flying reptiles). Why did these species die out when others, such as the mammals, survived?*

- **All dinosaurs on Earth** had died out, or become extinct, by 65 mya.

- **Many other reptiles**, such as pterosaurs and plesiosaurs, and many other animals and plants disappeared with the dinosaurs, in a 'mass extinction'.

- **A possible cause** of the mass extinction was a new kind of disease that swept across the land and seas.

> ... **FASCINATING FACT** ...
> Scientists found a huge crater – the Chixulub Crater – under sea-bed mud off the coast of Yucatan, Mexico. This could be where a giant meteorite hit Earth 65 million years ago.

- **The mass extinction** of the dinosaurs and other animals may have been due to a series of huge volcanic eruptions that filled the air with poisonous fumes.

- **Climate change** is another possible cause of the mass extinction – perhaps a period of global warming that lasted for a few hundred years, or even longer.

- **One theory** for the mass extinction is that a giant lump of rock from space – a meteorite – hit Earth.

▲ *A massive meteorite may have killed off the dinosaurs.*

- **A giant meteorite** 10 km across smashing into Earth would have set off earthquakes and volcanoes, and thrown up vast amounts of dust to darken the skies.

- **Skies darkened by dust for one year or more** would mean the death of many plants, and so the death of plant-eating animals, and consequently the meat eaters.

- **One great puzzle** about the disappearance of the dinosaurs is why similar reptiles, such as crocodiles, lizards and turtles, survived.

325

After dinosaurs

- **The Age of Dinosaurs** came to a fairly sudden end 65 mya. We know this from rocks and fossils, which changed dramatically at that time.

- **The Cretaceous Period** ended 65 mya.

- **There are no dinosaur fossils** after 65 mya.

- **Many animal groups**, including fish, crocodiles, turtles, lizards, birds and mammals, survived the extinction that took place 65 mya.

- **Birds and mammals** in particular underwent rapid changes after the dinosaurs disappeared.

- **Within 10 million years** of the dinosaurs' demise, bats, primates, armadillos, hoofed mammals and rodents had all appeared.

- **The land mammal** that came closest to rivalling the great size of the dinosaurs was *Indricotherium*, also known as *Baluchitherium*.

- *Indricotherium* was 8 m long, 5 m tall and weighed perhaps 25 tonnes.

- *Indricotherium* was less than half the size of the biggest dinosaurs.

... FASCINATING FACT ...
Some people believe that dinosaurs may still be alive today, deep in tropical forests or in remote valleys – but no firm evidence exists.

▲ *Baluchitherium was bigger than any land mammal alive today.*

Fossil formation

- **Most of the information** we know, or guess, about dinosaurs comes from fossils.

- **Fossils are the remains of once-living things** that have been preserved in rocks and turned to stone over millions of years.

- **Not just dinosaurs**, but many kinds of living things from prehistoric times have left fossils, including mammals, birds, lizards, fish, insects and plants such as ferns and trees.

- **The flesh, guts and other soft parts** of a dead dinosaur's body were probably eaten by scavengers, or rotted away, and so rarely formed fossils.

- **Fossils usually formed** when a dinosaur's remains were quickly covered by sediments such as sand, silt or mud, especially along the banks of a river or lake, or on the seashore.

- **The sand or other sediment** around a creature or plant's remains was gradually buried deeper by more sediment, squeezed under pressure, and cemented together into a solid mass of rock.

- **As the sediment turned to rock**, so did the plant or animal remains encased within it.

- **Information about dinosaurs** comes not only from fossils, but also from 'trace' fossils. These were not actual parts of their bodies, but other items or signs of their presence.

- **These include** egg shells, footprints, marks made by claws and teeth, and coprolites – fossilized dinosaur droppings.

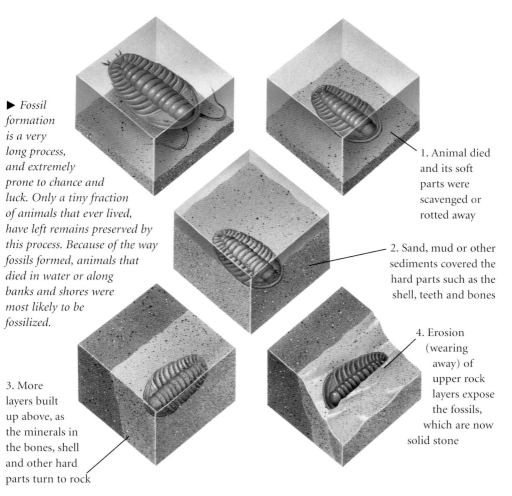

▶ *Fossil formation is a very long process, and extremely prone to chance and luck. Only a tiny fraction of animals that ever lived, have left remains preserved by this process. Because of the way fossils formed, animals that died in water or along banks and shores were most likely to be fossilized.*

1. Animal died and its soft parts were scavenged or rotted away

2. Sand, mud or other sediments covered the hard parts such as the shell, teeth and bones

4. Erosion (wearing away) of upper rock layers expose the fossils, which are now solid stone

3. More layers built up above, as the minerals in the bones, shell and other hard parts turn to rock

329

Dinosaur fossil-hunters

- **Many dinosaurs** were found in the USA in the 1870s–90s by Othniel Charles Marsh and Edward Drinker Cope.

- **Marsh and Cope** were great rivals, each one trying to find bigger, better and more dinosaur fossils than the other.

- **The rivalry between Marsh and Cope** extended to bribing people to smash each other's fossils with hammers, planting fake fossils, and damaging food, water and other supplies at each other's camps in the Midwest.

- **Cope and Marsh found and described** about 130 new kinds of dinosaurs between 1877 and 1897.

- **Joseph Tyrrell** discovered fossils of *Albertosaurus* in 1884, in what became a very famous dinosaur region, the Red Deer River area of Alberta, Canada.

- **Lawrence Lambe** found and described many North American dinosaur fossils, such as *Centrosaurus* in 1904.

- **German fossil experts** Werner Janensch and Edwin Hennig led expeditions to east Africa in 1908–12, and discovered *Brachiosaurus* and *Kentrosaurus*.

- **From 1933** Yang Zhong-jiang (also called CC Young) led many fossil-hunting trips in various parts of China.

- **José Bonaparte** from Argentina has found many fossils in that region, including *Carnotaurus* in 1985.

▲ *Othniel Charles Marsh (left) and Edward Drinker Cope (right) had a rivalry between them that came to be known as the 'Bone Wars'. Allegedly, this began when Marsh pointed out a mistake that Cope had made with the reconstruction of a plesiosaur skeleton. Cope never forgave him, but the rift led to the discovery of almost 140 new dinosaur species!*

> **FASCINATING FACT**
> One of the first great fossil-hunters in the USA
> was Joseph Leidy, who found *Troodon* in 1856.

Reconstructions

- **No complete fossilized dinosaur**, with all its skin, muscles, guts and other soft parts, has yet been found.

- **Most dinosaurs are reconstructed** from the fossil remains of their hard parts – chiefly teeth, bones, horns and claws.

- **The vast majority of dinosaurs** are known from only a few fossil parts, such as several fragments of bones.

- **Fossil parts** of other, similar dinosaurs are often used in reconstructions to 'fill in' missing bones, teeth, and even missing heads, limbs or tails.

- **Soft body parts** from modern reptiles such as lizards are used as a guide for the reconstruction of a dinosaur's muscles and guts, which are added to the fossils.

- **On rare occasions**, remains are found of a dinosaur body that dried out rapidly so that quite a few parts were preserved as mummified fossils.

- **One of the best-known**, part-mummified dinosaur fossils is 'Sue', a specimen of *Tyrannosaurus* found in 1990 in South Dakota, USA.

- **'Sue' is the biggest** and most complete preserved *Tyrannosaurus* ever found.

- **'Sue' was a female** *Tyrannosaurus*. It was named after its discoverer, fossil-hunter Susan Hendrickson of the Black Hills Institute of Geological Research.

▲ *Fossils must be handled very carefully to avoid any damage: remember, they are millions of years old! In the palaeontology laboratory, they are cleaned with special equipment*

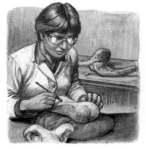

▲ *After cleaning, the fossils are laid out to show the dinosaur skeleton. Scientists then reconstruct body parts, such as skin and internal organs.*

▶ *Finally, the rebuilt skeleton is displayed in a museum*

Mysteries

▲ *When* Troodon's *tooth was first discovered, it was thought to belong to a carnivorous lizard such as this monitor lizard. However, scientists later discovered that it was from the most intelligent dinosaur ever!*

- **Some dinosaurs have been named** on very scant evidence, such as a single bit of fossil bone, or just one tooth or claw.

- **The small meat-eater** *Troodon* was named in 1856 on the evidence of a single tooth.

- **The first tooth** *Troodon* **tooth** was found in the Judith River region of Montana, USA.

- **At first,** the tooth of *Troodon* was thought to have come from a lizard such as a monitor lizard.

- **In the early 1900s,** more *Troodon*-like teeth were found in Alberta and Wyoming, and were believed to have come from a pachycephalosaur or 'bone-head' dinosaur.

- **In the 1980s,** a fuller picture of *Troodon* was built up by putting its teeth together with other fossils, including bones.

- **Only parts of the hands and arms** of *Deinocheirus* have been found. They were discovered in Mongolia, Central Asia, in the 1970s.

- **It is possible** that *Deinocheirus* was a gigantic ostrich-dinosaur, perhaps as tall as a giraffe, at 5–6 m.

- ***Therizinosaurus,* or 'scythe reptile',** was a huge dinosaur known only from a few parts of its limbs. It lived in the Late Cretaceous Period in Mongolia, Central Asia.

- **A mysterious fossil claw** was found, thought possibly to belong to *Therizinosaurus*, and measuring about 90 cm around its outer curve.

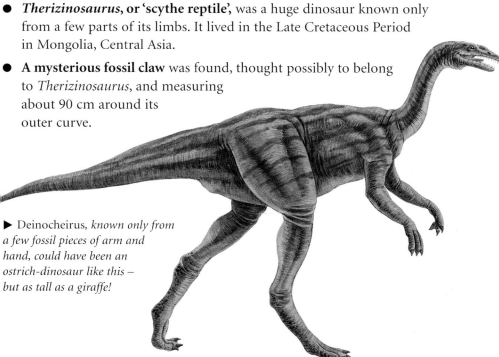

▶ Deinocheirus, *known only from a few fossil pieces of arm and hand, could have been an ostrich-dinosaur like this – but as tall as a giraffe!*

Inventing the 'dinosaur'

- **When fossils of dinosaurs were first studied** by scientists in the 1820s, they were thought to be from huge lizards, rhinoceroses or even whales.

- **The first dinosaur** to be given an official name was *Megalosaurus*, by English clergyman William Buckland in 1824.

- **Fossils of dinosaurs** were found and studied in 1822 by Gideon Mantell, a country doctor in Sussex, southern England.

- **In 1825,** Englishman Gideon Mantell named his creature *Iguanodon*, because its fossil teeth were very similar in shape to, but larger than, the teeth of the iguana lizard.

- **In the late 1830s,** British scientist Richard Owen realized that some fossils did not belong to lizards, but to an as yet unnamed group of reptiles.

- **In 1841–42,** Richard Owen invented a new name for the group of giant prehistoric reptiles – Dinosauria.

- **The name 'dinosaur'** means 'terrible reptile'.

- **Life-sized models** of several dinosaurs were made by sculptor Waterhouse Hawkins in 1852–54.

- **Hawkins' models** were displayed in the gardens of the Crystal Palace Exhibition in London, and caused a public sensation – the first wave of 'Dino-mania'.

  - **The three main dinosaurs** of the Dinosauria in the 1840s were *Iguanodon*, the big meat-eater *Megalosaurus* and the nodosaur *Hyaelosaurus*.

◄ *Even though* Iguanodon *is now one of the best known dinosaurs, it confused palaeontologists when its fossils were first discovered. They thought that its distinctive thumb claw belonged on its nose!* Megalosaurus, *a very early discovery, was the first dinosaur to be given an official scientific name, even though the term 'dinosaur' (meaning 'terrible reptile') was not invented until 1841.*

Recreating dinosaurs

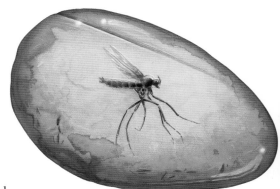

▶ *A mosquito perfectly preserved in amber is a reminder that many other creatures lived during the time of the dinosaurs. Recreating them, however, is beyond today's science.*

- **The *Jurassic Park* movies** showed dinosaurs being recreated as living creatures in the modern world.

- **The instructions**, or genes, of all animals, including dinosaurs, are in the form of the genetic substance known as DNA (deoxyribonucleic acid).

- **In *Jurassic Park,*** dinosaur DNA came not from dinosaur fossils, but from mosquitoes that had sucked the blood of living dinosaurs, and then been preserved in solidified amber.

- **Scientists** in *Jurassic Park* combined the DNA of dinosaurs with DNA from living amphibians such as frogs.

- **Tiny bits of DNA** have been recovered from fossils formed in the Age of Dinosaurs.

- **The bits of dinosaur DNA found so far** represent a tiny amount of the DNA needed to recreate a living thing.

▲ *The heroes of the movie* Jurassic Park *come face to face with a pack of* Velociraptors *which actually lived during the Upper Cretaceous Period, about 80-84 million years ago.*

- **Most scientists** doubt that living dinosaurs could really be made from bits of fossilized DNA.

- **Plants today** might not be suited to 'modern' dinosaurs.

- **'Modern' dinosaurs** might die from today's diseases.

- **The task of recreating** a living dinosaur from tiny fragments of DNA has been compared to writing all the plays of Shakespeare starting with a couple of words.

339

Bird fossils

▼ *Fossils of* Archaeopteryx, *such as this one, are some of the most famous fossils of all. They show the birds' feathers, clawed fingers, teeth-filled beak and long tail.*

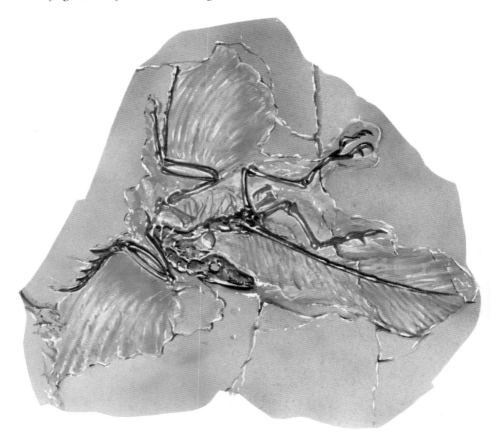

- **There are far fewer** fossils of birds than other animals because birds have very delicate skeletons.

- **Some species** of prehistoric birds are only revealed by the fossil impression of a feather or a fossilized footprint.

- **One of** the most-famous bird fossils is that of *Archaeopteryx*, which was discovered in Solnhofen, Germany, in 1861.

- **Lime-rich muds** slowly formed the limestone rock of Solnhofen. This process ensured *Archaeopteryx* was preserved in amazing detail, right down to the clear outline of its feathers.

- **Other famous** bird fossil sites have included the Niobrara Chalk of Kansas, and mudstone rocks of Utah and Wyoming.

- **The fossil site** at Messel in Germany also contains the skeletons of long-extinct birds as well as ones resembling flamingos, swifts, owls and nightjars.

- **The Messel bird fossils** are around 50 million years old and date from the Early Tertiary Period.

- **The flamingo fossils** at Messel proved that the modern flamingo is related to wading birds called avocets rather than ducks and storks, since they share a similar skeleton.

- **One quick way** fossil-hunters can identify bird bones is because they are hollow – unlike the bones of many prehistoric reptiles.

> **. . . FASCINATING FACT . . .**
> An example of a fossilized egg is one belonging
> to the giant extinct ostrich, *Aepyornis*. The egg
> was also huge – it could hold 8.5 litres of liquid!

341

Flight

- **Pterosaurs** (flying reptiles) evolved wings that consisted of a stretched membrane (a piece of thin skin).

- **The fourth finger** of flying reptiles was extremely long, and held up the wing membrane.

- **As well as the main** wing membrane, flying reptiles also had an additional flap of skin, stretched between the shoulder and wrist, that gave added stability during flight.

- **Over time**, the forelimbs of birds became elongated and developed into wings.

- **They also** developed feathers, which possibly evolved from the scales of their reptile ancestors.

- **Flying birds** have asymmetrical feathers, which have longer barbs on one side of the shaft than on the other. This helps to lift them up and allows them to move in the air. Flightless birds have symmetrical feathers – in which the shaft runs down the middle – which is why they cannot fly.

- **One theory** of how birds and reptiles developed flight is that as they ran along the ground, they flapped their arms to give them stability. Over time, these arms developed into wings.

- **Another theory** is that, before they could fly, some reptiles and birds glided from tree to tree in search of food. They then developed wings and flight.

- **The feathered wings** of birds survive injuries better than the more fragile skin wings of flying reptiles could have done. This may suggest why birds have outlived pterosaurs.

The reason why palaeontologists are confident that *Archaeopteryx*, the first known bird, could fly is because it had asymmetrical feathers.

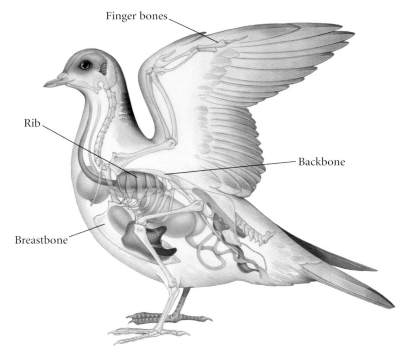

Finger bones

Rib

Backbone

Breastbone

▲ *Birds' skeletons, such as this modern-day pigeon's, are built for flight. The bones are lightweight and often hollow, the finger bones in the wing are joined to provide greater strength and the ribs, backbone and breastbone form a secure cage that supports powerful wings.*

Archaeopteryx

▲ Archaeopteryx *is the first known flying bird, but it would not have been a very efficient flyer because of its primitive skeleton and long tail.*

> ...FASCINATING FACT...
> The chick of the hoatzin bird, which lives in Venezuela and
> Guyana, has claws on each wing that are very similar to
> *Archaeopteryx's*. It uses them to climb and cling onto trees.

- *Archaeopteryx,* from two Greek words meaning 'ancient wing', is the earliest known flying bird.

- **It lived** in the Late Jurassic Period (159–144 mya).

- *Archaeopteryx* was roughly the size of a magpie – it would have weighed about 270 g and had a wingspan of approximately 60 cm.

- **Probably eight identified** *Archaeopteryx* fossils have been found, ranging from almost a whole skeleton to just one feather, all of them preserved in limestone, in Solnhofen, southern Germany.

- **The fossils reveal** that *Archaeopteryx* had feathers and that, like modern birds, they were asymmetrical – one side was thicker than the other.

- *Archaeopteryx* was therefore capable of flight, but could not fly long distances because it lacked a suitable skeleton.

- **Like carnivorous dinosaurs**, *Archaeopteryx* had jaws with teeth, and forelimbs (arms) that had separate fingers with claws.

- *Archaeopteryx* looks so similar to a small dinosaur that one museum labelled its *Archaeopteryx* fossil as such for decades until someone realized it had feathers.

- *Archaeopteryx* was a tree-dwelling creature. The big toe at the end of its hind legs pointed backwards, allowing it to grip branches.

Confuciusornis

- *Confuciusornis* was the first-known bird to have a true birdlike beak.

- **It lived in** the Late Jurassic to Early Cretaceous Periods (around 150–120 mya).

- **Unlike the slightly older** *Archaeopteryx,* which had a mouth filled with teeth, *Confuciusornis,* had a toothless beak, like modern birds.

- **This beak** had an upwards curve – a fact that has led palaeontologists to argue about this bird's diet. Some think it ate seeds and others that it hunted fish.

- *Confuciusornis* was approximately 60 cm long.

- **It had** lightweight bones, a deep chest and a short, rudder-like tail. All of this means it was probably a better flyer than *Archaeopteryx.*

- **Like *Archaeopteryx***, it had a backwards-pointing big toe on its hind feet, which suggests it lived in trees.

- **The remains** of *Confuciusornis* were discovered at the Liaoning Fossil Beds, in northeast China, in the mid 1990s.

- **The Liaoning Fossil Beds** were the site of a prehistoric lake. Fossil-hunters have found so many *Confuciusornis* fossils at this site that the bird probably lived in large colonies on the lakeshore.

- *Confuciusornis* means 'Confucius bird'. It is named after the ancient Chinese philosopher Confucius.

▼ *A male* Confuciusornis. *Scientists think that males had long tail feathers, but females had much shorter tails.*

Terror birds

- **After the dinosaurs** became extinct (about 65 mya), huge flightless birds – known as terror birds – seized the opportunity to become the dominant predators of their day.

- *Gastornis* was one such terror bird. It had an enormous head and powerful legs, like those of its dinosaur ancestors, so it could outrun its prey.

- **Some experts** believe that *Gastornis* is the ancestor of ducks, geese and other related birds.

- **Even though these birds** could be huge, they were also light-footed, quick runners. This is because, like all birds, they had hollow bones.

- **The diets** of terror birds included small and medium-sized mammals, such as prehistoric rodents and horses.

- **During the Late Eocene** and Oligocene Epochs (40–24 mya), the big carnivorous mammals became more powerful and better hunters and so more dominant, taking over.

- **However, in South America,** which was cut off from North America and the rest of the world for much of the Tertiary Period (65–1.6 mya), terror birds managed to stay dominant for a longer period of time.

▼ Gastornis *was about 2 m tall, with a head the size of a horse's. Around 50 mya it was one of the top hunters in Europe and North America.*

- **One South American** terror bird was *Phorusrhacus*, which grew up to 1.5 m tall.

- ***Titanis*** was another South American terror bird, and the biggest of all – it was 2.5 m tall and weighed 150 kg.

▶ Phorusrhacus *probably hunted on open grasslands, seizing goat-sized mammals with its huge beak.*

Other flightless birds

- **Most prehistoric** flightless birds were giants, but not all of them were terror birds.

- *Shuvuuia,* which lived about 80 mya, was an early, flightless bird. Like the terror birds, it was very large.

- *Shuvuuia* was about 1 m high. It probably fed on insects and small reptiles.

- **The name** *Shuvuuia* comes from the Mongolian word for 'bird'. It lived on the plains of Central Asia and had the long, thin legs of a fast runner.

- **For a long time,** palaeontologists thought that *Shuvuuia* was a reptile, but in fact its skull is much more similar to a modern bird's than a reptile's.

- **Much later giant** birds grew to incredible sizes. *Dinornis,* for instance, was the tallest flightless bird ever at 3.5 m tall.

- *Dinornis* lived in New Zealand. It first appeared about 2 mya and survived until 300 years ago!

- **At 450 kg,** *Aepyornis* was the heaviest bird ever to have lived. It lived on the island of Madagascar between 2 million and 500 years ago.

- **Both** *Dinornis* **and** *Aepyornis* were herbivores. Their diet consisted of seeds and fruit.

> **FASCINATING FACT**
> *Dinornis* was a type of moa bird. The only survivor of this group is the kiwi.

Ostrich

Rhea

Emu

Cassowary

Bennet's
cassowary

Kiwi

▲ *These modern flightless birds are descendants of prehistoric flightless birds. The collective name for flightless birds is ratites, from the Latin* ratis *meaning 'raft'. Unlike flying birds, ratites have flat, raftlike breastbones that cannot support the muscles needed for flight.*

Water birds

- *Ichthyornis* was a prehistoric seagull, which first appeared in the Late Cretaceous Period (85–65 mya).

- **It was similar in size** to a modern seagull, but had a much larger head and a beak full of very sharp teeth.

- *Presbyornis* was a prehistoric duck. Like *Ichthyornis*, it evolved in the Late Cretaceous Period and was abundant in the Early Tertiary Period (65–40 mya).

- *Presbyornis* was much bigger than a modern duck – it stood between 0.5 m and 1.5 m tall.

- **It had much longer legs** than its modern relative and so may have been a wading bird rather than a diving bird.

- *Presbyornis* lived in large flocks on lake shores, like modern flamingos.

- *Osteodontornis* was a huge flying bird, with a wingspan up to 5.2 m across.

- **It lived in the Miocene Epoch** (24–5 mya), and would have flown over the North Pacific Ocean.

- *Osteodontornis* had a long bill, lined with toothlike bony spikes. Its diet probably included squid, seized from the surface of the sea.

. . . FASCINATING FACT . . .
The skull of *Presbyornis* most closely resembles that of the living Australian duck *Stictonetta*.

▶ *Some experts believe that* Palaelodus *was a prehistoric flamingo that lived in France about 26 mya.*

Hesperornis

- *Hesperornis* was a flightless seabird, a bit like a modern penguin but it lived only in the northern hemisphere.

- **It lived between** 120 and 65 mya, in the Middle and Late Cretaceous Period.

- *Hesperornis* was about 2 m long, with tiny, useless wings and a long neck.

- **It had a long beak** filled with teeth, which it used to stab and then crunch up its diet of fish and squid.

- **This tooth-filled beak** shows that *Hesperornis* was a primitive bird – later birds, and all modern ones, have toothless beaks.

▶ Hesperornis' *wings had evolved into tiny stubs, which were useless for flying, but good for steering while swimming.*

- **It had large**, webbed feet, which probably meant it swam well in the sea, but waddled like a penguin on land.

- **Another indication** that it waddled on land was the position of its legs, which were situated far back on its body.

- **These legs**, however, were strong and would have made *Hesperornis* a powerful diver, thrusting under the waves.

- **Fossil hunters** have unearthed *Hesperornis* remains in northern USA, including parts of Alaska.

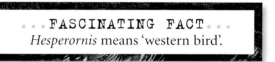

FASCINATING FACT
Hesperornis means 'western bird'.

Land birds

● **Land birds** are flying birds that fly in the skies over land and hunt or feed on the ground, unlike water birds.

● **Fossils** of prehistoric land birds are rare because their bones were light and would not have fossilized well.

● **As a result**, there are big gaps in palaeontologists' knowledge of the evolution of many species of birds. However, there are some early land birds they do know about.

◄ *No one knows for certain when parrots first evolved, but fossils date back to at least 20 mya. Some bird experts think that parrots were once much more plentiful than they are today.*

> ··· **FASCINATING FACT** ···
> *Neocathartes* was an early vulture-like bird. There are similarities between its skeleton and that of storks, which suggests vultures and storks are closely related.

- **Archaeopsittacus** was an early parrot of the Late Oligocene Epoch (28–24 mya).

- **Ogygoptynx** was the first-known owl. It lived in the Palaeocene Epoch (65–58 mya).

- **Aegialornis** was an early swiftlike bird, which lived in the Eocene and Oligocene Epochs (58–24 mya). It may be the ancestor of swifts and hummingbirds.

- **Gallinuloides** was an early member of the chicken family. *Gallinuloides* fossils have been found in Wyoming, USA, in rock strata of the Eocene Epoch (58–37 mya).

- **The earliest-known vultures** lived in the Palaeocene Epoch (65–58 mya).

- **The earliest-known hawks**, cranes, bustards, cuckoos and songbirds lived in the Eocene Epoch.

▶ *This vulture's earliest ancestors were the very first birds of prey. Scientists think that* Lithornis, *a bird of prey that lived around 65 mya, was a type of vulture.*

Argentavis

- *Argentavis* was an enormous bird of prey – the largest one ever discovered.
- **Its wingspan** was more than 7 m across, which is double the size of the largest modern living bird, the wandering albatross.
- **Individual** *Argentavis* feathers were up to 1.5 m long!
- *Argentavis* lived between 8 and 6 mya.
- **It looked similar** to a modern vulture, and may have had a similar scavenging lifestyle.
- **Its huge size** and weight (up to 80 kg) suggests that it was more of a glider than an active flier.

- *Argentavis* was possibly bald-headed, with a ruff of feathers around its neck, much like a modern vulture or a condor.

- **It had a large**, hooked beak, which was probably more effective at grabbing hold of prey than its feet.

- *Argentavis* means 'bird of Argentina' and it is so-called because its remains were first discovered there.

- *Argentavis* belonged to a family of extinct flying birds called teratorns.

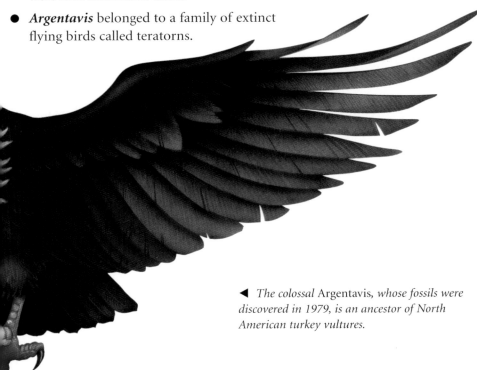

◀ *The colossal* Argentavis, *whose fossils were discovered in 1979, is an ancestor of North American turkey vultures.*

Mammal fossils

- **There are few fossil** remains of the earliest mammals because scavengers would usually have eaten their bodies.

- **However** coprolites (fossilized dung) of predators and scavengers sometimes contain undigested parts of the early mammals themselves, such as their teeth.

- **Palaeontologists** can tell a lot from a mammal's molar (cheek tooth). They can work out its species and the period it lived in from the pattern of ridges and furrows on its surface.

- **Palaeontologists** can also estimate the age of a mammal when it died by looking at the wear and tear on its teeth.

- **Some mammals** are preserved in tar pits – prehistoric pools that were full of a mixture of hydrocarbons that formed sticky tar, which preserved fossils.

- **Tar pits** at Rancho La Brea, near present-day downtown Los Angeles, USA, contained a perfectly preserved skeleton of the sabre-tooth carnivore *Smilodon*.

- **Freezing** is another very effective way of preserving animals. Remains of frozen mammoths have been discovered in near-perfect conditions in Siberia.

- **Explorers** using dog sledges discovered some of the first frozen mammoths. Their remains were so well preserved that the dogs were able to eat the meat on their bones.

▶ *The remains of a woolly mammoth, preserved in frozen soil. Besides bones, palaeontologists have discovered skin, hair and other body parts of mammoths in Siberia.*

- **The most complete** frozen mammoth find occurred in 1977, with the discovery of the 40,000-year-old baby male mammoth, which people named Dima.

- **Fossil finds** of prehistoric mammals include skulls, teeth, jawbones, ear bones, horns, tusks and antlers.

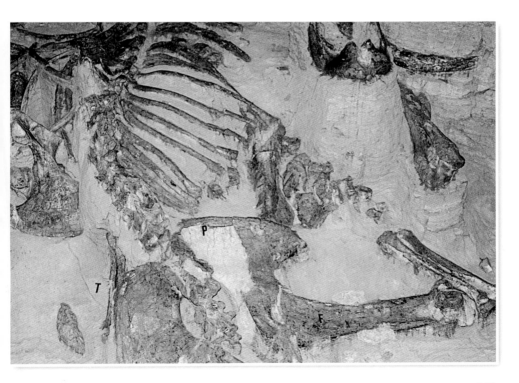

Rise of
the mammals

- **The earliest mammals** were small, shrewlike creatures that appeared in the Late Triassic Period (220–208 mya).

- **After their initial emergence**, mammals developed little in the two periods following the Triassic, Jurassic and Cretaceous Periods (208–65 mya).

- **This is because dinosaurs** dominated the land at this time. Mammals had to remain small and hidden to avoid becoming dinner!

- **It was only after dinosaurs** became extinct around 65 mya, that mammals started to evolve into larger and more varied forms.

- **Mammals** (and birds) have bigger brains than reptiles, and are also warm-blooded.

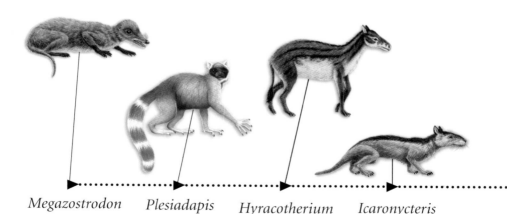

Megazostrodon
220 mya

Plesiadapis
60 mya

Hyracotherium
60–50 mya

Icaronycteris
55–45 mya

- **These abilities** meant that mammals could be adaptable – something that ensured their success in the changing climates of the Tertiary and Quaternary Periods (65 mya to the present).

- **The rise of mammals** to the top was not instant – during the Early Tertiary Period, (65–58 mya), the major killers were the giant flightless terror birds.

- **During the Eocene Epoch**, (58–37 mya), mammals became the most dominant animals on land.

- **Eocene mammals** also took to the air in the form of bats – and the seas in the form of whales – and later, dolphins and seals.

- **Mammals have been** – and still are – the most adaptable of all backboned animals.

Basilosaurus
40 mya

Paraceratherium
30 mya

Smilodon
1 mya

Woolly Mammoth
120,000 years ago

Early mammals

- *Megazostrodon* was one of the first true mammals. It appeared at the end of the Triassic Period (about 220 mya).

- **It was a shrewlike insectivore** (insect-eater) and about 12 cm long. It had a long body that was low to the ground and long limbs that it held out to the side in a squatting position.

- *Eozostrodon* was another very early mammal, which emerged about the same time as *Megazostrodon*.

- **It had true mammalian teeth**, including two different sorts of cheek teeth – premolars and molars – which were replaced only once during its lifetime.

- **Its sharp teeth** suggest it was a meateater, and its large eyes suggest that it hunted at night.

- **A further early mammal** was *Morganucodon*. It too had premolars and molars and chewed its food in a roundabout motion, rather than the up-down motion of reptiles.

- *Sinoconodon* was yet another early mammal that lived in the Early Jurassic Period (about 200 mya). It was probably covered in fur.

- **These early mammals** also had three middle ear bones, which made their hearing more sensitive than reptiles.

- **They also had whiskers**, which suggests they had fur, which in turn suggests they were warm-blooded.

- **All true mammals** are warm-blooded, which means they maintain a constant body temperature. Fur helps mammals keep warm when it is cold – at night, for instance.

▲ *Like other small, early mammals,* Megazostrodon *was probably a nocturnal animal, coming out to hunt at night.*

365

Leptictidium

- *Leptictidium* was a small carnivorous mammal that lived 50 to 40 mya.

- **Its name** means 'delicate weasel'. It grew up to 90 cm long.

- *Leptictidium* had long hind legs and moved by hopping, a bit like a kangaroo.

- **It was an insectivore**, or insect eater. However, it also fed on small lizards, mammals and invertebrates.

- *Leptictidium* belonged to a group of insectivores called leptictids.

- **All leptictids** had three-cusped molars – or three grinding points on the surface of each cheek tooth.

- **Leptictids** died out when the tropical rainforests in which they lived began to disappear.

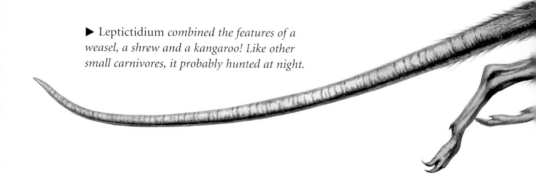

▶ Leptictidium *combined the features of a weasel, a shrew and a kangaroo! Like other small carnivores, it probably hunted at night.*

- **Leptictids** are the ancestors of modern insectivores such as hedgehogs, shrews and moles. Some palaeontologists also think they are the ancestors of hoofed mammals and primates.

- **The best examples** of *Leptictidium* fossils come from Messel, near Frankfurt in Germany – the site of a lake 50 mya, which was surrounded by a subtropical forest.

- **Some *Leptictidium* fossils** at Messel even show the outline of the animal's fur, as well as the contents of its stomach.

Mammal offspring

- **Mammals** developed a very different way of producing young, compared to reptiles and birds, which both lay eggs.

- **Instead, most mammals** are viviparous, which means they give birth to live young.

- **One unusual group of mammals**, the monotremes, defy this rule by laying eggs. There are five surviving monotremes – the duck-billed platypus and four species of echidna.

▲ *All mammal offspring such as these lambs, feed on their mother's milk, which contains a rich source of nutrients to help them to grow quickly.*

- **After the young** of mammals are born, their mothers feed them milk, produced in their mammary glands.

- **The word 'mammal'** comes from the mammary glands – the part of female mammals' bodies that secretes milk.

- **The first mammals,** such as *Megazostrodon, Eozostrodon* and *Morganucodon* grew a single set of milk teeth, which suggests that the young fed on breast milk.

- **Milk teeth** are temporary teeth that grow with the nutrients provided by milk, and prepare the jaw for later teeth.

- **Mammals** can be divided into three groups depending on how they rear their young – placentals, marsupials and monotremes.

- **In placental mammals**, the offspring stays inside its mother's body, in the womb, until it is a fully developed baby – at which point it is born.

- **Marsupial mammals** give birth to their offspring at a much earlier stage. The tiny infants then develop fully in their mothers' pouch, called a marsupium.

◄ *Marsupial mammals, such as this kangaroo and its joey (infant), give birth at an earlier stage than other mammals.*

Rodents

- **In terms of their numbers**, variety and distribution, rodents are the most successful mammals that have ever lived.

- **Squirrels**, rats, guinea pigs, beavers, porcupines, voles, gophers and mice are all types of rodent.

- **Rodents** have been – and still are – so successful because they are small, fast-breeding and able to digest all kinds of foods, including substances as hard as wood.

- **The first-known rodent** was *Paramys*, which appeared about 60 mya.

- *Paramys* was a squirrel-like rodent that could climb trees. It was 60 cm long, and had a long, slightly bushy tail.

- **Modern squirrels** evolved from *Paramys* around 38 mya. These mammals have one of the longest ancestries that we know of.

- **Another early rodent** was *Epigaulus,* which was a gopher with two horns.

- *Epigaulus* was 26 cm long and lived in North America in the Miocene Epoch (24–5 mya). It probably used its horns for defence or digging up roots.

- **Prehistoric rodents** could be massive. *Castoroides* was an early beaver that was over 2 m long – almost the size of a black bear.

> ... **FASCINATING FACT** ...
> Rabbits and hares are descended from rodents.
> Modern hares first appeared around 5 mya.

▼ Platypittamys *was a prehistoric, ratlike rodent. Rodents became plentiful during the Oligocene Epoch (37–24 mya).*

Carnivores

- **The first carnivorous mammals** were the creodonts, which ranged in size from the cat-like *Oxyaena* to the wolflike *Mesonyx*.

- **In the Late Eocene Epoch** (around 40 mya) large hoofed carnivores began to appear, such as *Andrewsarchus*.

- **Modern carnivores** are descended from a seperate group called miacids.

- **Modern carnivores** belong to the order Carnivora.
  This order had two subgroups – the fissipeds, which include the cat and dog families and the pinnipeds (seals, sea lions and walruses). Now many classification schemes put pinnipeds in their own mammal group, seperate from the fissiped carnivores.

- **In the Oligocene Epoch** (37–24 mya), fissipeds began to replace creodonts as the dominant carnivores.

- **Fissipeds** were smarter, faster, and deadlier than creodonts, and were the only predators that could catch the new fast-running herbivores.

- **Faster mammals** evolved in the Oligocene Epoch as thick forests changed into open woodlands, with more space to run after, and run from, other creatures.

Allodesmus was a prehistoric seal. It had flippers, large eyes
and spiky teeth, which it used to impale slippery fish.

- **As carnivores evolved**, so they developed bigger brains, more alert senses,
  sharper claws and teeth, and stronger jaws and limbs.

- **The pinnipeds** are carnivorous mammals that, like whales and dolphins
  (and reptiles before them), reinvaded the seas.

◀ Dinictis *was a fissiped carnivore
and member of the cat family,
which lived in North America
about 30 mya. Fissipeds
were superbly adapted for
hunting fast-running
mammals.*

Creodonts

- **Creodonts** were the first flesh-eating mammals. They lived in the Eocene Period (58–37 mya).

- **They came in many different shapes** and sizes. Some were as small as weasels, while others were bigger than bears.

- **Many creodonts** were flat-footed, and walked on short, heavy limbs tipped with claws.

- **They caught early herbivores** that, like these early carnivores, had not yet evolved into quick runners.

▶ Sinopa *was a creodont – an early carnivore. It would have been a little bigger than a domestic cat.*

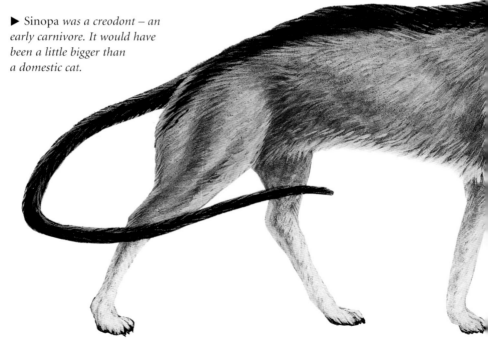

- **Creodonts had smaller**, more primitive brains than later carnivores – these were cleverer, faster hunters than the creodonts, and forced them into decline.

- **Another way** in which creodonts were less successful than later carnivores was with their teeth, which were less effective at stabbing or slicing.

- **Creodonts were**, however, the top predators of their day. The wolf-sized *Hyaenodon* was particularly successful.

- **Fossils of *Hyaenodon* skulls** show that they had a very highly-developed sense of smell, as well as powerful, bone-crushing jaws.

- **Fossils** of male *Hyaenodon* teeth reveal grinding marks, which palaeontologists think means they ground their teeth to ward off rivals, like some modern animals.

... FASCINATING FACT ...
Hyaenodon species ranged in size from
30 cm high at the shoulders to 1.2 m high
– the size of a small rhinoceros.

Herbivores

- **The first specialist herbivores** (plant eaters) appeared in the Late Palaeocene Epoch (around 60 mya).

- **They ranged in size** from the equivalent of modern badgers to pigs.

- **These early herbivores** were rooters or browsers – they foraged for food on the floors of their forest homes.

- **It was not until** the very end of the Palaeocene Epoch (58 mya) that the first large herbivores evolved.

- **Large herbivores** emerged before large carnivores. They must have had a peaceful life – for a while!

- *Uintatherium* was one of the large early herbivores. It was the size of a large rhinoceros, with thick limbs to support its heavy body.

- *Uintatherium* had three pairs of bony knobs protruding from its head. Males had very long, strong canine teeth, which they would have used if attacked by creodont carnivores.

- **The growth of grasslands** and the decline of forests in the Miocene Epoch (24–5 mya) speeded up changes to herbivores' bodies.

- **They developed** faster legs to outrun carnivores in open spaces. They also developed better digestive systems to cope with the new, tough grasses.

376

● **The most important** requirements for a herbivore are complex teeth and digestive systems to break down plant food and release its energy.

▲ Merycoidodon *was a herbivore that lived around 30 mya. It was about the size of a sheep, with a large head and a long body.*

377

Ruminants

- **Ruminants** are a very successful group of plant-eating mammals that first appeared about 40 mya.

- **Modern ruminants** include cattle, sheep, deer, giraffes, antelopes and camels.

- **All these animals** can eat quickly, store plant material in the stomach and then bring it back to their mouths again, to chew it and break it down. This process is called 'chewing the cud'.

- *Archaeomeryx* was an early, rabbit-sized ruminant, which lived in Asia. It is the ancestor of the chevrotain – a small, hoofed mammal also known as the mouse deer.

- *Archaeomeryx* had a three-chambered stomach, each of which broke down its plant food a little bit further.

- **Camels** were the next ruminants to evolve. One large prehistoric camel was *Aepycamelus*, which had a very long giraffe-like neck.

- **They were followed** by cattle, sheep and deer, which were more advanced ruminants because they had four-chambered stomachs.

- **The four chambers** of ruminants' stomachs are called the rumen, the reticulum, the omasum and the abosmasum.

- **Ruminants' big advantage** over other plant eaters was that they could decide when to digest their food. If they sensed a threat while they were eating they could run away and digest their meal later.

- **Camels and chevrotains** are the only surviving ruminants with three-chambered stomachs.

▶ *Like other ruminants, these Arabian camels, or dromedaries, use urea, a bodily waste product, to feed the bacteria in their stomach chambers that break down plant matter. Less urea waste means less urine and so less water loss – which is why camels can cope with desert conditions.*

Condylarths

- **Condylarths** were the first hoofed mammals.

- **They lived** in the Early Tertiary Period, between 65 and 40 mya.

- **All later hoofed mammals**, from horses to pigs, are descended from condylarths.

- **The earliest condylarths** had claws as opposed to hooves.

- **Later ones** evolved longer limbs, tipped with nails or hooves, for running away quickly from carnivores.

- **The first-known** condylarth was *Protungulatum*, a rabbit-sized plant eater.

▶ *All hoofed mammals descend from condylarths, such as this* Hyopsodus. *The rat-sized, forest-dwelling* Hyopsodus, *however, had claws rather than hooves.*

- **A slightly later** condylarth was *Phenacodus*, which palaeontologists think was an insectivore (an insect eater).

- ***Phenacodus*** was the size of a small sheep, and had clearly-developed hooves.

- **Condylarths** spread over most of the world, including Europe, Asia, South America and Africa.

FASCINATING FACT
Early condylarths were also rabbit-sized.
Later ones, however, were as big as bears.

Perissodactyls

▼ *These horses are perissodactyls –*
they have one toe (a hoof) on each
foot. Early horses had three toes.

- **Perissodactyls** are plant-eating, hoofed mammals with an odd number of toes (either three or one) on their feet.

- **The three** living groups of perissodactyls are horses, tapirs and rhinoceroses.

- **The two** extinct groups of perissodactyls are brontotheres and chalicotheres.

- **Brontotheres** included massive beasts, such as *Brontotherium*, which had elephant-like limbs and a blunt, bony prong jutting from its nose. It ate only soft-leaved plants.

- *Chalicotherium* was a chalicothere. It lacked front teeth, and ate by placing soft plant shoots in the back of its mouth, like a modern panda.

- **The earliest ancestors** of modern horses, tapirs and rhinos appeared about 50 mya.

- *Miotapirus* was an ancestor of modern tapirs. It lived in North America about 20 mya.

- **Perissodactyls' feet** carried the weight of the animal on the middle toe, either in a single hoof, as in horses, or a big toe with one on each side, as in tapirs and rhinos.

- **For much of the Tertiary Period** (65–1.6 mya), perissodactyls were the most abundant form of hoofed mammals. They then declined, however, and artiodactyls (even-toed mammals) became dominant.

. . . FASCINATING FACT . . .

Chalicotheres had long front legs and long curved claws, which they could not place flat on the ground. Instead, they walked on their knuckles, like apes.

Artiodactyls

- **Artiodactyls** are hoofed mammals with an even number (either two or four) of toes on their feet.

- **Pigs**, camels, giraffe, sheep, goats, cattle, hippopotamuses, deer, antelopes and their ancestors are all artiodactyls.

- **Like the perissodactyls**, artiodactyls first appeared about 50 mya.

- *Dichobune* was an early artiodactyl, which lived between 40 and 30 mya. It had short limbs and four-toed feet.

- **In smaller artiodactyls**, such as sheep and goats, the foot is often cloven into two parts (toes).

- **In very heavy artiodactyls**, such as hippopotamuses, there are four toes to carry the animal's weight.

- **At least two** of the middle toes on artiodactyls' feet carry an equal weight.

- **During the Miocene Epoch** (24–5 mya), artiodactyls became the most successful hoofed mammals.

- **Their success** lay more in their stomachs than in their feet. Artiodactyls evolved more advanced digestive systems, which allowed them to process the tough grasses that had replaced the earlier, softer, forest plants.

- **Another difference** between artiodactyls and perissodactyls is their ankle bones. Artiodactyls' ankle bones have more rounded joints at both ends, which means they provide more thrust when they run.

▶ *This cow and her calf are members of the most successful group of hoofed mammals to have evolved – the artiodactyls. There are around 150 living species of artiodactyl.*

Cats

- **Cats** are the most highly developed carnivores. They are the fastest and most intelligent land hunters, with the sharpest claws and teeth.

- **Cats** evolved along two lines. One group was the sabre-tooths, which included *Smilodon* (see pages 142–143). This group is extinct today.

- **Sabre-tooths** specialized in killing large, heavily-built animals with thick hides, which explains their long canine teeth.

- **The other group** of cats is the felines, which are the ancestors of all modern cats, from lions and cheetahs to your pet cat.

- **The felines** were faster and more agile than the sabre-tooths, who became extinct because their prey became faster and able to outrun them. The felines, however, continued to be successful hunters.

- **One prehistoric feline** was *Dinictis* (see pages p132–133), a puma-sized cat that lived in the Oligocene Epoch (37–24 mya).

- **A later feline** was *Dinofelis,* which lived between 5 and 1.4 mya.

- **The name *Dinofelis*** means 'terrible cat'. It looked like a modern jaguar, but had stronger front legs that it used to press down on its victims before stabbing them with its teeth.

- ***Dinofelis'*** diet included baboons, antelope and australopithecines – our human ancestors.

> **· · · FASCINATING FACT · · ·**
> Prehistoric cats' ability to unsheathe and retract their claws
> provided them with one of their deadliest weapons – and one
> that cats still have.

▶ *The terrifying sabre-tooth cat* Smilodon
*was not the ancestor of modern tigers, lions or
domestic cats. It belonged instead to a different
branch of the cat family known as achairodonts.*

Dogs

▲ *Part of a pack of* Hesperocyon *dogs, tracking the scent of their prey. Organized hunting in packs is an example of dogs' intelligence.*

- **Early dogs** hunted in a similar way to modern wild dogs – in packs.

- **Dogs** developed long snouts, which gave them a keen sense of smell, and forward-pointing eyes, which gave them good vision.

- **Dogs** also developed a mixture of teeth – sharp canines for stabbing, narrow cheek teeth for slicing and, farther along the jaw, flatter teeth for crushing.

- **These different teeth** meant that dogs could eat a variety of different foods, including plants, which they might have had to eat if meat was in short supply.

- **One of the ancestors** of dogs, as well as bears, was the bear-dog *Amphicyon*. Its name means 'in-between dog'.

- *Amphicyon* lived between 40 and 9 mya.

- **Trace fossils** of *Amphicyon*'s footprints show that it walked like a bear with its feet flat on the ground.

- *Hesperocyon* was one of the earliest dogs, living between 37 and 29 mya.

- *Hesperocyon* was the size of a small fox. It had long legs and jaws, forward-pointing eyes and a supple, slender body.

> **FASCINATING FACT**
> Hunting in packs allowed *Hesperocyon* to catch large animals
> that it would not have been able to kill on its own.

Andrewsarchus

- *Andrewsarchus* is one of the largest meat-eating land mammals that has ever existed.

- **It lived in East Asia** in the Late Eocene Epoch (around 40 mya).

- **No complete** *Andrewsarchus* skeleton has ever been found – only its skull, which measured 83 cm long.

- **Palaeontologists** have built up an impression of the rest of the animal's body from knowledge of its skull, and its relation to the earlier, bearlike *Mesonyx*.

- **If their impression** is correct, *Andrewsarchus* was 1.8 m high and 5 m long.

- **It had long**, strong jaws, which it used to eat a variety of foods.

- *Andrewsarchus* was a scavenger and an omnivore – it would eat anything.

- **It belonged** to a group of carnivorous hoofed mammals known as mesonychids.

- **Fossil-hunters** have found most mesonychid remains near prehistoric rivers and coasts, suggesting that this was where they lived and hunted.

▶ *The colossal* Andrewsarchus *lived a bit like a bear. It hunted hoofed mammals but would also have scavenged other predators' leftovers and eaten leaves, berries and insects.*

····· FASCINATING FACT ·····
Andrewsarchus means 'Andrew's flesh-eater'. It was named after the naturalist, explorer and writer Roy Chapman Andrews (1884–1960).

Smilodon

▲ Smilodon *was a fearsome predator. It became extinct because it was not fast enough to catch the quick-running mammals that evolved at the end of the last Ice Age, about 11,000 years ago.*

- *Smilodon* was a terrifying predator that belonged to a group of cats called sabre-tooths.

- **It lived** between 1 million and 11,000 years ago in North and South America.

- **One of *Smilodon*'s** most distinctive features was its huge, curved canine teeth, which could be up to 25 cm long. It could also open its jaws to an angle of about 90 degrees!

- **The first** sabre-tooth was *Megantereon*. It lived about 30 mya.

- *Smilodon* was only a little larger than a big lion, but was around twice its weight at 200 kg.

- **Its 'design'** was more like a bear's than a modern cat's – it had very powerful forelegs, a thick neck, and a short spine.

- **Because of its shorter spine** and heavier build, *Smilodon* was not as fast as feline cats (the ancestors of modern cats). But it made up for this with its power and its teeth.

- *Smilodon* preyed on large and slow-moving creatures, such as prehistoric bison, mammoths, giant camels and ground sloths.

- *Smilodon* was truly a top predator, with no real enemies and no direct competitors – until the emergence of modern humans.

... FASCINATING FACT ...
Smilodon's large canines were very delicate. They could break when stabbing thick-skinned animals, such as bison.

Entelodonts

- **Entelodonts** were large piglike mammals that lived in Asia and North America in the Miocene Epoch (25–4 mya).

- **They are** the ancestors of modern pigs.

- **One entelodont** was *Dinohyus*, which probably fed off plant roots or scavenged for prey.

- *Dinohyus* was one of the largest entelodonts, standing at least 2 m tall at the shoulder with a skull that was around 1 m long.

- *Dinohyus* had very distinctive teeth. Its incisors (front teeth) were blunt, but the teeth next to them, the canines, were sturdy and substantial, and could have been used for defence.

- **Another entelodont** was the scavenger *Entelodon*, the largest of which was about the same size as *Dinohyus*.

- **There are** severe wounds in the fossils of some *Entelodon* skulls, such as a 2-cm-deep gash in the bone between its eyes. Palaeontologists think these were caused by the animals fighting amongst themselves.

- *Entelodon* means 'perfect-toothed', and this mammal had a thick layer of enamel on its teeth.

- **However**, many fossil remains of *Entelodon* have broken teeth – a result of the tough, varied diet of this scavenger.

> ... **FASCINATING FACT** ...
> *Entelodon's* face had bony lumps all over it.
> One reason for this is that they protected
> its eyes and nose during clashes with rivals.

▲ *The fierce-looking* Dinohyus, *also known as* Daeodon, *may well have scavenged for its food like modern hyenas. Its powerful neck muscles and large canine teeth suggest it could have broken bones and eaten flesh.*

Paraceratherium

- *Paraceratherium* is the largest land mammal ever to have lived.

- **It was a gentle giant**, which could be as tall as 5.5 m at the shoulder.

- *Paraceratherium* belonged to the group of mammals called perissodactyls – hoofed mammals with an odd number of toes.

- **It was also** an early rhinoceros, but unlike its living relatives, had no horns on its snout.

- **Remains** of this huge beast have been discovered in Europe and Central Asia, where it lived between 30 and 16 mya.

- **Until recently** this beast was known as *Indricotherium*, but it is now more commonly known as *Paraceratherium*.

- *Paraceratherium* had long front legs and a long neck, which it used like a giraffe to reach leaves on the high branches of trees.

- **Males** were larger than females, and had heavier heads with more dome-shaped skulls.

- **In comparison** with the rest of its body, *Paraceratherium*'s skull was quite small.

> **. . . FASCINATING FACT . . .**
> Male *Paraceratherium* could be as heavy as 30 tonnes
> – four times the weight of a modern elephant!

▼ Paraceratherium – *also known as* Indricotherium – *was a giant, hornless, long-necked rhinoceros. Although it was massively heavy, its long legs probably meant that* Paraceratherium *was capable of running.*

Brontotherium

▼ *Male* Brontotheriums *had larger two-pronged horns than females, which suggests that males used them for display and for fighting.*

● *Brontotherium* was a large herbivore, whose name means 'thunder beast'.

 ● **It lived in North America** and central Asia around 40 mya.

 ● *Brontotherium* was somewhere between a rhinoceros and an elephant in size. It was 2.5 m tall at its shoulders.

● **It belonged** to the group of mammals called perissodactyls – hoofed mammals with an odd number of toes.

● *Brontotherium* had thick legs and short, broad feet with four toes on its front feet and three toes on its hind feet.

● **It had a thick**, Y-shaped horn on the top of its snout.

● **Palaeontologists** think that *Brontotherium* used its horn to ward off predators and to fight rival males.

● *Brontotherium* lived in herds on grassy plains and in forests.

● **It had big**, square molar teeth that crushed the soft leaves it fed on.

> ...FASCINATING FACT...
> *Brontotherium* is a distant cousin of
> modern horses, tapirs and rhinoceroses.

South American mammals

- **South America** was separated from the rest of the world for much of the Tertiary Period (65–1.6 mya).

- **Like Australia**, South America's isolation meant that certain mammals evolved there and nowhere else.

- **The main difference** between them was that South America had placental mammals as well as marsupials.

- **Placental mammals** included the giant ground sloths, such as *Megatherium*, and huge rodents the size of bears.

▶ Protypotherium *was a rabbit-like rodent that was about 50 cm long. It was related to hoofed mammals, but had claws instead of hooves.*

- **Marsupial mammals** included the marsupial carnivores, such as *Thylacosmilus*.

- **Evolutionary convergence**, whereby different species can come to look very similar, happened in South America just as in Australia. One example was *Thoatherium*, which looked very much like the small horses that were evolving in other parts of the world.

- **The formation** of the Panama isthmus (a strip of land) reconnected South America to North America about 3 mya.

- **Many South American mammals** journeyed north. Some, such as armadillos, porcupines and guinea pigs, were very successful in their new homes.

- **Others**, like the glyptodonts, eventually died out. This might be because of climate change – or because humans hunted them to extinction.

...FASCINATING FACT...
An example of evolutionary convergence was the *Pyrotherium*, which had the trunk, cheek teeth and tusks of an early elephant – except that it wasn't one!

401

Megatherium

▶ Megatherium, *meaning 'great beast' was identified and named by the French naturalist Georges Cuvier (1769–1832).*

- *Megatherium* was a giant ground sloth – an extinct type of sloth that lived about 5 mya.

- *Megatherium* stood about 7 m tall. It had huge, extremely strong arms and massive claws, which it used to pull down branches and even uproot trees.

- **It had short** hind legs and a powerful tail that it used for extra support when it stood up on its rear legs to reach the tallest branches.

- *Megatherium* walked on its knuckles on its forelimbs and on the side of its feet on its hind legs.

- **The sheer size of** *Megatherium* would have put off most predators, but it also had very tough skin – an extra defence.

- **The remains** of ground sloth skin found in caves in South America show that its was made even stronger by tiny lumps of bone.

- *Megatherium* lived in parts of South America, such as present-day Bolivia and Peru.

- **When South America** became joined to North America about 3 mya, *Megatherium* spread northwards.

- *Megatherium* is thought to have become extinct 11,000 years ago, but some people in Argentina claim it lived until 400 years ago. If this is so, it is likely that humans killed off the last of these giants.

. . . **FASCINATING FACT** . . .
Megatherium belonged to a group of mammals
called edentates, which lacked front teeth.

Glyptodonts

▲ Glyptodon, *means 'grooved tooth'. It was named by the English scientist Richard Owen (1804–1892) from fossilized bones that the English naturalist Charles Darwin (1809–1882) brought back with him from South America.*

- **Glyptodonts** were giant armadillos that lived in South America between 5 million and 11,000 years ago.

- **They had domelike shells** and armoured tails that ended in a spiked club.

- **Their tail** also served as an extra support when they reared up on their hind legs – either to defend themselves against attackers or to mate.

- **They also had** powerful jaws and huge cheek teeth that could constantly be replaced, unlike most other mammals.

- **These constantly** growing teeth meant they could chew through the toughest plants without wearing down their teeth.

- *Glyptodon* was a 3 m-long glyptodont. Like other glyptodonts, it was an edentate – in other words, it did not have front teeth.

- *Doedicurus* was an even bigger glyptodont. It weighed 1400 kg and was 4 m long – the size of a big car!

- *Doedicurus* is the most heavily-armoured planteater ever to have lived. A sledgehammer would have made little impression on its massive, bony shell.

- **The body armour** and weaponry of glyptodonts were designed to protect them against predators such as *Thylacosmilus*.

...**FASCINATING FACT**...
Glyptodonts' armour and tails were similar to those of ankylosaur dinosaurs. This is another example of evolutionary convergence – when separate groups of animals develop similar characteristics.

Toxodon

- *Toxodon* was a very unusual mammal that evolved in isolation in South America. It combined the features of several other animals.

- **It was a hoofed animal** the size of a rhino – but with very short legs. It had a trunk like an elephant's, but had other features that were more like those of a rodent!

- *Toxodon's* **ears**, eyes and nose were all on the top of its head. This suggests it lived like a hippo, spending most of the time wading in rivers and lakes with only the top of its head sticking out.

- *Toxodon* **lived** in the Pleistocene Epoch (1.6 million– 10,000 years ago).

- **Given the large number** of *Toxodon* fossils that have been found, it was probably one of the most common large hoofed mammals in South America at one point.

- *Toxodon* had large gaps between its front teeth, and even larger gaps between its cheek teeth.

- **These teeth** were continually growing and being replaced, which suggests that its diet included tough grasses.

- *Toxodon* was a notoungulate, a type of hoofed mammal that evolved in isolation in South America.

- **After the naturalist** Charles Darwin (1809–1882) saw *Toxodon's* fossils he wrote that it was 'perhaps one of the strangest animals ever discovered'.

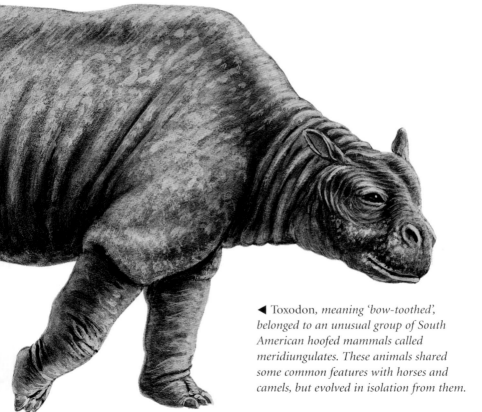

◀ Toxodon, *meaning 'bow-toothed', belonged to an unusual group of South American hoofed mammals called meridiungulates. These animals shared some common features with horses and camels, but evolved in isolation from them.*

407

Bats

- ***Icaronycteris*** is the earliest-known bat. Its fossil remains are between 55 and 45 million years old.

- **Despite its age,** *Icaronycteris* looks very similar to a modern bat. It has a bat's typically large ears, which it probably used as a sonar, like modern bats.

- **One difference** from modern bats was that *Icaronycteris'* tail was not joined to its legs by flaps of skin.

- **Palaeontologists** think that there must have been earlier, more primitive-looking bats from which *Icaronycteris* evolved.

- **The chance of finding** earlier prehistoric bat fossils is very small – like birds, bats have very fragile skeletons that do not fossilize well.

- ***Icaronycteris*** ate insects. Palaeontologists know this because they have found insect remains in the part of the fossil where its stomach would have been.

- ***Icaronycteris*** fossils have been found in North America.

- **The fossil remains** of another prehistoric bat, *Palaeochiropteryx,* have been found in Europe.

- **Like *Icaronycteris*,** this bat seems to have been an insectivore (insect eater).

▶ *Like this living bat, prehistoric bats such as* Icaronycteris *probably used sonar to sense nearby objects and hunt for prey. Bats use sonar by making a high-pitched sound and then listening to its echoes.*

Bats are the only mammals that are known to have
reached Australia after it became isolated from the
rest of the world around 40 mya.

Marsupials

- **Marsupials** are mammals that give birth to their offspring at a very early stage in their development – when they are still tiny.

- **After being born**, the infant crawls through its mother's fur to a pouch called the marsupium, where it stays, feeding on milk, until it is big enough to leave.

- **Palaeontologists** think that the first marsupials evolved in North America and then spread to South America and Australia.

- *Alphadon,* meaning 'first tooth', was an early marsupial, which emerged around 70 mya. It lived in North and South America

- *Alphadon* was 30 cm long and weighed 300 gm. It would have lived in trees, using its feet to climb and fed on insects, fruit and small vertebrates.

- **When Australia** became isolated from the rest of the world about 40 mya, its marsupials continued to evolve – unlike the rest of the world, where they fell into decline.

- **Marsupials** continued to exist in South America, which was also isolated from the rest of the world, during much of the Tertiary Period (65–1.6 mya).

- **But when South America** became reconnected with North America, about 3 mya, the arrival of placental mammals from the north led many marsupials to become extinct.

- **Today,** there are only two surviving groups of marsupials in the Americas: the opossums found throughout America and the rat opossums found in South America.

- **Australia** has many living marsupials, from kangaroos to koalas. However it had a much greater marsupial population in the Tertiary Period – we know this from fossil sites such as Riversleigh in northwest Queensland.

▶ Procoptodon *was a giant kangaroo that stood around 3 m tall. In Australia, plant-eating marsupials such as kangaroos and wallabies occupied the position taken by hoofed mammals in other parts of the world.*

411

Australian mammals

- **Australia** has a unique natural history because it became isolated from the rest of the world around 40 mya.

- **Australia's native mammals**, living and extinct, are mostly marsupials – mammals that give birth to tiny young, which then develop in their mother's outside pouch.

- **The earliest Australian marsupials** date from the Oligocene Epoch (37–24 mya). Most fossils come from the Miocene Epoch (24–5 mya) or later.

- **These fossils** show that there were giant kangaroos, called *Procoptodon*, as well as giant wombats, called *Diprotodon*.

- **Two marsupial carnivores** preyed on these giant herbivores. One was the lion-like *Thylacoleo*, the other was the smaller, wolf-like *Thylacinus*.

- **Palaeontologists** are very interested in *Thylacoleo* and *Thylacinus* because they both demonstrate how different species can come to look very similar – the process known as evolutionary convergence.

- **Although they had different** ancestors and lived on different continents, *Thylacoleo* came to look like a placental lion, while *Thylacinus* came to look like a placental wolf.

- **The Miocene fossil site** in Riversleigh, northern Queensland, has revealed the extent and variety of prehistoric marsupials in Australia.

- **Among the fossils** are many long-extinct marsupials. One of these was so unusual that at first palaeontologists called it a 'thingodont', although now it is known as *Yolkaparidon*.

- ***Thylacinus*** continued to exist in Australia into the 20th century, but the last one died in a zoo in Tasmania in 1936.

◀ *At 3.4 m long, the giant wombat* Diprotodon *was the largest marsupial ever to have lived. It had tusks for its front teeth, but its cheek teeth were like a kangaroo's.*

Thylacosmilus

- *Thylacosmilus* was a carnivorous marsupial. It belonged to a family of South American marsupials called the Borhyaenidae, all of whom had large skulls and teeth.

- **It lived and hunted** on the grassy plains of South America in the Pliocene Epoch (5–1.6 mya).

▶ *While* Thylacosmilus *had much in common with sabre-tooth cats, it had some differences too. Unlike true cats, it was a marsupial, its sabre-teeth never stopped growing and it could not retract its claws.*

- *Thylacosmilus* **was about the size** of a modern jaguar, growing up to 1.2 m long and weighing about 115 kg.

- **There are some** amazing similarities between *Thylacosmilus* and the sabre-tooth cats, such as *Smilodon*.

- **Like *Smilodon*,** *Thylacosmilus* had very long, upper canine teeth, which it used to stab its prey.

- **Also like *Smilodon*,** *Thylacosmilus* had very powerful shoulder and neck muscles, which meant it could press its huge canines down with great force.

- **This is remarkable** because the sabre-tooths were placental mammals that evolved in North America and *Thylacosmilus* was a marsupial that evolved in South America at a time when the two continents were not connected.

- **It is another example** of evolutionary convergence – when separate groups of animals develop similar characteristics.

- **Unlike the sabre-toothed cats,** however, *Thylacosmilus*' teeth continued to grow throughout its life.

- *Thylacosmilus* became extinct after the land bridge between North and South America was re-established. It could not compete with the more powerful carnivores that arrived from the north.

415

Elephant evolution

- **Elephants** and their ancestors belong to an order of animals called Proboscidea, meaning 'long-snouted'. Another word for elephants is proboscideans.

- **The ancestors** of elephants appeared around 40 mya. They were trunkless and looked a bit like large pigs.

- *Moeritherium* is the earliest known of these elephant ancestors. Its name comes from Lake Moeris in Egypt, where fossil-hunters first discovered its remains.

- **It was 3 m long** and weighed 200 kg, and probably spent much of its life wallowing in rivers or shallow lakes, like a hippopotamus.

- **The next step** in the development of elephants was taken by *Phiomia*, which lived about 36 mya.

- *Phiomia* had a well-formed trunk as well as two pairs of tusks – a pair on its upper jaw, projecting out and then down, and a pair on its lower jaw.

- *Phiomia* is the first-known of a group of elephants called mastodonts. Its shoulder height could be up to 2.4 m, and it lived in swampy areas.

- **One group** of elephants that descended from *Phiomia* were the deinotheres, which had one pair of enormous downward curving tusks in the lower jaw.

- **The other groups** that evolved from the mastodonts were the true elephants (which resemble living elephants) and the mammoths. These animals appeared in the Pliocene Epoch (5–1.6 mya).

...FASCINATING FACT...
Mammoths were giant elephants. The first
mammoth was possibly *Stegodon*, which had very
long tusks and lived in Asia and Africa.

▼ *The hippopotamus-like* Moeritherium. *The American palaeontologist Henry Fairfield Osborn (1857–1935) described it as 'a missing link' between elephants and other mammals.*

Platybelodon

- *Platybelodon* was an early – but not the first – member of a group of prehistoric elephants called mastodonts.

- **It lived about** 25 mya in the cold northern regions of Europe, Asia and North America.

- *Platybelodon's* lower jaw ended in two very wide, flat tusks – like a pair of spades.

- *Platybelodon* is known as 'shovel-tusker', because palaeontologists think it used its tusks as a shovel to scoop up plants.

- **It also** had flat cheek teeth, sharp front teeth, and a very wide trunk.

- **This mastodont** had a pair of tusks on its upper jaw, too. They slotted into an indentation near the top of its lower tusks when *Platybelodon* closed its mouth.

- *Platybelodon* **was 6 m long** and weighed between 4 and 5 tonnes.

- **The time period** in which *Platybelodon* lived was quite short compared to other animals, and other species of elephant in particular.

- **This is probably** because *Platybelodon* was a very specialized feeder and was vulnerable to any climate change that would affect the sort of plants it ate.

> ...FASCINATING FACT...
> The first elephants lived in Africa but – as discoveries of
> *Platybelodon* fossils have shown – they migrated to Europe,
> Asia and then North America.

▲ *Scientists used to think that* Platybelodon *fed on soft water plants. Recent research on its fossilized tusks suggests that it ate much tougher material, such as the branches of trees.*

Woolly mammoth

▶ In 1994, scientists discovered DNA, or genetic material, in the fossil remains of a woolly mammoth. They found that it was nearly identical to the DNA of living elephants.

. . . .

. . .FASCINATING FACT. . .

People often think the woolly mammoth had red hair, but in fact this colour was a chemical reaction that happened after the animal died.

- **Woolly mammoths** (scientific name *Mammuthus primigenius*) lived between 120,000 and 6000 years ago.

  - **They lived** on the steppes of Russia and Asia and the plains of North America during the ice ages of the Quaternary Period (1.6 mya to the present).

    - **To survive** these cold places, woolly mammoths were designed for warmth and insulation.

      - **Their woolly coats** were made up of two layers of hair – an outside layer of long, coarse hairs, and a second layer of densely packed bristles.

      - **They also had** very tough skins – up to 2.5 cm thick – beneath which was a deep layer of fat.

      - **Male woolly mammoths** could grow up to 3.5 m long and 2.9 m high at the shoulder, and weigh up to 2.75 tonnes.

      - **They had** long tusks that curved forward, up and then back. They used their tusks to defend themselves against attackers and – probably – to clear snow and ice to reach low-lying plants.

        - **Some cave paintings** by Cro-Magnon humans clearly depict woolly mammoths.

          - **Many excellently preserved** woolly mammoth remains have been discovered in the permanently frozen ground of Siberia.

Columbian mammoth

- **The Columbian mammoth** (scientific name *Mammuthus columbi*) was an even bigger species than the woolly mammoth.

- **Its coat** was not as thick as the woolly mammoth's, and it lived in warmer regions, including North America and Mexico.

- **The Columbian mammoth** grew up to 4.2 m high at the shoulder, and weighed over 10 tonnes – the equivalent of 130 adult humans!

- **It needed to eat** more than 350 kg of plant food every day to keep itself going, and to drink about 160 litres of water.

- **It used** its powerful trunk for feeding, as well as for moving and breaking things.

- **This trunk** was like an extra arm. It had two finger-like projections at the end, which could grab hold of objects.

- **Its tusks** could grow up to 5 m long. It used these for fighting rival mammoths and defending themselves against predators.

- **Some scientists** think that the Columbian mammoth was actually the same species as the imperial mammoth (scientific name *Mammuthus imperator*). The imperial mammoth was one of the largest mammoths ever to have lived, estimated by some to have stood 4.8 m high at the shoulder.

- **Both the Columbian** and the imperial mammoths lacked thick coats and lived in relatively warm climates.

- **The imperial mammoth's** tusks, however, were much more twisted than those of the Columbian mammoth.

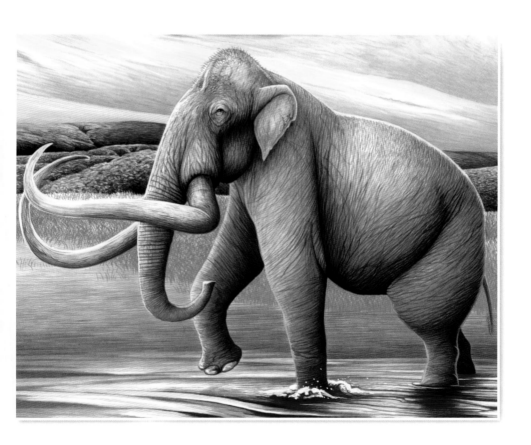

▲ *Early humans in North America hunted the Columbian mammoth, a fact known from finds of tools and building materials made out of the mammoth's bone.*

Rhinoceroses

- **Rhinoceroses** were a very important group of mammals in the Tertiary Period (65–1.6 mya).

- *Hyracodon* was an early rhino that lived in North America about 30 mya.

- *Hyracodon* **had long**, slender legs and would have been a fast runner. It grew to about 1.5 m long.

- **Amynodonts** were a group of prehistoric rhinos that experts believed evolved from *Hyracodon*.

- *Metamynodon* was an amynodont rhino. It was as large as a hippopotamus and may have had a similar lifestyle to one, wading in rivers and lakes.

- **True rhinoceroses**, the ancestors of modern rhinos, were another group that descended from early rhinos such as *Hyracodon*.

- **One of the first** true rhinos was *Trigonias*, which had four toes on its front feet but three on its hind feet. It lived in the Oligocene Epoch (37–24 mya).

- *Caenopus*, another true rhino, had three toes on all four feet. This was the pattern for all later rhinos.

- *Indricotherium* was another prehistoric rhino, and the most amazing of all. It was the largest rhino ever, growing up to 5.5 m tall.

- **Rhinos became extinct** in North America between 5 and 1.6 mya, and later in Europe. But they survived in Asia and Africa and continue to do so today, although they too are threatened by extinction.

▶ *Hunted for their horns, which some people value as medicine, all the world's rhinoceroses are endangered.*

Woolly rhinoceros

- **The woolly rhinoceros** (scientific name *Coelodonta*) lived between 1.8 million and 10,000 years ago.

- **It had thick**, long fur, short legs and small ears – all of which helped it survive the ice-age times it lived through.

- **Woolly rhinoceroses** lived on the plains of northern Europe, Russia and northern China.

- **They were herbivores**, feeding on low-growing plants such as mosses, herbs and dwarf shrubs.

- **Woolly rhinoceroses** had a pair of horns on their snout, which were made of matted hair.

- **The front horn** could grow up to 1 m long on adult males.

- **Woolly rhinoceroses** could grow up to 3.5 m long, and weighed up to 4 tonnes.

- **Their closest** living relative is the Sumatran rhino.

- **Early human cave paintings** of woolly rhinoceroses suggest that they had a band of darker hair around the middle of their bodies.

- **When woolly rhinoceros** horns were discovered in Russia in the 19th century, many people thought they were the claws of a giant bird.

▼ *Palaeontologists have a good idea of what woolly rhinoceroses looked like – both from prehistoric cave paintings and discoveries of the animals' remains, preserved in frozen soil.*

Propalaeotherium

- ***Propalaeotherium*** was one of the earliest ancestors of the horse.

- **Its name means** 'ancestor to the ancient beast'. *Palaeotherium* ('ancient beast') was another early horse, but *Propalaeotherium* was even earlier.

- *Propalaeotherium* lived in thick forests between 49 and 43 mya in the Early Tertiary Period.

- **There were two species** of this little animal. One stood 30–35 cm tall at its shoulders, the other stood 55–60 cm tall.

- *Propalaeotherium*, like other horses, was a perissodactyl, or odd-toed hoofed mammal. Other perissodactyls include tapirs and rhinoceroses.

- *Propalaeotherium* had four small hooves on its front feet, and three hooves on its back feet. It walked on the pads of its feet, like a dog or a cat.

- **It would have looked** a little like a duiker, a modern, small antelope that lives in Africa.

- **The fossil remains** of more than 70 *Propalaeotherium* individuals have been found at Messel, Germany, which was the site of a lake 50 mya.

- **Other *Palaeotherium* fossils** have been unearthed at Geiseltal, which is also in Germany.

...FASCINATING FACT...
Palaeontologists discovered leaves and fruit in the stomachs of the Messel fossils, suggesting that *Propalaeotherium* foraged on the ground for its food.

◄ *Tiny* Propalaeotherium *was a forest-dweller, but as forests gave way to grasslands its descendants became much bigger, developing longer legs and necks.*

429

The first horses

▼ Hyracotherium *is the earliest known horse.
Over time, horses became the best-adapted of
all hoofed animals for life on the open plains.*

- **Horses** have one of the best fossil records of any animal, so palaeontologists have been able to trace their evolution from the earliest horselike mammals to the modern horse.

- *Hyracotherium* is the first-known horse. It lived in forests in North America and Europe in the Late Palaeocene and Early Eocene Epochs (60–50 mya).

- **Another name** for *Hyracotherium* is *Eohippus,* which means 'dawn horse'.

- *Hyracotherium* was the size of a fox. It had a short neck, a long tail and slender limbs. It also had three toes on its hind feet and four toes on its front feet.

- *Mesohippus* was one of the next horses to evolve after *Hyracotherium,* between 40 and 25 mya. Its name means 'middle horse'.

- *Mesohippus* had longer legs than *Hyracotherium* and would have been a faster runner.

- **It would also** have been better at chewing food, because its teeth had a larger surface area.

- **An improved** chewing ability was important for horses and other plant-eaters as forests gave way to grasslands, and more abundant but tougher plants.

- *Mesohippus* had also evolved three toes on its front feet to match the three on its hind feet.

- **As horses** evolved, they migrated from North America and Europe to Asia, Africa and South America.

The first whales

- **The very first whales** looked nothing like the enormous creatures that swim in our oceans today.

- *Ambulocetus*, one of the first members of the whale family, looked more like a giant otter. It lived about 50 mya.

- *Ambulocetus* means 'walking whale', and it spent more time on land than in water.

- **It would**, however, have been a good swimmer. Fossil remains show that *Ambulocetus* had webbed feet and hands.

- **An even earlier** whale ancestor than *Ambulocetus* was *Pakicetus*, which lived about 52 mya.

- *Pakicetus* is named after the country Pakistan, where a fossil of its skull was found in 1979.

▼ Pakicetus *could run fast and swim well. It probably lived alongside rivers and streams and hunted animals both in and out of the water.*

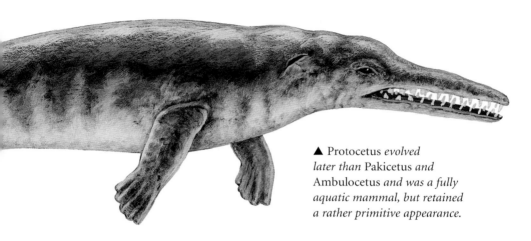

▲ Protocetus *evolved later than* Pakicetus *and* Ambulocetus *and was a fully aquatic mammal, but retained a rather primitive appearance.*

- *Pakicetus* was around 1.8 m long. *Ambulocetus,* at 3 m, was bigger.

- **Palaeontologists** think that whales evolved from carnivorous hoofed mammals called mesonychids.

- **Around 40 mya**, the first true whales, which swam only, evolved from their half-walking, half-swimming ancestors.

...FASCINATING FACT...
Only the back of *Pakicetus*' skull and part of its lower jaw have been found. From this, however, palaeontologists can tell it was not able to dive very deeply.

Later whales

- *Basilosaurus* which first appeared about 40 mya, closely resembled whales we are familiar with today, more so than its ancestors *Pakicetus* and *Ambulocetus*.

- **It was also enormous!** It measured between 20 and 25 m long – the same as three elephants standing in a row.

- **It had** a variety of teeth in its mouth – sharp teeth at the front for stabbing, and saw-edged teeth at the back for chewing.

- *Basilosaurus* ate large fish, squid, and other marine mammals.

...FASCINATING FACT...
Cetotherium was a prehistoric baleen whale that first appeared 15 mya. Instead of teeth, these whales had hard plates in their mouths called baleen that filtered plankton and small fish.

▼ *The prehistoric whale* Basilosaurus, *which means 'king of the lizards', was so named because the first person to examine its remains thought it was a gigantic plesiosaur – a prehistoric marine reptile.*

- **There were some** big differences between *Basilosaurus* and modern whales. For a start, it had a slimmer body.

- **It also lacked** a blowhole, a nostril on the top of modern whales' heads that they breathe out of when they come to the surface. Instead, *Basilosaurus* had nostrils on its snout.

- ***Prosqualodon*** did have a blowhole and was a more advanced whale than *Basilosaurus*. It lived between 30 and 20 mya.

- **It may have been** the ancestor of toothed whales, a group that includes sperm whales, killer whales, beaked whales and dolphins.

- ***Prosqualodon*** looked similar to a dolphin. It had a long, streamlined body and a long, narrow snout, which was full of pointed teeth.

437

Dolphins

- **All modern dolphins**, whales and porpoises come from common ancestors, which were called Protocetidae and which lived around 45 mya.

- **Recognisable dolphins** first appeared in the Early Miocene Epoch (23.7–16.4 mya).

- **Alongside the dolphins** that would evolve into the types living today were other dolphin families that later became extinct.

- **One of the most common** Miocene dolphins was *Eurhinodelphis*, which means 'true-nosed dolphin'.

- *Eurhinodelphis'* **ear** structure suggests it had evolved an echo hearing system, like modern dolphins.

- *Eurhinodelphis* grew up to 3.7 m long. It had a long snout, which it may have used to strike at its prey, and strong flippers.

- **As dolphins evolved**, their bodies became more streamlined and the vertebrae in their necks became fused together.

- **Dolphins** also developed a different blood-supply route to the brain than land mammals. This supply passed through an artery in the fused vertebrae and not outside the neck.

- **This artery** gives dolphins a constant blood supply when they dive to great depths.

> **...FASCINATING FACT...**
> Like whales and porpoises, dolphins also evolved
> large brains, which scientists believe they use to
> communicate with each other in complex ways.

▼ *Bottlenose dolphins. Dolphins are relatives of whales and, like them, have evolved from meat-eating land mammals.*

Megaloceros

▲ *Scientists used to believe that, because* Megaloceros' *antlers were so big, they could only have been used for display purposes – to scare off rivals. In the 1980s however, research proved that these antlers were used for fighting.*

- *Megaloceros* is one of the largest species of deer ever to have lived. Adult males were 2.2 m long, 2 m tall at the shoulders and weighed 700 kg.

- **This deer** lived between 400,000 and 9000 years ago.

- *Megaloceros* is known as the Irish elk because a large number of fossils of the species have been discovered in Ireland, particularly in peat bogs.

- **But *Megaloceros*** lived all over Europe, the Middle East, China and North America, too.

- *Megaloceros* had a much broader, flatter snout than modern deer, which suggests it was a less fussy eater and just hoovered up plant food in enormous quantities.

- **Like modern deer,** *Megaloceros* males shed their antlers and grew another pair every year. For antlers as big as *Megaloceros'*, this required a huge intake of nutrients and minerals.

- **About 10,000 years ago**, falling temperatures led the dwarf willow bush – a major source of the nutrients *Megaloceros* needed to grow its antlers – to decline.

- **This food shortage** is one theory as to why *Megaloceros* became extinct.

- **Another theory** is that early humans, who greatly prized *Megaloceros'* antlers, hunted it to extinction.

. . . FASCINATING FACT . . .
Megaloceros was a fast runner – it could move at around 80 km/h. It used this turn of speed to escape from predators such as wolves.

Hominid fossils

- **The fossil record** of hominids (human ancestors) is very patchy.

- **Most early hominid fossils** have been discovered in the Great Rift Valley region of East Africa, which stretches through Ethiopia, Kenya and Tanzania.

- **Probably the most important** site for evidence of human ancestors is Olduvai Gorge in northern Tanzania.

- **Archaeologists** have discovered fossils from more than 50 hominids at the Gorge, including *Australopithecus boisei*, *Homo habilis*, *Homo erectus* and a 17,000-year-old *Homo sapiens*.

- **Complete hominid skeletons** are very rare. Archaeologists usually have to rely on skulls, knee joints or even single teeth.

- **Another type of fossil** remain is a trace fossil, such as tracks and footprints.

- **The most famous hominid** trace fossil is the footprints that were left by two *Australopithecus afarensis* individuals. The prints were made in wet, sandy ground and were then covered in ash from an erupting volcano.

- **This fossil footprints were discovered** in 1978 by the archaeologist Mary Leakey (1913–1996). They are known as the Laeotoli footprints, after the site in Tanzania where she found them.

- **Caves** are second only to rivers and lakes as good sites for fossils, since bodies are less likely to be disturbed there. Most hominid fossils in southern Africa are from caves.

- **Scientists** can tell from hominids' teeth what they ate. Unlike earlier hominids, *Homo erectus* was a meat eater because its teeth are scratched and damaged.

◀ *The Laeotoli footprints left by two* Australopithecus afarensis *individuals were proof that early hominids walked on two legs.*

Early primates

- **The primates** are a group of mammals that include lemurs, monkeys, apes and humans.

- **Primates** have a much greater range of movement in their arms, legs, fingers and toes than other mammals.

- **They also have** a more acute sense of touch because their fingers and toes end in flat nails, not curved claws – so the skin on the other side evolved into a sensitive pad.

- **The ancestors** of primates were small insectivorous (insect-eating) mammals that looked like shrews.

- **The first known primate** was *Plesiadapis,* which lived about 60 mya in Europe and North America. It was a squirrel-like tree climber.

- **More advanced primates** developed about 10 million years later. They looked a bit like modern lemurs.

- *Notharctus* was one of these lemur-like primates. It ate leaves and fruit, was about 40 cm long, and had a grasping thumb that would have gripped well to branches.

- **Other more advanced** – but still early – primates includes *Smilodectes* and *Tetonius.* They had larger brains and eyes, longer tails and smaller snouts than *Plesiadapis.*

- **These animals** were the ancestors of tarsiers, lemurs and lorises, but not the higher primates – the monkeys, apes and humans. Palaeontologists believe that role belongs to the omomyid primates.

- **One early monkey** was *Mesopithecus,* which lived 8 mya in Greece and Turkey. It was similar to modern monkeys in many ways, but had a longer tail.

▲ *The early primate* Plesiadapis *had a long tail and claws on its fingers and toes – unlike later monkeys and apes, which had nails.*

Apes

▶ *The early ape* Dryopithecus *stood about 1 m tall. It had the largest brain for its size of any mammal and flourished in open grassland regions in Africa, Asia and Europe.*

- **Apes** are primates that have more complex brains than monkeys and no tails. Hominids (early humans) evolved from apes.

- ***Aegyptopithecus*** was one of the ancestors of apes. It lived in Egypt in the Oligocene Epoch (37–24 mya). It was small and had a short tail.

- *Proconsul,* which lived between 23 and 14 mya, was an early ape. Its body size varied from that of a small monkey to that of a female gorilla, and had a larger brain than *Aegyptopithecus.*

- *Proconsul* was a fruit eater. Palaeontologists think that it walked on four limbs with part of its weight supported by the knuckles of its hands, like modern chimpanzees and gorillas.

- **Two lines of apes** developed after *Proconsul.* From one line came gibbons and orang-utans, from the other chimpanzees, gorillas and humans.

- *Dryopithecus* was a chimp-like ape that evolved after *Proconsul* and lived in the Miocene Epoch (24–5 mya). It may have stood on two legs but climbed using all four.

- *Ramapithecus* was an ape that lived in the Middle and Late Miocene Epoch. It is now thought to be part of the chain of evolution of Asian apes and is possibly an ancestor of the orang-utan.

- **Australopithecines** were a further step in the evolution from apes to humans. Australopithecines (meaning 'southern apes') walked on two legs.

- **The biggest-ever ape** was *Gigantopithecus,* which lived in China until around 1 mya. It may have been up to 2.5 m tall and weighed 300 kg.

... FASCINATING FACT ...
Proconsul was named in 1927 after Consul, a performing chimpanzee that appeared on stage smoking a pipe and riding a bicycle.

Walking upright

- **Hominidae** is the 'human family' of ourselves and our ancestors and prehistoric relatives. Hominids (humans) differed from apes by walking on two legs, rather than four.

- **Fossils** of hominids' backbones, neck, foot and leg bones demonstrate their evolution from apes that walked on all fours.

- **Hominids'** spines developed an S-shaped curve so that the hips supported the weight of the upper body. Apes' spines have just one curve.

- **The heads of the hominids** evolved to sit on the top of the spine, while apes' heads sit at the front of the spine.

- **Hominids'** feet became long and flat to support the rest of the body when they walked. Apes' feet have curved toes to grasp onto branches for climbing.

- **The leg bones of hominids** became longer and straighter than those of apes, so they could walk greater distances more effortlessly.

- **Walking on two legs** helped hominids cover greater distances in the open grasslands of Africa where they lived.

- **It also allowed them** to see above tall grasses, an advantage when it came to looking for food or keeping a lookout for danger.

- **Upright walking** also freed their arms to do other things, such as carrying babies or food.

> ...FASCINATING FACT...
> The first fossilized footprints of an upright walker
> were discovered in 1978. They belong to
> *Australopithecus afarensis*, which lived 3.8 mya.

448

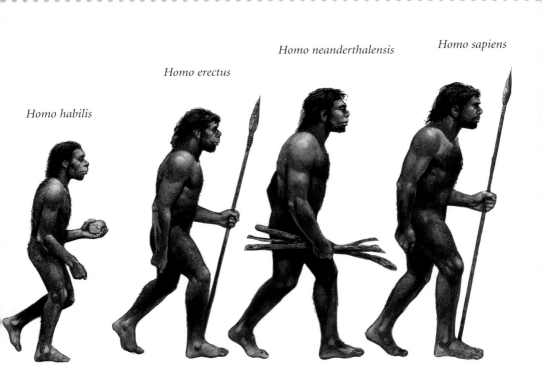

Homo habilis

Homo erectus

Homo neanderthalensis

Homo sapiens

▲ *Experts agree that the adoption of upright walking was one of the most important developments in the history of hominids. It freed the arms and hands to carry objects, making the body look bigger to potential predators and keeping it cool in the hot Sun.*

Human offspring

- **Human parents** look after their children for a longer period than any other animal.

- **A close bond** between parents and children is also a feature of modern primates – and would have been so for prehistoric primates, too.

- **This is because humans** and primates have small numbers of infants compared to many other animals, and females are pregnant for longer.

- **There is also** a longer period of upbringing for humans and primates than for other animals – during which time offspring learn survival and social skills.

- **As with apes**, the pelvises of early hominids were quite wide, which meant that their offspring were quite large when they were born.

- **Like modern humans**, later hominids – from *Homo ergaster* on – had smaller pelvises, which meant that their babies were smaller and less developed when born.

- **Smaller** and less developed babies require more nurture and protection – as a result, childcare became an even bigger concern for hominids.

- **This change** led to other ones. Hominid groups increased in size, so that the responsibility for childcare could be spread around.

- **There was also** more cooperation between males and females and they began to pair-up in partnerships.

- **Such partnerships** were mutually beneficial – the female could look after the offspring while the male provided food. In turn, the male could be certain that the offspring was his own.

▲ *A female orang-utan with its infant. Primates have closer relationships with their young than other animals, but this is particularly true for humans. Unlike monkeys and apes, human babies cannot move around independently soon after birth and are very dependant on their mothers.*

Early hominids

▲ Ardipithecus ramidus. *Scientists gave it its name from the Afar language of Ethiopia – 'ardi' means 'ground' while 'ramid' means 'root' – words that express its position at the base of human history.*

- **One of the earliest-known** hominids (early humans) is *Ardipithecus ramidus,* which lived about 4.5 mya.

- **It would have looked** similar to a chimpanzee in many ways, except for one major difference, *Ardipithecus ramidus* walked on two legs.

- **It lived** in woods and forests, sleeping in trees at night, but foraging on the ground for roots during the day.

- **A full-grown** *Ardipithecus ramidus* male was about 1.3 m tall and weighed about 27 kg.

- **Archaeologists** discovered the teeth, skull and arm bone fossils of *Ardipithecus ramidus* in Ethiopia in 1994.

- **In 2001**, archaeologists in Ethiopia found the remains of an even older hominid, *Ardipithecus ramidus kadabba*, which lived between 5.6 and 5.8 mya.

- **The fossils** of *Ardipithecus ramidus kadabba* are similar to those of *Ardipithecus ramidus,* so it is possible both are very closely related.

- **Some scientists argue,** however, that *Ardipithecus ramidus kadabba* is closer to an ape than a hominid.

- *Australopithecus anamensis* is a later hominid than *Ardipithecus ramidus.* Its fossils date to between 4.2 and 3.9 million years old.

- **A fossil** of one of *Australopithecus anamensis'* knee-joints shows that it shifted its weight from one leg to the other when it moved – a sure sign that it walked on two legs.

Sahelanthropus tchadensis

- **In 2002**, a team of French archaeologists announced the discovery of a new species called *Sahelanthropus tchadensis,* which may be a missing link between apes and early hominids.

- **The archaeologists** discovered a near-complete fossil skull of *Sahelanthropus tchadensis*, which has been dated to between 7 and 6 million years old.

- **They also** found the fossils of two pieces of jawbone and three teeth.

- **The French team** found the skull not in East Africa, like all the other early hominids, but in Chad, in central Africa.

- **Finding the skull** in Chad indicates that early hominids ranged well beyond East Africa, where scientists previously believed all early hominids lived.

- **The archaeologists** who discovered the skull nicknamed it Toumaï, meaning 'hope of life' in Goran, an African language.

- **Despite its great age,** *Sahelanthropus tchadensis'* skull suggests that it had a surprisingly human face, which protruded less than apes.

- *Sahelanthropus tchadensis* also had heavy ridges for its eyebrows. Some archaeologists believe that, because of this, it was closer to an ape than a hominid, since female apes have similar heavy ridges.

- **Like later hominids**, *Sahelanthropus tchadensis* had small canine teeth and did not grind its teeth in the same way as apes.

- *Sahelanthropus tchadensis* lived alongside a diverse range of animals. Other fossil finds in the same region include more than 700 types of fish, crocodiles and rodents.

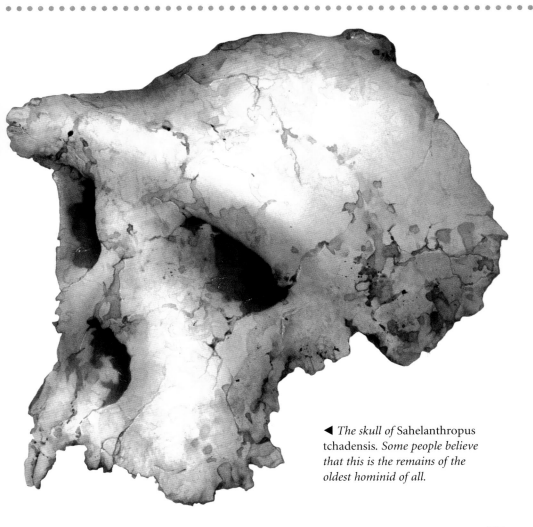

◄ *The skull of* Sahelanthropus tchadensis. *Some people believe that this is the remains of the oldest hominid of all.*

Australopithecus afarensis

- *Australopithecus afarensis* was an early hominid that lived 3.5 mya.

- **Its brain** was the size of a modern chimpanzee's, and it had the short legs and long arms of modern apes.

- *Australopithecus afarensis* was small, only measuring between 90 and 120 cm.

- **Like other** australopithecines, it walked on two legs. This was the most efficient way for it to move over grassland in search of food.

- **It had a wider pelvis** and shorter legs than modern humans. This may have made it a more efficient walker than modern humans.

- *Australopithecus afarensis* ate seeds, fruits, nuts and occasionally meat.

- **These hominids** had a brief childhood, reaching adulthood at the age of 11 years old. They lived for a maximum of 50 years.

- **Fossil footprints** of *Australopithecus afarensis* show that their feet were similar to ours, although their big toes may have been more apelike.

- **The first fossils** of *Australopithecus afarensis* to be discovered belonged to a female. They were found by American anthropologists Donald Johanson and Tom Gray in 1974, at Hadar in Ethiopia.

> **. . . FASCINATING FACT . . .**
> Johanson and Gray named the female 'Lucy' after the Beatles' song 'Lucy in the Sky with Diamonds', which they listened to on the day of their discovery.

▲ Australopithecus afarensis *spent its days on the ground, foraging for food, but at night may have slept in trees.*

Australopithecus africanus

- *Australopithecus africanus*, which means 'the southern ape of Africa', was an early hominid that emerged between 2.8 and 2.3 mya.

- *Australopithecus africanus* was the first australopithecine to be discovered.

- **The Australian-born** scientist Raymond Dart made the discovery of this important fossil in South Africa in 1924.

- **The fossil** Dart identified was found in a quarry near the village of Taung, on the edge of the Kalahari Desert.

- **It was the fossil** of a skull, belonging to a child around 2 or 3 years old. The fossil became known as the Taung child.

- **Many people** didn't believe in Dart's discovery – they thought the find was an ape, not a hominid. But one person did believe it – the archaeologist Robert Broom.

- **In 1947** Broom himself found a skull of an adult *Australopithecus africanus*.

- **The adult skull** became known as 'Mrs Ples' because Broom first thought it belonged to a different species, *Plesianthropus transvaalensis*.

- **By the 1950s** other parts of *Australopithecus africanus*' skeleton had been unearthed, including a pelvis and a femur.

- **They proved** beyond doubt that *Australopithecus africanus* was an upright-walking hominid.

▶ *The Taung child may have looked like this. Marks on the skull, and remains of a large eggshell nearby, suggest a large bird killed the child.*

Paranthropus
boisei

● *Paranthropus boisei* was a hominid that lived between one and two mya.

● **It had much bigger** jaws and teeth than modern humans but much smaller bodies. Males grew to about 137 cm tall.

● **Male skulls** were more than twice as big as female skulls because they had large crests of bone on the top, to which powerful chewing muscles were fixed. Females did not have these muscles.

● *Paranthropus boisei* was one of several different hominid groups that developed in East Africa between 2.8 and 2.5 mya in response to climate change.

● **Different hominids** developed to exploit different resources. *Paranthropus boisei* evolved as a specialist eater of very hard, abundant, but low-quality plant foods like roots and tubers.

● **In contrast**, more advanced hominids such as *Homo habilis* and *Homo rudolfensis* evolved to vary their diets and to seek out high-quality foods.

● **Because it was such a successful** plant eater, *Paranthropus boisei* forced other hominids to become omnivores, eating whatever they could find.

● **The first *Paranthropus boisei*** was discovered in Tanzania in 1959 by the archaeologists Louis and Mary Leakey.

● **The Leakeys** named their find after the businessman Charles Boise who had supported their work. Paranthropus means 'near man'.

● **Unlike modern humans**, there were no whites to *Paranthropus boisei's* eyes, so one individual could not tell where another was looking, or what it was feeling.

◄ *These* Paranthropus boisei *hominids were another species of australopithecine ('southern ape'). The males had particularly large jaws and robust skulls.*

461

Homo habilis

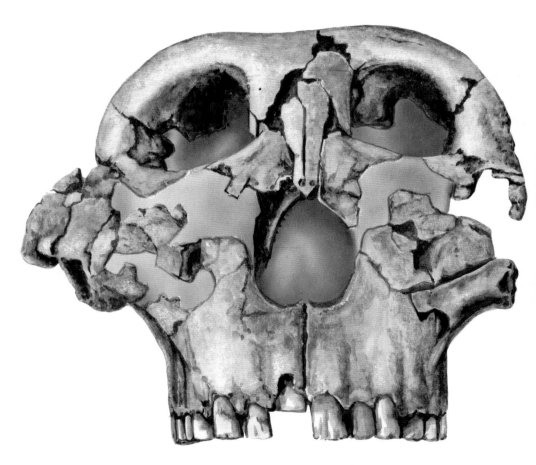

▲ *The first* Homo habilis *skull found by Louis and Mary Leakey in Tanzania.* Homo habilis *had a bigger brain than any previous hominid.*

- *Homo habilis* is one of the earliest-known members of the genus *Homo*, to which we also belong.

- *Homo habilis* lived between 2.4 and 1.6 mya.

- **The archaeologists** Louis and Mary Leakey first discovered its remains at Olduvai Gorge in Tanzania, in 1961.

- **Fossils** of *Homo habilis*' skulls have since been found around Lake Turkana in Kenya, one of the richest sites for hominid fossils in the world.

- **The skulls** show that *Homo habilis* had a flat face with prominent cheekbones, similar to australopithecines, which it would have lived alongside.

- *Homo habilis* was much more ape-like than its successor, *Homo ergaster*. It had fur and lacked any form of language.

- **But it did have** a bigger brain than any australopithecine. It also had more flexible hands and straighter, more sensitive fingers.

- *Homo habilis* means 'handy man' – it could use its hands to gather fruit and crack nuts. It also created the first stone tools.

- **A fully grown** *Homo habilis* male was around 1.5 m tall and weighed about 50 kg.

...FASCINATING FACT...
Homo habilis used stone tools to crack open animal bones so it could eat the nutritious marrow inside.

Homo ergaster

- *Homo ergaster* was the first 'human-looking' early human. It first appeared about 1.9 mya.

- **Adult males** grew to approximately 180 cm tall, with long, slender limbs and a straight spine.

- *Homo ergaster* was the first smooth-skinned hominid, unlike its hairy ancestors. Like us it cooled down by sweating, not panting, which is how earlier hominids cooled themselves.

- **It was also** the first hominid to have a protruding nose – previous hominids merely had nostrils on the surface of their face.

- *Homo ergaster* was generally a scavenger, although it would hunt and kill older or weaker animals.

- **Scientists** know that it ate a lot of meat because one of the skeletons that have been found shows evidence of a bone disease caused by eating too many animal livers.

- **Fossil remains** of *Homo ergaster* were first discovered in 1975. But the most complete skeleton was found in 1984.

- **The skeleton** belonged to a teenage boy named Nariokotome Boy after the site in Lake Turkana, Kenya, where it was found.

- **The structure** of Nariokotome Boy's bones suggest that he was much stronger than modern humans.

- *Homo ergaster* was the first hominid to travel beyond Africa. One place where its remains have been found is Dmanisi, in the Republic of Georgia, near Russia.

► Homo ergaster *was different from any previous hominid. It was taller, with a face that was more lightly built and had smaller cheek teeth.*

Homo erectus

- *Homo erectus* may be a descendant of *Homo ergaster*.

- **It was** virtually identical to its immediate ancestor, except that it had thicker bones in its skull and a more protruding eyebrow ridge.

- *Homo erectus* and *Homo ergaster* lived alongside each other for 2 million years.

- **But while *Homo ergaster*** became extinct about 600,000 years ago, *Homo erectus* survived until less than 50,000 years ago.

- *Homo erectus* spread beyond Africa and settled in Europe and Asia.

- **In the late 19th century,** Eugène Dubois discovered *Homo erectus* fossils on the Indonesian island of Java. He was a famous Dutch palaeoanthropologist (someone who studies hominid fossils).

- **In the 1930s,** archaeologists discovered more than 40 *Homo erectus* skeletons in China.

- **The archaeologists** also found evidence that *Homo erectus* used fire and practised cannibalism!

- **For a long time**, people called the human to which the Chinese fossils belonged 'Peking Man'. It was much later that palaeoanthropologists realized it was, in fact, *Homo erectus*.

...FASCINATING FACT...
The 'Peking Man' fossils disappeared at the beginning of the World War II and have never been found. They were confiscated by Japanese troops just when they were about to be shipped to the USA.

▲ *Stone hearths in caves that were used by* Homo erectus *prove that it had mastered fire. Fire provided warmth, light, protection and the means to cook food.*

Homo
heidelbergensis

▲ Homo heidelbergensis *was a superb hunter who used stones, wooden spears and even stone blades to capture food.*

- *Homo heidelbergensis* lived between 600,000 and 250,000 years ago in Africa and Europe.

- **It was the first** hominid to settle in the cold territories of northern Europe.

- **Homo heidelbergensis** had a body much like ours, but its head was rather different, with a heavier jaw, a minimal chin, a flat nose and thick eyebrow ridges.

- **The teeth** of *Homo heidelbergensis* were 50 percent longer than ours.

- **They also** had a much thicker covering of enamel, which suggests that this species ate the tough parts of animals' flesh and maybe used its teeth for gripping objects.

- **Towards the end** of its existence, *Homo heidelbergensis* would have lived alongside Neanderthals in the same territories.

- *Homo heidelbergensis* is named after the city of Heidelberg in Germany. It was near there that one of the hominid's jawbones was found in 1907.

- **The greatest find** of *Homo heidelbergensis'* fossils was made in a cave system in the Atapuerca hills of northern Spain, in 1976. Archaeologists discovered the remains of 32 individuals.

- **In the mid 1990s**, archaeologists unearthed *Homo heidelbergensis* bones, tools and animal carcasses in Boxgrove, England. The carcasses had been expertly stripped of all their meat.

> . . . FASCINATING FACT . . .
> Unlike the Neanderthals that came later, there is no
> evidence that *Homo heidelbergensis* buried its dead.

Homo neanderthalensis

- *Homo neanderthalensis* – or Neanderthals – lived between 230,000 and 28,000 years ago across Europe, Russia and parts of the Middle East.

- *Homo neanderthalensis* **means** 'man from the Neander Valley', which is the site in Germany where the first of its fossil remains were found in 1865.

- **Neanderthals** are our extinct cousins rather than our direct ancestors – they are from a different branch of the human family.

- **They were** about 30 percent heavier than modern humans. Their bodies were more sturdy and they had shorter legs.

- **Neanderthals'** shorter, stockier bodies were better suited than modern humans to life in Europe and Russia during the ice ages of the Pleistocene Epoch (1.6 million to 10,000 years ago).

- **Their faces** were also different, with sloping foreheads and heavy brow ridges.

- **They buried** their dead, cooked meat and made various tools and weapons.

- **Neanderthals** made the first ever spears tipped with stone blades.

- **For about 10,000 years** Neanderthals lived alongside modern humans in Europe, before becoming extinct.

. . . FASCINATING FACT . . .
Many people think that Neanderthals were slow and stupid, but in fact their brains were at least as big as modern human's.

471

Homo floresiensis

- **In 2004**, Australian palaeoanthropologists discovered an entirely new species of human, *Homo floresiensis,* which lived on the Indonesian island of Flores between 95,000 and 13,000 years ago.

- **In total**, palaeoanthropologists have unearthed the remains of seven individuals.

- **The most complete**, although still partial, skeleton, is that of a female. Study of one of its leg bones shows that it was an upright walker.

- **The discovery** changes scientists' understanding of human evolution – beforehand, it was assumed that *Homo sapiens* had been the sole remaining human species since the disappearance of Neanderthal humans about 30,000 years ago.

- **Palaeoanthropologists** nicknamed *Homo floresiensis* 'hobbit man' because of its tiny size. It was about one metre tall, and had a brain the size of a chimpanzee's.

- **Its small brain size** does not seem to have reflected its intelligence however – *Homo floresiensis* was a skilled toolmaker, producing finely crafted stone tools.

- **Flores**, off the coast of mainland Asia, has been an island for over a million years. Being small represents an adaptation to living on an isolated island, where resources were limited.

- ***Homo floresiensis'*** small size challenges the accepted belief that humans modify their surroundings to suit themselves. It is believed that, on the contrary, this human species evolved into a smaller creature to cope with its island habitat.

- **Local inhabitants** of Flores have long told stories of little hairy people called *ebu gogo*, meaning 'grandmother who eats anything', which used to live on the island.

- ***Homo floresiensis*** was a hunter. One of the animals it preyed on was the pygmy elephant. Both *Homo floresiensis,* and the pygmy elephants seem to have become extinct after a volcanic eruption about 12,000 years ago.

▲ *Two* Homo floresiensis *hunters prepare to attack a pygmy elephant. The discovery of this new species of human challenges our ideas of human evolution.*

473

Homo sapiens

- *Homo sapiens* – meaning 'wise man' – first appeared in Africa around 150,000 years ago. This is the species to which human beings belong.

- **The first** *Homo sapiens* outside Africa appeared in Israel, 90,000 years ago.

- **By 40,000 years ago**, *Homo sapiens* had spread to many parts of the world, including Europe and Borneo.

- **We call the humans** that settled in Europe Cro-Magnons. They dressed in furs and hunted with spears and nets.

- **Cro-Magnons** had a basic language and culture, which included painting images on cave walls.

- **They were** very similar to modern humans, but with marginally bigger jaws and noses and more rounded braincases (the part of the skull that encloses the brain).

- *Homo sapiens* probably arrived in North America about 30,000 years ago.

- **They would have** crossed the Bering land bridge – formed by shrunken sea levels during the then ice age – from present-day Siberia to present-day Alaska.

- **The earliest known** human culture in North America is that of the Clovis people, which is thought to be around 11,500 years old.

. . . **FASCINATING FACT** . . .
Humans living today have evolved only slightly from the earliest *Homo sapiens*. Our full scientific name is *Homo sapiens sapiens*, which means 'the wise wise man'.

▲ *Cave painting, cooking and complicated tool-making are all features of early* Homo sapiens. Homo sapiens *also look different from other human species, having a higher forehead and a more prominent chin.*

475

Brains and intelligence

- **Primates,** from which hominids descended, had bigger brains in relation to their body size than other mammals.

- **Primates developed** larger brains – and more intelligence – because living in and moving between trees required a high degree of balance, coordination and the skilful use of hands and feet.

- **Once hominids' brains** started getting bigger, so their skulls began to change. Bigger brains led to the development of foreheads.

- *Homo habilis'* **brain** was 50 percent bigger than its australopithecine predecessors. It had a brain capacity of 750 ml.

- **The structure** of its brain was different to that of earlier hominids. It had much bigger frontal lobes – the parts of the brain associated with planning and problem-solving.

- *Homo habilis* put its greater intelligence to use in the quest to find meat, which it scavenged from other animals' kills to supplement its diet.

- **Eating more meat** allowed hominids' brains to get even bigger. Breaking down plant food uses up a huge amount of energy, so the fewer plants hominids ate, the more energy was available for their brains.

- *Homo ergaster* had an even bigger brain, with a capacity of around 1000 ml. It could use this intelligence to read tracks left by animals – a major development in hunting.

- **The brain** of *Homo erectus* became larger during its existence. About 1 mya its brain capacity was 1000 ml; 500,000 years later it was 1300 ml.

- **Our brain capacity** is 1750 ml.

*Australopithecus
afarensis*

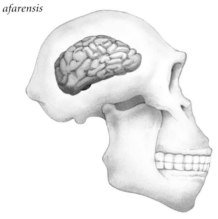

◀ *Brain size is linked to
intelligence, but size isn't
everything! What makes
humans and our ancestors
intelligent is our brain's
complex structure.*

Homo habilis

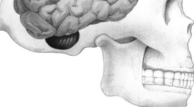

Homo sapien

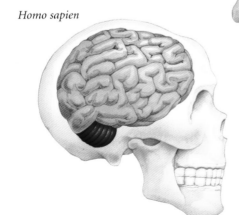

Language

- **Language** may go back as far as *Homo erectus* or even *Homo ergaster* – although this would have been a very, very simple form of communication.

- **Language developed** as a way of maintaining relationships within groups.

- **Language** is different from cries of alarm or mating calls. It involves a system for representing ideas and feelings.

- **Speech** requires a long pharynx – a tube in the neck that runs up from the vocal cords (contained in the larynx) to the mouth.

- **In other primates** the pharynx is too short to produce complex modifications of sound.

- *Homo ergaster* had a longer pharynx than earlier hominids, suggesting that it was able to produce some basic speech.

- *Homo heidelbergensis* had an even longer pharynx and would have been able to produce complex sounds. However, its speech would have differed from ours because of the different shape of its face.

- **Neanderthals** would also have been able to speak. The fossil remains of a Neanderthal hyoid bone, which supports the larynx, is almost identical to a modern human's.

- **Modern speech** only developed with the arrival of *Homo sapiens*.

- **Some experts** think that modern speech first took place 100,000 years ago – others think it did not happen until around 40,000 years ago.

▶ *The differences between a chimpanzee (top) and a modern human (bottom) mean that the human is capable of speech, but the chimpanzee is not. Unlike chimpanzees and early hominids, we have long throats and shorter muzzles. Therefore our pharynxes can produce a range of sounds and our tongues can move backwards and forwards in our mouths to utter these sounds.*

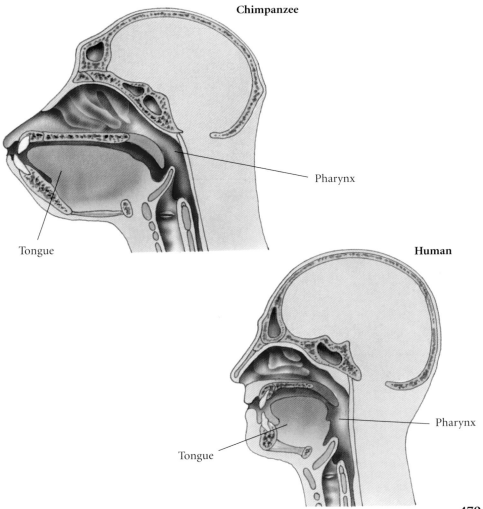

Chimpanzee

Pharynx

Tongue

Human

Pharynx

Tongue

479

Tools

▶ Homo habilis *produced flakes of stone, such as this one, by striking one stone against another, called a hammerstone.*

- **The greatest number** of *Homo habilis* tools has been found in the Olduvai Gorge in Tanzania. They include rocks that were used as hammers, flakers, choppers and scrapers.

- ***Homo habilis*** used these tools to cut meat and, especially, to scrape open animal bones to eat the marrow inside.

Stone tool

- **The stone tools** used by *Homo habilis* are crude and basic. This hominid was the first toolmaker, but, hardly surprisingly, it was not a skilled one.

- **But making** these early stone tools was still a challenging task – the toolmaker needed to strike one rock with another so that it would produce a single, sharp flake rather than shattering into many pieces.

- **Toolmaking requires** considerable intelligence. It involves the use of memory, as well as the ability to plan ahead and to solve abstract problems.

▶ Homo ergaster *used hammers made of bone to produce thinner and sharper flakes of stone.*

- *Homo ergaster's* tools were much more advanced. This hominid made tear-drop shaped, symmetrical hand axes called 'Acheulean axes', after the place in France where similar axes have been discovered from a later period.

- **Neanderthals** developed a method for producing razor-sharp flakes of stone, called Levallois flakes, which could be placed on the end of spears.

Flint axe

- **This method** required great precision and dexterity. While modern humans have a much broader range of skills, they would be very hard pushed to produce such tools themselves.

- **Modern humans** developed the greatest variety of tools. Cro-Magnon tools include knives, spearpoints and engraving tools.

- **Cro-Magnon humans** also began to make tools from materials other than stone, including wood, bones, antlers and ivory.

▶ Homo sapiens' *tools became more and more complex. They incorporated different materials, such as twine in the axe (above) and, in this saw (right), flint teeth held in place by resin.*

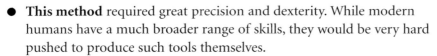

481

Groups

- **Early hominids**, such as *Australopithecus afarensis*, came together in groups at night to sleep, but spent their days in smaller foraging parties.

- **Other early hominids**, such as *Paranthropus boisei*, spent more time in larger groups because their food – roots and tubers – was more widely available.

- **Like apes and chimpanzees**, the main form of bonding between early hominids was grooming.

- **Grooming** among apes and chimpanzees involves cleaning, stroking and picking ticks off one another.

- **There could** be a lot of tension in groups, especially when males competed with each other for females.

- **As hominids** evolved they gave birth to smaller children.

- **Smaller children** were more vulnerable and required more co-operation between group members to help raise them.

- **This co-operation** also led to partnerships between mothers and fathers.

- **Hunting** also developed co-operation between group members. Hominids realized the advantage of working together to hunt animals that were too big for them to kill on their own.

. . . **FASCINATING FACT** . . .
Just like us, our ancestors were social creatures.
They lived in groups and benefited from the
protection and sense of well-being this brought.

▼ *The social behaviour of early hominids would have been similar to that of these chimpanzees – the closest living relative of modern humans.*

Hunting

- *Homo erectus* was one of the earliest human hunters. Other hominids that came before it, like *Homo habilis,* may have hunted small or lame animals, but they mostly scavenged other animals' kills.

- *Homo erectus* used fire to drive animals into traps. They also developed handaxes, which they used to kill animals or butcher them once they were dead.

- **But it was the Neanderthals** that excelled in hunting – a skill they developed during the ice ages of the Pleistocene Epoch (1.6–0.01 mya).

- **Hunting** developed into a way of providing not only food, but also clothing (animal skins) and materials for tools (bones, horns and hooves).

- **Neanderthals** used nets or spears to catch spawning fish. They also hunted seals by spearing them through holes in the ice or by throwing spears at them.

- **In the 1990s,** finds of Neanderthal weapons in Boxgrove, England, showed the full range of this species' hunting arsenal. They include axes, slicing knives, cutting blades and slashing blades.

- **As well as hunting** for meat, hominids also gathered wild fruits, vegetables and nuts.

- **Another Neanderthal site**, at Schöningen in Germany, preserved the remains of nine polished wooden spears, made from a spruce tree.

- **Each of these spears** was over 2 m long, and was designed to be thrown like a javelin.

- *Homo sapiens* developed new weapons for hunting, including the bow and arrow, the blowpipe and the boomerang.

▶ *Early humans developed more and more sophisticated methods of killing animals, including weapons, traps and fire.*

Cave paintings

- **Cro-Magnon** people produced many cave paintings.

- **One of the best** examples is the Grotte de Chauvet in the Ardeche, France, which was discovered in 1994.

- **The Grotte de Chauvet** caves contain more than 300 drawings of animals, from lions and deer to buffalos and woolly rhinoceroses.

- **People** used to be very sceptical that early humans could have produced cave paintings and thought they were hoaxes.

- **Another magnificent example** of cave painting is that of the Altamira cave in northern Spain, which has an 18-metre-long ceiling covered with red-, black- and violet-coloured paintings of bison.

- **Most cave paintings** date from around 20,000 to 15,000 years ago, when Cro-Magnon man lived in Europe and elsewhere.

- **Some cave paintings** may be much older. Some archaeologists think that the Grotte de Chauvet paintings are 33,000 years old.

- **No one can say** for sure what cave art means. Many appear to represent hunting scenes, but there are also many symbols in caves, including patterns of squares and dots.

- **Another very common image** in caves is that of a human hand.

> **...FASCINATING FACT...**
> Cro-Magnon people made hand outlines by
> blowing a sooty pigment over their hand as
> they pressed it against the cave wall.

▲ *A series of cave paintings known as the Great*
Hall of Bulls in Lascaux, south-west France.
The paintings are around 15,000 years old.

Index

A

acanthodians 64,65, 72
Acanthostega 74, *75*, 80, **82–83**, 84
acraniates 60
adders 119
Aegialornis 357
Aegyptopithecus 446
Aepycamelus 378
Aepyornis 341, 350
Africa 145, *148*, 149, 181, 188, 196, 197, 200, 206, 207, 211, 216, 220, **300–301**, *300*, *301*, 319, 320, 330
age **280–281**, 290, *291*
Aglaophyton 20
agnathans 62, 72
air passages 241, 292
Alamosaurus 295
Alaska *285*
Albertosaurus 144, *144*, 295, 330
algae 16, *17*, 18, *19*
blue-green (cyanobacteria) 18
Algeria 187
alligators 154
Allodesmus 373
Allopleuron 128
Allosaurus **148–149**, *148*, 149, 155
Carnotaurus 152
claws 254
Eustreptospondylus *175*
noses 240
pack-hunters 155
Alphadon 410

Altamira cave paintings, Spain 486
amber 35
amphibian fossils 74
spiders 55
Ambulocetus 434, *435*, 436
American Museum of Natural History 302
ammonite fossils 34, 35
ammonites **44–45**
amphibian fossils **74–75**
amphibians, breathing 80
eggs 96, *96*, 97
epospondyls 89
jaws 98
limb evolution 72
modern 90
obe-finned fish 70
reptiles 94
tetrapods 78, *78*, 79
Amphicyonid 388
amynodont rhinoceroses 424
anapsids 98
Anatosaurus 203
ancestors **140–141**, 316
Anchiceratops 213
Anchisaurus 181, 216–217, *216*, *217*, 301
Andrews, Roy Chapman 390
Andrewsarchus 372, **390–391**
Andrias scheuchzerii 91
angiosperms **28–29**

ankylosaurs **192–193**, *192*
armour 258
beaks 244
nodosaurs 226, *226*, 227
Scelidosaurus 214
tails 269
Ankylosaurus *192*, *193*, *258*, *259*, 315
Anning, Mary *125*, 127
Anomalocaris 39
Antarctica *286*
ant eater 229
antelopes *242*, 378, 384
antiarchs 66, *66*, 67
antlers 440, *441*
antlers, mammal fossils 361
ants, giant 56
Apatosaurus, feet *265*
sauropods 184, *184*, 185, 186, 186
teeth *247*
apes 444, **446–447**
group living 482
hominids 448, 452, 454, 456
offspring 450
aquatic mammals *435*
aquatic reptiles *see also* marine reptiles 120, 122, *123*
arachnids 40
Arandaspis 62
Araucaria 26
Archaefructus 28, *29*
archaeocyathids 38
Archaeomeryx 378
Archaeopsittacus 357
Archaeopteris 30

Archaeopteryx 133,168, 169, 298, *317*, *340*, 341, 343, **344–345**, 346,
Archelon **116–117**
archosaurs 102, **112–113**, **316–317**
Arctic Circle *285*, 287
Ardipithecus ramidus 452, *453*
Ardipithecus ramidus kadabba 453
Argentavis **358–359**
Argentina 296, 297
Carnotaurus 152, *152*
earliest dinosaurs 142, 143
fossil-hunters 330
Herrerasaurus 312
meat eaters 144
prosauropods 181
Saltasaurus 258
Argentinosaurus 184, *185*, 297
armadillos 401, 405
armour **258–259**
ankylosaurs 192, 193
fossil fish 58
nodosaurs *226*, 227
Sauropelta 231
Scelidosaurus 215
Tuojiangosaurus 222
armoured dinosaurs, beaks 244
horns 243
nodosaurs 226, *227*
Sauropelta 230, *231*
Scelidosaurus 214
tails 269
arms,
Coelophysis 151
Deinocheirus 254, 335, *335*

501

503

507

Acknowledgements

The Publishers would like to thank the following artists whose
work appears in this book:

Martin Camm, Eric Rowe, Mike Saunders, Mike White, Rudi Vizi

All other artworks are from Miles Kelly Artwork Bank

The Publishers would like to thank the following picture sources
whose photographs appear in this book:

Science Pictures Limited/Corbis: Page 148, 303
Kobal Collection/Amblin/Universal: Page 339

All other photographs from:

Castrol, CMCD, Corbis, Corel, DigitalSTOCK, digitalvision,
Flat Earth, Hemera, ILN, John Foxx, PhotoAlto, PhotoDisc,
PhotoEssentials, PhotoPro, Stockbyte